For Sandy,
Thank you so much
for getting me started
in environmental
political theory—
Yours,
Joan

PROVISIONAL
POLITICS

PROVISIONAL POLITICS

kantian arguments
in policy context

elisabeth ellis

yale university press / new haven and london

Published with assistance from the foundation established in memory
of Philip Hamilton McMillan of the Class of 1894, Yale College.

Set in Minion and Franklin Gothic types by The Composing Room of Michigan,
Inc.
Printed in the United States of America.

Library of Congress Cataloging-in-Publication Data

Ellis, Elisabeth.
    Provisional politics : Kantian arguments in policy context / Elisabeth Ellis.
        p. cm.
    Includes bibliographical references and index.
    ISBN 978-0-300-12522-1 (cloth : alk. paper)
    1. Kant, Immanuel, 1724–1804—Political and social views.   2. Political
science—Philosophy.   I. Title.
    JC181.K284E55 2008
    320.01—dc22
                                                                    2008017701

A catalogue record for this book is available from the British Library.

This paper meets the requirements of ANSI/NISO Z39.48-1992 (Permanence of
Paper). It contains 30 percent postconsumer waste (PCW) and is certified by the
Forest Stewardship Council (FSC).

10 9 8 7 6 5 4 3 2 1

For Allison

Sigh no more, ladies, sigh no more,
Men were deceivers ever,
One foot in sea and one on shore,
To one thing constant never:
Then sigh not so, but let them go,
And be you blithe and bonny,
Converting all your sounds of woe
Into Hey nonny, nonny.

—William Shakespeare, *Much Ado about Nothing (2.3.61–76)*

CONTENTS

ACKNOWLEDGMENTS

This book could not have been written without the enthusiasm and encouragement of my students, colleagues, friends, and family. My first thanks are due to the students in my honors courses in Environmental Political Theory and Contemporary Political Thought, for reading and arguing with me about topics covered in this book. Graduate students Hassan Bashir, Sara Jordan, Roberto Loureiro, Sibel McGee, and Annie Wilson contributed essential bibliographical research and literature reviews. The intellectual curiosity of graduate student Sung Ho Park pushed me to learn more about democratic theory in the early stages of this project. My colleague Cary Nederman generously read repeated drafts of portions of the book and offered invaluable suggestions. Judy Baer, Ed Portis, and Diego von Vacano joined Cary and the Texas A&M political theory graduate students in listening to me defend parts of my argument over several years of convocation meetings; their patience and support are very much appreciated.

I am grateful for the time and energy my fellow political theorists have devoted to this work. Martin Burke, Joshua Dienstag, Doug Dow, Steve Forde, Jeff Isaac, Jim Johnson, David Johnston, David Kettler, Sharon Krause, Chris Laursen, Mika LaVaque-Manty, Kirstie McClure, David Miller, Jennifer Pitts, Andrew Sabl, Melissa Schwartzberg, Brian Shaw, Melvin Richter, and Michael Walzer generously offered criticisms and comments at various stages of the work's progress. Sandy Hinchman encouraged me to pursue environmental political theory and gave me my starting point with a selection of readings that formed the basis of my later work. Dwight Allman listened to me talk about provisionality over a period of years, and kindly invited me to discuss democratic theory at the Baylor University Department of Political Science. I am especially grateful to Amy Borovoy and Kristen Ghodsee for a very fruitful series of conversations about anthropology and political theory.

Members of the Lone Star Chapter of the Conference for the Study of Political Thought and panelists at recent meetings of the Association for

Political Theory, the American Political Science Association, and the Western, Southern, and Midwest Political Science Associations all generously listened to and commented on drafts of the material in this book. The participants in the conference "Problems and Methods in the Study of Politics," sponsored by the Departments of Political Science at Yale University and the University of Pennsylvania, provided the first forum for my early work on provisional theory, along with very useful comments and encouragement. The Workshop on German History, Literature, and Culture at the University of Texas at Austin provided an especially congenial group with whom to discuss *geschichtliche Grundbegriffe.* I am grateful to the political theorists at the University of California, Los Angeles, the Columbia Seminar on Political and Social Thought, and the School of Social Sciences at the Institute for Advanced Study in Princeton for opportunities to present my work in progress.

Parts of an article published by the *Journal of Politics* as "Citizenship and Property Rights: A New Look at Social Contract Theory" (August 2006) appear, in different form, in portions of chapters 1, 3, and 4. My first attempt to use the idea of provisional right in connection with democratic theory was published as "Provisionalism in the Study of Politics," in *Problems and Methods in the Study of Politics,* edited by Ian Shapiro, Rogers M. Smith, and Tarek E. Masoud, published by Cambridge University Press in 2004.

Work on this project has been possible thanks to the generous support of the Glasscock Center for Humanities Research, the Office of the Vice President for Research, and the Department of Political Science at Texas A&M University. Completion of the project in its final stages was supported by a grant from the National Endowment for the Humanities. I am grateful to the School of Social Science at the Institute for Advanced Study for providing me with ideal circumstances under which to complete this work. I would like to thank John Kulka, for his encouragement of this project from the beginning, and Keith Condon, whose generous stewardship brought it to fruition. Otto Bohlmann has, for the second time, applied his incomparable editorial judgment to my work, for which I am very grateful.

As anyone who has read Ian Shapiro's *Democratic Justice* will recognize, this book could not have been written without it. Puzzles from Shapiro's work on democracy, as well as some of his remarks on the history and particularly the practice of political theory, provided the starting points for most of the chapters and for the book as a whole. The structure of the book as a series of mutually interacting theoretical and empirical discussions is a response to the challenge that Shapiro implicitly makes to political theorists with the epigraph at the start of *Democratic Justice*. If I am reading the lines (by the poet Zbigniew Herbert) in the proper spirit, we theorists are being asked to look out at the political world and then to see whether the evidence offered by the world corresponds to our expectations. This can be a difficult and painful process, as I know all too well. My original expectations for this book were disconfirmed by a summer of research into the history of contract theory, where I found very little precedent for Kantian provisionalism. By the final chapter of the final product, however, this back-and-forth process of characterizing the object of study through theory, looking out to see what can be learned through those categories, and revising the theory accordingly should have yielded a few generalizable insights about provisionality as well as some sobering suggestions about the limits of politics. Needless to say, neither Shapiro nor any other generous interlocutor listed or not listed in these acknowledgments is responsible for the errors in this book.

I have been lucky not only in my professional but also in my personal circumstances during the writing of this book. Thanks are due to Allison Cruse, Courtney Golden, Terrie Burchett, and Kim Davis for providing the love and care that made my daughters happy while I was writing. I would like to thank Lydia Cumings, who taught Susie and Allison pretty much everything, but especially to love learning. My friend Joan Wolf listened to me with patience and sympathy, for which I am very grateful. My family has supported me throughout this project. My mother was always there when I needed help or encouragement; my sister-in-law, Claire LeBuffe, provided friendship through the most intense periods of writing the book, plus a very timely reference; some of my relatives actually read my first book and expressed a touching if incredible eagerness to read this next one. Most of all, my husband, Mike LeBuffe, is the rock on whom I and the rest of the family rely, and for that I am profoundly grateful.

1

introduction to provisional theory

Why do we fail so often to explain ourselves as a polity? Why is there such an enormous gap between our professed principles and our practical action? It is not simply that our political principles are mere feel-good balm, meant to soften the reality of interest-based politics. If this were so, we would behave very differently. Nor does this problem reflect any genuine divide between realists and idealists, fighting for temporary advantage and muddling our policies as we go. The problem, I argue in this book, is that our language of competing conclusive political principles is inadequate to the immense complexity, uncertainty, and dynamism of the world of politics.

We speak the language of timeless principles and use it as best we can to make sense of our moral intuitions and political decisions. It is certainly better than the usual alternative: the language of realpolitik made famous by hard-nosed men from Cleon to Henry Kissinger. Neither extreme, however, provides an adequate picture of political life. Both idealists and realists are unrealistic. If we want to speak more accurately about political morality and about politics generally, we ought to learn to use provisional rather than conclusive reasoning.

As I write these lines, I can see the brushy scrub surrounding a lagoon outside the study window. Living there are a pair of birds, California gnatcatchers, that will soon be replaced by a condominium complex despite their status as members of an endangered species. The language of conclusive right has reduced debate around the bird and its habitat to a pair of absolute claims, one for property rights, the other for ecological values.

This discourse, as we shall see in chapter 5, has little to do with the real politics of species preservation. The very distance between our conclusive modes of public discourse and the dynamic moral-political reality of practice makes those operating under realistic conditions of principled uncertainty less willing to engage politically.

The norms of conclusive argument force us to choose between hypocritical moralism that exaggerates our certainty, on the one hand, and amoral disengagement that denies our interest in justice, on the other. Provisional theory, however, should allow us to speak of ourselves accurately, along multiple dimensions: as members of groups, as individuals, as predictable according to reductive statistics, and as exercising free choice. Many of the aporias to which political discourse leads us these days come from the application of an inappropriate language to the context at hand. Provisional theory can, for example, recognize the goal of increasing the scope of individual free choice without denying the powerful realities of group membership and social determination. Take the example from the contemporary United States of claims by white students to have suffered reverse discrimination. If the question is whether racial diversity in higher education serves a compelling state interest, then provisional theory directs us to consider the recipients of higher education as members of society, not as individual agents more or less deserving of rewards meted out by the state. Provisionalism can recognize the long-term ideal of a system of meritocratic placement in education without having to deny itself the social-scientific means to move toward that goal, means that would rightly fail to pass muster under a conclusive, fully individualized standard. Having to realize the principle of state recognition of individual merit before an appropriate context for such merit exists—a description, I would argue, of most present-day systems of admissions to higher education in the United States—not only deprives us of justice from a group-rights perspective but also deprives us of the possibility of approaching realization of the original, individualistic principle.

Immanuel Kant frequently used asympotitic imagery to describe the human political condition in which we may hope to approach ideals but never to achieve them conclusively. He summarized this same provisional insight with the maxim that one should always seek to promote the conditions of justice; as he put it in *The Metaphysics of Morals*, "Always leave open the possibility . . . of entering a rightful condition."[1] Now, Kantian political ethicists have rightly been criticized for using abstraction to create an empty subject of political agency. Michael Sandel has famously argued that the Kantian liberal self abstracts from the very ties that make us human, for example.[2] 'Kantian' has practically become a term of abuse among political theorists interested in understanding the world as it really is lived: multifariously, with deep moral and even epistemological pluralism. Kant's ethics may not in fact be as empty and rigoristic as these critics assume, but this is irrelevant to my argument. In his specifically political works, Kant describes a world in which moral argument is ubiquitous, but inconclusive, concretely effective, but only indirectly. Kantian political theory does rest on abstraction, but not on abstraction from the historical and cultural specificity of the moral subject, as we find in the ethical theory. Instead, given the context dependence of political argument as such, Kantian provisional theory abstracts from the particular contents of any given moral principle to the general fact of moral principles and their political importance. *What matters for politics is not the conclusiveness of any particular ethical system, even Kant's own, but the abstract ubiquity of moral argument in political life.*

Though his political works contain no major philosophical volumes on the order of any of the *Critiques,* and though Kant considered his political work unfinished, still he managed to provide a few important hints about how to understand political life.[3] First, Kant developed the concept of provisional right in the context of social contract theory, after experimenting with it in his earlier work on international right. Second, Kant argued for the concrete historical effects of argument in public, pioneering the concept of the public sphere and providing an initial template for the dynamics of discourse in the public sphere that is still of considerable interest. Third, Kant attempted to theorize provisionally about major political institutions, such as property and citizenship, rather than applying conclusive principles without attention to context. Fourth, throughout his work, Kant experimented with a variety of modes for the application of reason to political decision-making in practice (he explicitly contrasted this effort with the "castles in the air" approach of designing rational political systems in the abstract). Fifth, Kant developed a dynamic account of public reason and political life that, though hampered with an indefensible teleology, still remains more empirically interesting than ahistorical accounts.

This is not a book about Kant, but I do refer to him thoughout it for insights and arguments about provisionality in politics. I argue that the right kind of Kantian abstraction can allow us to make context-sensitive, provisionally legitimate arguments about hypothetically granted principles, and that these kinds of arguments are far more defensible generally than our usual competing conclusive principles. This tack may frustrate anyone looking for general defenses of particular policies. Provisional theory cannot provide policy prescriptions that transcend historical context; thus this book will disappoint readers looking for the next clever philosophical argument to bolster their preexisting political commitments. However, and to a degree which began to surprise me several years ago and which amazes me still, provisional theory can reach substantive conclusions about a number of political questions at a degree or two of abstraction higher than on-the-ground policy. Moreover, provisional theory can defend robust hypothetical statements about the compatibility of particular principles and institutions. Provisional theory allows us to speak accurately about the relationship between political morality and political practice. Finally, and even more surprisingly, provisional theory can lead us to a few broad institutional generalizations about the conditions enabling different political goals. In the chapters that follow, I illustrate several of these rare, substantive conclusions from provisional theory (which is not, believe it or not, an oxymoron).

What, then, does it mean to theorize provisionally? As I have said, for Kant, provisional right means roughly, "always leave open the possibility of entering into a rightful condition." In *Toward Perpetual Peace,* for example, Kant discusses the various crimes that states sometimes commit, using this provisional standard to distinguish among temporarily permissible and absolutely forbidden crimes.[4] Damaging international trust through the use of spies, assassins, or false promises undermines the possibility that a country may enter into peaceful relations with others later; thus these sorts of practices must be fought implacably. On the other hand, there are practices in clear violation of any reasonable (that is, for Kant, any enlightened protoliberal) view of right that may still be tolerated, such as treating the state as personal patrimony. It is clearly wrong, argues Kant, to treat the entity justified by its protection of the welfare of its members—the state, that is—as if it were personal property. But even though the practice is wrong, its continuation for a time may not undermine, and may even promote, the possibility of more general right (more peace) in the future. For example, a ruler who has been given her domain as a present would be wrong to refer to her illustrious family, to divine right, or to any other traditional justification for her reign. Treating the state as personal property cannot be justified, for Kant. However, if the ruler is working to promote the rule of law and the conditions of progress toward more rightful circumstances, her reign might well be provisionally justifiable. As we shall see in chapter 3, Kant uses similar arguments with regard to the institution of private property. Throughout his writings, he argues against violent revolution on the provisional grounds that quick transitions are generally counterproductive, and also that revolution undermines the condition for progress toward more republican (more accountable) government. Thus toleration of a conclusively unjust domestic situation may be provisionally legitimate, according to Kant.

Kant did not have the last word on provisional right. But already some of the advantages of a broadly Kantian view of provisional right for political argument are apparent. With some hypothetical goal in view, the provisional theorist may calculate sets of arguments that can promote the goal without having to make untenable philosophical commitments on the way. Imagine that one makes an empirical study of the development of the concept of human rights, for example. One might discover that the concept of human dignity has far more actual purchase in the world, even today, than the concept of human rights. One might further discover that the idea of a right has a culturally and historically particular history, perhaps one that has exclusive consequences that are less emancipatory than one might originally have thought. A little more philosophy, and one could begin to interpret the language of rights as part of a hegemonic scheme, as a dominant discourse, or even as a set of deliberate lies. All this research would move our conception of human rights closer to the empirical bone: these historical stories are too good at explaining outcomes to be dismissed. But what should a theorist conclude from this hard-won wisdom about the particularity of the concept of a human right?[5]

So long as rights-based argument remains only provisionally authoritative in some contexts, this new knowledge of the shaky origins of rights-based arguments should not lead us to reject them on the basis of their inconclusiveness. In some contexts, use of rights talk serves worthy purposes, purposes whose utility cannot be undermined by the particular genealogy of rights-based argument itself. Consider the following example. The Inuits of the International Circumpolar Conference have filed a complaint against the United States with the Inter-American Commission on Human Rights, arguing that the results of global warming driven by U.S. carbon emissions violate their human rights.[6] As the ice pack on which their way of life depends melts, the lawsuit contends, Arctic natives suffer injuries to their livelihoods and even to their cultural identities. They seek redress for these losses from the largest group of those responsible for causing climate change: the citizens of the United States. Now, when representatives of this Inuit group argue that their human rights have been violated by global carbon emitters, they are not victims of false consciousness or dupes of a slave morality; they are savvy political agents operating flexibly in a dynamic moral-political environment. Provisional theory asks not whether Inuit Circumpolar Conference representative Sheila Watt-Cloutier can defend the idea of human rights as such but whether her engagement in human rights discourse multiplies rather than constrains political possibilities.

Provisional theory takes two basic conditions of politics as given: agency and plurality. The values of agency and plurality are conditions of principled political action as such, rather than particular conditions reified to absolute precepts. In other words, though it is certainly possible to imagine a world without agency and plurality, it is very hard to imagine moral argument in politics without them. As Hannah Arendt once wrote, "The trouble with modern theories of behaviorism is not that they are wrong but that they could become true."[7] For Kant, and for provisional theory generally, a realistic view of politics must take moral argument and its concrete effects into account.[8]

SOME KANTIAN BACKGROUND

Kant's politics should not be derived from his ethics.[9] Anyone reading Kant's political essays even casually will notice that they are filled with fascinating arguments and hypotheses about the practice of politics, even though most of the secondary literature on Kant limits itself to formalistic abstractions illustrated by ill-chosen examples from ethical treatises like the *Groundwork of the Metaphysics of Morals*.[10] In his political essays, Kant gives us arguments about live political questions: how to trick the monarch into making himself obsolete; why permanent rule-giving of any kind is illegitimate; why freedom of expression matters; why gradual-ism is to be preferred to revolution; why the intelligentsia should get spe-cial rights; how regime change occurs; what institutions promote inter-national peace; how one should treat foreigners; and so forth. True, Kant takes the conclusions of his ethical work for granted in his political theo-rizing; he treats corollaries of the categorical imperative as conclusive principles of political right. However, in his political theory his concern is not simply to lay out another ideal system of politics, however well or ill grounded, but to understand the relationships among pragmatic politics, public applications of moral judgment to political practice, and the processes of political change.[11] Kant does construct an ideal republican political system, but his main theoretical innovation lies elsewhere, in his account of provisional right. Provisional right, as I explain below, em-phatically does not mean a temporary free pass for wrongdoing in the name of pragmatic political ends. Instead, it is something much subtler and more interesting: provisional right is a response to the inevitable un-certainties that arise from the hybrid, half-ideal, half-empirical world of politics. It would be a misunderstanding to confuse provisionality with relativism. Research in the history of political thought and observation of contemporary political behavior reveal the near-ubiquity of conclusivist moral argument in political life. As Kant famously puts it, "True politics can . . . not take a step without having already paid homage to morals" (8:380; 347). Moral arguments with conclusive ambitions compete for temporary advantage in the public sphere, constraining what it is possible to defend in any given context. Thus Kant can analyze, even celebrate, the moral element in political life without retreating to the usual castle in the air built by conclusive theory in spite of reality.

It is one thing, however, to posit that morality matters for politics and quite another to argue that a particular set of moral principles is conclu-sively authoritative.[12] Political theorists who place Kant's ethics at the center of his politics make a mistake: they take the *content* of Kant's moral system to be critical, when what matters for politics is the *fact* of human morality itself. Since human beings are capable of agency, any politics that ignores the role of judgments about the right made by political agents will be inaccurate: political ideals have concrete political effects. Kant argues that a single moral law governs all human agents, but even so, as a clear-eyed interpreter of the political world, he knows that the sources of political authority in really existing societies vary. Thus he argues for provisional rather than conclusive political right: right that applies in the absence of universally authoritative political judgment. A general formulation for provisional right in specifically Kantian language is: "Always leave open the possibility of . . . entering a rightful condition" (6:347; 485). Kant identifies the distinction between provisional and conclusive right and applies it to a variety of political topics, including the idea already mentioned here, the determination of which violations of international right are immediate threats to the possibility of world peace, and which might be provisionally tolerated (8:343–349; 317–322). Even as Kant presumes in his ethics that he has identified a universally authoritative set of moral rules, in his politics he recognizes *both* human agency *and* plurality. For example, Kant argues in "An Answer to the Question: What Is Enlightenment?" that any group of authorities attempting to set down conclusive moral rules for posterity necessarily violates future generations' human agency (8:39; 20).

Obviously, there are plenty of tensions in Kant's work. The political theory Kant and others derive straight from his ethical first principles is a nice, moderate republican social contract view of some historical importance.[13] Even Patrick Riley, whose seminal work of the 1970s and 1980s renewed interest in Kant's political thought, can generate only moderate enthusiasm for the ideal theory, calling it "the most adequate of the social contract theories."[14] It was not news, even in Kant's time, that a republican system of government ought to respect basic freedoms, ought to separate the executive and legislative authorities, ought to guarantee equal protection under the law.[15] These views amount to a static, rather than a dynamic, political theory. Kant himself plays down the value of this type of intellectual labor, saying in *The Conflict of the Faculties* that building ideal republics is ultimately irresponsible (7:92).

Instead, strangely ignored by nearly everyone but Habermas (whose *Structural Transformation of the Public Sphere* contains a brief but brilliant exposition of Kant's theory of publicity), Kant struggles in a series of efforts to come up with a dynamic theory of politics appropriate to limited rational beings interacting with each other.[16] His formal contract theory is set out in the *Rechtslehre*, the first half of the *Metaphysics of Morals,* and begins with an account of property rights that starts out as conventional and becomes a radical departure from the contractarian tradition. With regard to property rights, Kant's provisional contractarianism turns conventional wisdom on its head. Kant does not accord priority to the status quo in property holding, but neither does he posit a radical break between the state of nature and the civil state. Instead, given the clay feet of every existing state, he argues for *provisional recognition* of property rights. Kant avoids the traps of according absolute priority either to a "baseline" state of nature or to the state (more particularly: either to individual property rights or to redistribution according to some general interest [6:323–324; 465–467]).

Kant developed the concept of provisional right in the course of a series of works, and he first made sustained use of it in *Toward Perpetual Peace,* two years before setting out the social contract theory of the *Rechtslehre.* For Kant, the concept of provisional right applies to institutions that imperfectly mirror their own normative principles; since all existing political institutions do this, pragmatic politics must follow a rule of provisional rather than conclusive right. In his *Rechtslehre,* Kant claims that the right that applies in real-world civil societies must be "provisional" (*provisorisch*) rather than "conclusive" (*peremptorisch):* provisional right holds in anticipation of and preparation for the more perfect state of conclusive right (6:257; 410). As I have already mentioned, Kant uses an early version of this distinction in his famous essay on international politics, *Toward Perpetual Peace,* where he argues that even though many types of state action are in blatant violation of universal moral norms, only some of those violations must cease immediately. States that make peace treaties while secretly preparing for war, that forcibly interfere in the domestic affairs of other states, and that use methods that poison the possibility of future trust, such as assassination, not only violate moral norms but also by their conduct prevent the possibility of future peaceful relations; these types of violation must not be tolerated. On the other hand, international actors that violate moral norms by treating the state as personal patrimony, maintaining standing armies, or using national debt to promote military adventure ought to cease such practices, but they may do so gradually, since these three violations do not prevent the possibility of progress as such (8:343–347; 317–321). For Kant, the primary rule of provisional right, which is the rule that applies to all societies between the state of nature and the ideal republic, is to promote the possibility of progress. This pragmatic norm is at odds with the received wisdom on

Kant's politics, which distills a rigoristic set of political principles out of his ethical works. Readers of Kant's *political* works will enjoy a very different sort of argument, one that is context sensitive and attentive to modern concerns like the difficulty of constructing a predictive science of politics.

Provisional political arguments are not devoid of moral force. In fact, as I shall argue, they are the only means for plural political agents to realize their moral claims in the political sphere. The impossibility of conclusive legitimacy—of rightness across contexts of time, place, and policy—does not rob provisional claims of their authority in context. Instead, it is the would-be conclusive arguments that are self-undermining.

Readers may wonder how such a position can square with Kant's famous assertion in *Toward Perpetual Peace,* "fiat iustitia, pereat mundus" (let there be justice, even if the world should perish). Kant's view would seem to support the morally rigoristic position, in which one is at least certain about one's own principles, let the consequences be as they may. In fact, as I have already mentioned, Kant is widely associated with such a morally rigoristic view not only of ethics but also of political morality. Sissela Bok's reading of Kant on the maxim is typical: since Kant's moral theory is "absolutist," and since Kant cannot admit that moral duties might conflict with each other, he is forced to weaken the strength of the maxim by denying that justice could ever threaten the world.[17] If Bok's reading is correct, then Kant's commitment to provisional political right is at least compromised, if not contradicted, by his position in the first appendix to *Toward Perpetual Peace.*

Let us see, then, what exactly Kant argues there: "The proposition that has become proverbial, *fiat iustitia, pereat mundus,* or in German, 'let justice reign even if all the rogues in the world perish because of it,' sounds rather boastful but it is true; it is a sturdy principle of right, which bars all the devious paths marked out by cunning or force, provided it is not misinterpreted and taken, as it might be, as permission to make use of one's own right with utmost rigor (which would conflict with ethical duty) but is taken instead as the obligation of those in power not to deny anyone his right or to encroach upon it out of disfavor or sympathy for others" (8:378–379; 345).

"Let there be justice, even if the world should perish" and its classical predecessor "let there be justice, even if the heavens should fall" remain popular maxims today among political activists and public moralizers.

They exemplify a radical commitment to moral principle over pragmatic consequence. Taken to the extreme, they can justify courses of action that achieve expressive moral purity by sacrificing the possibility of physical endurance. "Fiat iustitia et pereat mundus" was adopted by the Holy Roman Emperor Ferdinand I (1558–1564) as his motto, and it was leveled by Erasmus at Christian princes tempted by what passed for Machiavellian ideals.[18] If the motto is popular among activists today, it is decidedly unpopular among scholars and pundits, who generally find moral absolutism abhorrent. Even scholars interested more in disclosing political dynamics than in judging them have associated fiat iustitia with the justification of extreme policies. Slavoj Žižek, for example, calls it the "motto of divine violence" and associates it with Robespierre.[19]

The popular discourse touting fiat iustitia calls for political leaders to be prevented from avoiding their duty through ad hoc excuses. Kant, too, supports the motto because it "bars all the devious paths marked out by cunning or force," constraining leadership to adhere to a just if difficult policy. This "no excuses" motto seems to stand in direct contradiction to Kant's arguments in the first section of *Toward Perpetual Peace*, where he distinguishes between violations of right that must cease immediately and those that may be tolerated provisionally in the name of stable progress toward just political arrangements. How can the Kant who is willing, at least provisionally, to allow rulers to treat societies of human beings as patrimony, to maintain standing armies, and to use national debt to finance aggressive adventure be the same Kant who mere pages later denies that any deviation from justice is acceptable? Bok suggests in a note that Kant's position on political rigorism shifts over the course of his career; this reading of *Toward Perpetual Peace* suggests that it shifts over the course of a single essay.[20]

Fortunately, we need not adhere to this initial reading of Kant's position in the first appendix to *Toward Perpetual Peace*. Note that Kant immediately points out that he does not mean fiat iustitia to justify the dogmatic promotion of one's own right. Instead, Kant directs the motto against rulers who would otherwise behave with *partiality:* it should be seen "as the obligation of those in power not to deny anyone his right or to encroach upon it out of disfavor or sympathy for others." The difference between Kantian provisional permission in the first section of preliminary articles and the Kantian fiat iustitia of the first appendix is that the former permission promotes the universal value of perpetual peace, while violation of the second would only benefit the particular interests of the ruler in question.

In his writings on politics, Kant is consistently aware of the relation of moral arguments to the context in which they are made, and in particular to the power differentials in operation in any given situation. Kant himself rarely forgets to think about the political dynamics affecting questions of public ethics. His interpreters, however, focused as they generally are on his moral philosophy and reading the political philosophy as an ethically derived side product, consistently miss them. Not only is Kant directing the fiat iustitia against powerful political rulers, he specifically forbids them to create classes among their subjects or to otherwise violate the principle of legal equality ("not to deny anyone his right or to encroach upon it out of disfavor or sympathy for others"). Most commentators notice that Kant narrows the sense of the Latin phrase in his rendering of it into German, but few realize that this rather free reading of the motto serves the purpose of setting its application into a power-political context. Kant was no slouch as a Latinist. His apparent mistranslation of "pereat mundus," or "even if the world should perish," as "even if *all the rogues* in the world perish" is no mistake but a gloss of the sense in which Kant wishes to take the motto. Those who would except themselves from the rule of justice are those rogues ("*Schelme*") whose partial interests contradict everyone's interest in achieving peace and justice. Far from promoting a moral rigorism of the particular against the well-being of the world (which would indeed be the moral fanaticism that worries Bok), Kant insists on the vindication of universal ends against would-be self-excepters.

"The world will by no means perish by there coming to be fewer evil people," Kant continues a little further down the page (8:379; 346). For Bok, this move represents a dodge, a failure on Kant's part to face up to the real conflict between moral rigorism and global survival.[21] Strangely, given the priority she accords to Kant's ethical over his political philosophy, Bok misses the connection Kant is drawing here between rulers who would violate principles of justice to pursue their own goals and his doctrine of radical evil from *Religion within the Boundaries of Mere Reason*. Human beings who would except themselves from universal ethical principles are "radically evil," for Kant; they place their particular interests

above the imperatives of morality. Kant is thinking of the political counterpart to radical evil here: placing the interests of a particular state, and
even of an individual ruler, above the imperatives toward peace and justice that ought to bind everyone. "Political maxims must not issue from
the welfare or happiness of *each state* ["eines jeden Staats"] that is to be
expected from following them, and so not from the end that each of them
makes its object" (8:379; 345; emphasis mine). *Pace* Bok, Kant does not
intend to exchange the survival of the world for the vindication of some
particular personal right (this, he explicitly says, would be unethical). Instead, the subjective perspective of the ruler, whose personal world may
indeed be shaken by the rule of justice, must submit to the objective ends
of universal humanity.

In keeping with his political philosophical principles, Kant insists
that concrete institutions are required for the realization of the norms of
peace and justice: "For this there is required, above all, a constitution or-
ganized in accordance with pure principles of right within a state, and
then too the union of this state with other neighboring or even distant
states for a lawful settlement of their disputes (by analogy with a universal state)" (8:379; 345). Bok complains that Kant cannot claim both that
the rule of justice requires currently unavailable institutions (domestic
republicanism and an international pacific federation) and that his
proposition is "true."[22] Placed within Kant's political thought, however,
the two claims are perfectly compatible. For Kant, ideal considerations
lead us to true principles of right, to which the provisional arguments
that apply to existing institutions must refer. Fiat iustitia thus requires
rulers to abide by provisional principles that promote the establishment
of institutions undergirding justice; for Kant these principles would
never entail self-serving exceptions that treat subjects unequally or pursue unilateral goals.

As I have already argued, though Kant does not use the specific language of provisional right in *Toward Perpetual Peace* (but only two years
later in the *Rechtslehre*), already in this text Kant presumes its political
logic. He provides one of his clearest statements of this view early in the
first appendix. Writing about the "moral politician" for whom political
prudence and ethics must coexist, Kant argues that though rulers are
obliged to redress policies that contradict political right, and though considerations of particular interest offer no reason to delay such reform,

there are cases in which gradual rather than sudden changes are called for. "Since the severing of a bond of civil or cosmopolitan union even before a better constitution is ready to takes its place is contrary to all political prudence, which agrees with morals in this, it would indeed be absurd to require that those defects be altered at once and violently; but it can be required of the one in power that he at least take to heart the maxim that such an alteration is necessary, in order to keep constantly approaching the end (of the best constitution in accordance with the laws of right)" (8:372; 340). Kant goes on to argue that toleration of an imperfect regime depends on the local conditions, and particularly on whether the alternative to toleration would be anarchy. He concludes that both rational reform and the quasi-natural event of revolution are paths to "a lawful constitution based on principles of freedom, the only kind that endures" (8:374; 341).

Thus we see that Kant's two views—provisional permissiveness in the first section of preliminary articles and fiat iustitia, pereat mundus in the first appendix—do not in fact conflict with one another. Though most readers have interpreted Kant as endorsing a morally rigoristic view of political right in this passage, we have seen that in fact Kant rejects narrowly rigoristic enforcement of particular rights. Instead, for Kant fiat iustitia, pereat mundus bars individual states and their rulers from taking "devious paths" away from the justice that serves everyone. The "no excuses" rule applies to all policies that serve merely particular interests, even if Kant is willing to find provisional justification for those practices whose temporary continuation serves the universal cause of international peace.[23]

Bok would have Kant revise his fiat iustitita to distinguish between cases in which justice does not threaten the world with annihilation and those in which it does. In the latter case, she argues, no one could reasonably will that the maxim become a universal law, since this would mean to will the destruction of everything.[24] The source of Bok's mistaken reading is now clear: she presumes that for Kant "iustitia" refers simply to the personal ethics Kant expounds in the second *Critique,* the *Groundwork of the Metaphysics of Morals,* and elsewhere. But Kant is talking here about moral politics, not personal duties viewed in social isolation. Political justice prima facie rules out truly world-devastating maxims, as Kant has already insisted in his gloss of the motto. Bok is thinking of examples such as Kant's notorious unwillingness to allow consequentialist reasoning to affect our response to the famous "murderer at the door" (in his essay "On a Supposed Right to Lie from Philanthropy," Kant argues that even a lie to protect a friend from a murderer seeking to discover him is wrong).[25] Such examples lead her to conclude that justice, read as Kant's most rigoristic personal ethics, could require decisions that lead to the destruction of the world, as surely as a truthful answer to the murderer at the door will lead to the death of a friend. Kant says explicitly, however, that fiat iustitia must *not* be taken "as permission to make use of one's own right with utmost rigor" (8:379; 345). Instead, the justice in question is political justice.

KLOSKO ON PLATO AND PROVISIONALITY

Kant, of course, is not the only philosopher in the canon to have thought about provisionality and politics. It is true, however, as I have already mentioned, that I did find a great deal less about provisionality in the tradition, and especially in the social contract tradition, than I had expected at the outset of this project. It is hard to explain the absence of a thing. Part of the explanation for the lack of sustained consideration of the problem of provisionality in the canon of political thought surely has to do with the genre in question: a treatise justifying a particular set of political principles is an unlikely place for speculation undermining the conclusiveness of those or any other principles as such. More scholarly works, historical approaches, and other studies that view theories at a distance are much more likely to adopt a provisional standpoint than a book expounding a canonical (or would-be canonical) point of view. Thus Thucydides, Michel Foucault, Max Weber, Michael Oakeshott, and Alexis de Tocqueville have all written in a mode I would call provisional, while Thomas Hobbes, John Locke, Adam Smith, Jean-Jacques Rousseau, and Karl Marx have not.[26]

George Klosko, however, has identified a provisional streak in Plato, who would seem the most conclusive of political philosophers, with his doctrine of forms and his blueprint for the ideal republic.[27] Klosko's argument is important, and I shall take a few lines to review it. Klosko begins with the copious literature documenting Plato's conclusive arguments about political right. However, Klosko notes, the Socrates of the early dialogues takes an explicitly provisional attitude toward knowledge.[28] "In the simplest of terms, 'provisionality' is an attitude of extreme openmindedness. It is the willingness constantly to re-examine one's convictions, especially one's moral convictions, to make sure that they are the best available. The Socrates of Plato's early dialogues became a firm adherent of provisionality as a result of his distinctive mission."[29]

Klosko easily demonstrates the Socratic commitment to provisionality in this context with reference to Socrates' insistence that every argument stand up to rational scrutiny in every context, to his skepticism with regard to received wisdom, and to his willingness to reinvestigate every question, even the ones in the *Crito* that bear on his imminent death. "Thus Socrates holds his beliefs, even his deepest beliefs, only provisionally. But so long as a given conviction proves worthy, his commitment to it is absolute."[30] Note, by the by, that Klosko's Socrates seems to agree with my contention that moral arguments made provisionally nevertheless demand firm commitment. Moral authority should not have to rest on excessive certainty, and a recognition of human fallibility ought to enhance, rather than degrade, the weight of the speaker's words. Similarly, the provisional nature of moral principles in politics ought not to undermine the legitimacy of moral arguments in politics as such.

Having demonstrated Socrates' provisionality in the early dialogues, Klosko moves on to the much tougher argument that the Plato of the *Republic* is likewise committed to provisionality. His Plato rings downright Kantian as Klosko argues that since eternal principles must be applied to changing political conditions, continuous rational judgment will be required of the philosopher-kings. The need to apply principles in context leads to a "crucial element of provisonality... built into the ideal state."[31] Klosko reminds us of the places in the *Republic* where future revisions of stated policies on education, and even on poetry, are said to be expected. "Thus we see that the central elements in the ideal state undoubtedly are maintained provisionally."[32]

PREVIEW OF THE ARGUMENT

Philosophers as different as Plato and Kant, then, have looked at political right and found provisionality. This is encouraging, but not definitive for my argument. Before I can say with some confidence that arguments about political right ought necessarily to be made in the provisional mode, I shall have to engage with the real world of political discourse. The book, therefore, moves through a series of policy areas as provisionalism applies to them. Part of the point of this structure is to demonstrate the futility of noncontextual application of conclusive principles. Moreover, we must be sensitive to shifts in context not only across temporal and geographic boundaries but also across policy areas. Different kinds of state activities offer different kinds of constraints. As we shall see in chapter 5, for example, a principle appropriate to increasing substantive democratic participation may work far less well when the goal is species preservation.

Another thing to notice about the movement of the book is that it proceeds, roughly, from cautious optimism to muted pessimism, at least about the capacity of political agents for substantive self-rule in a plural environment. The dynamics of discourse can be encouraged, I argue in chapter 2, with context-sensitive development of institutions that will promote protected discursive enclaves, overlapping authoritative institutions, and empowered citizens with the leverage to make a political difference. These three structures, I argue, are likely candidate conditions for the promotion of multiplied rather than reduced political possibility. Even across inevitable if unpredictable setbacks, if enclaves, overlapping authorities, and some citizen leverage remain, political opportunities for vindicating agency and plurality will continue to be possible under all sorts of conditions. The examples in chapter 2 show political agents in democratic environments both constrained by discursive judgments of right, and actively engaged in revising those public judgments. Legislators are forced to engage with the consequences of inadequate budgets; proponents of school voucher schemes are constrained to recognize the effects of their policies on the community as a whole; would-be counter-revolutionary Frenchmen are prevented from turning the clock back on emancipation. Though most of the examples of discursive dynamics in chapter 2 exhibit flaws of some kind, together they point to modes of reason-giving in politics that satisfy provisional theory's demands for effective moral-political argument.

I am also relatively optimistic about the prospects for provisional theory in the area of property rights over the first half of chapter 3, where I show that provisionalism can dispel some of the most pernicious reified conclusive principles limiting political possibility in the present-day developed world. However, this optimism reaches its limit when confronted with the same sorts of questions in a less-developed context. Provisionalism provides no neat solution to the stark choices offered in the case of the clash between widow's rights and the rights of the clan in parts of present-day Kenya. Kant's concept of the *globus terraqueus* (a world of permanent potential interaction of each with all), so valuable for vindicating the principle of affected interests across plural boundaries in chapter 4, offers no such solace in this case. Instead, relations in the interdependent world offer sharply *reduced* political possibilities for the collective determination of an economic system. Moreover, the three candidates for generalizable conditions of agency and plurality from chapter 2—protected enclaves, citizen capacity, and overlapping institutions—offer only mixed results in the context of Kenyan women's property rights. For example, the Kenyan legal system is a near-textbook example of overlapping authority, and yet it has certainly not led to the widespread vindication of women's property rights at this writing (though it has had some successes in this area). However, the Kenyan example does confirm some of the basic political dynamics that provisional analysis can reveal. Reified conditions of property holding, converted to conclusive policies and applied without attention to context, tend to limit political possibilities. On the other hand, property rights discourse, wielded provisionally in the service of agency and plurality, did sometimes function as a powerful weapon against domination.

Chapter 4's account of citizenship and provisional theory presents a similar dynamic: optimism with regard to the political potential of citizen leverage appropriate to context, but pessimism when citizenship runs up against indefensibly conclusive political boundaries. Here chapter 1's optimism regarding the concrete effectiveness of moral-political discourse reaches a serious obstacle, since the ideal-typical path from enclave incubation to widespread linguistic constraint seems to be running behind rather than in front of conventional aggregations of interest (and relatively undemocratic ones at that). Just as inclusive discourses with regard to Native Americans existed during the American Indian genocide but only became dominant after the damage was irreversible, so other discourses of inclusion seem only to cover over accomplished relations of domination and assimilation. The structure of interest conflicts seems to determine the cases in which increased citizen leverage may be effective; such leverage seems to have more potential effectiveness in cycles of inequality and polarization in the United States and other rich democracies, but less potential effectiveness in cases of widespread short-term collective interest, as in the expropriation of native lands or the exploitation of noncitizen labor. In these cases, the most conventional political science, pointing us to policy divisions according to the concentration or dispersion of interests, seems to explain outcomes sufficiently. Discursive dynamics still matter, but they are not dominant.

Finally, with chapter 5's analysis of species conservation policies, the book arrives at its most pessimistic moment for the vindication of agency and plurality. Here, as with the discourse of native citizenship, the discourse of species conservation seems to serve a sort of mourning rather than a policy-constitutive function. Once the hard choices about species preservation are made in favor of short-term development of the dominant interests, then the discourse of the value of species may safely disperse beyond enclaves. Even more troubling for provisional theory than the discursive sequence we observe in this case, however, are the structural barriers preventing substantive collective decision-making in this area. The irreversibility of decisions against species protection, for one thing, leads policy in this area to a sort of ratchet dynamic in which proconservation decisions only temporarily prevent degradation, while anticonservation decisions ratchet the policy arena toward reduced possibility (that is, toward extinctions). Even if the arguments against irreversibility prevail, however, the very institutions that in the present-day U.S. context seem best suited to vindicate agency and plurality turn out inexorably to reduce the scope of political possibility. The same institutions that a provisional theorist would rely upon in this context to maximize future political possibility end up reducing it, in fact, by a drastic measure.

This conclusion, however sobering from the environmental point of view, reaffirms some of provisional theory's basic insights. Provisionalism counsels us to promote the conditions of possibility for the political vindication of agency and plurality in multifarious contexts. It cannot guarantee that democratic institutions will produce desirable policy outcomes; indeed, if it could, it would be engaging in exactly the kind of paternalism that undermined conventional and deliberative democratic theory in the first place. If democratically appropriate provisional institutions produce policies that undermine future freedom of choice, this should only remind us of the importance of maintaining the conditions of dynamic political decision-making in the hope that some better set of conditions will be constructed, not by political theorists but by agents in a plural environment themselves.

PROVISIONAL THEORY AND MORAL ARGUMENT IN POLITICS

One way to understand this book is as a response to the following conundrum: despite the impossibility of conclusive moral principles for politics, moral argument is ubiquitous in politics. As Michael Walzer argues in the context of war, our very deceptiveness and hypocrisy point to the reality of moral judgment. "If we had all become realists . . . there would be an end alike to both morality and hypocrisy. We would simply tell one another, brutally and directly, what we wanted to do or have done. But the truth is that one of the things most of us want . . . is to act or seem to act morally."[33] Everyone differs about the content of political moral reasons, but only a Foole would deny that moral reasons matter. Though I found very little precedent for Kantian provisionalism in the history of contract theory, there are a number of recent attempts to come to terms with this conundrum. Rawlsian overlapping consensus, Cass Sunstein's notion of incompletely theorized agreement, Kantian provisional theory: all of these are efforts to vindicate moral reasoning without calcifying it—and thus handing a victory to the (crude) realists.[34]

Provisional theory seeks to investigate the conditions under which the realization of political principles in general is possible. Unlike most political philosophy, provisional theory does not seek to ground conclusive political principles, imagine political institutions that embody them, or provide strategies for their realization. Instead, provisional theory begins with agency and plurality as broad background conditions for politics as such. Since concrete institutional suggestions from provisional theory always take the form of hypothetical imperatives, the provisional theorist will necessarily focus on the conditions that multiply rather than foreclose political possibilities.

This is not to say that provisional theory would always condemn particular political developments that foreclose some possibilities while instituting others in the name of justice. Some political possibilities themselves militate against agency and plurality as conditions of politics; the institution of slavery is the classic example. In chapter 2, I discuss Reinhard Koselleck's analysis of the development of the concept of emancipation; he argues for a point in the discursive development of the concept after which it became practically impossible to defend old-regime institutions. However, this specific development in the history of political discourse is of interest to the provisional theorist not for its concrete contents, however inspiring; instead, provisional theory focuses on the conditions that made such a conceptual change possible in the first place.

Provisional theory is what Amy Gutmann and Dennis Thompson would call a "second-order" rather than a "first-order" theory.[35] Instead of positing some foundational basic principles of justice, provisional theory seeks to examine the conditions under which any political principles may be discussed and put into practice. There are other strategies available to political theorists interested in the political consequences of moral arguments. Walzer, for example, also declines to "expound morality from the ground up," noting that were he to begin with ethical foundations, he "would probably never get beyond them."[36] However, rather than turning as I do to the conditions of moral argument in politics themselves, Walzer makes a practical case for one set of posited values shared by a group: "I try to make a case for that assumption [of a common morality]. But it's only a case; it's not conclusive. Someone can always ask, 'What is this morality *of yours?*'"[37] Another strategy for political theory is to expound foundational arguments that are unabashedly particular to a single tradition. In *Sources of the Self,* for example, Charles Taylor contends that Western intellectual history has provided a concrete set of values that are binding for its inheritors.[38] Others, including especially John Rawls, strive for maximum ethical neutrality while preserving the idea of justice. Even the most morally pluralistic arguments of this sort have to make some basic contestable presuppositions, however. Rather than taking some baseline ethical principles and spinning them into a political system, provisional theory takes abstract conditions of political interaction —agency and plurality—and uses them to understand outcomes. The distinction between these two strategies is similar to the distinction between the traditional use of Kantian ethics for politics (through the positing of an abstract liberal subject) and my focus on Kant's actual political writings (in which the fact of moral reason's ubiquity rather than its content is what matters).[39]

This book is an effort to illustrate the consequences of some very basic political dynamics. In a similar vein, Philip Pettit has applied his theory of resilience in political institutions to the explication of present-day criminal sentencing practices in the United States. By analyzing the risks facing political agents and the way agents evaluate those risks, Pettit shows that a particular policy—harsh sentencing practices—is likely to prevail even when public and expert opinion are united against the policy.[40] Another example of this kind of effort would be Jane Mansbridge's recent argument that a "logic of formal justice" promotes human equality as a kind of default supposition in the absence of any overriding argument in a particular context.[41] Mansbridge uses this "logic" to explain the development of increasingly inclusive public discourse; once activists have undermined a set of worn-out reasons for maintaining inequality, she argues, political argument naturally moves toward formal equality; this dynamic results in sort of pro-equality ratcheting effect, at least in the limited context of the twentieth-century United States that Mansbridge and her colleagues have studied. Both Pettit and Mansbridge are conducting what provisional theory identifies as the right kind of abstraction: not from circumstances (this produces what Sandel objects to in liberalism) but from the specific contents of moral-political principles in practice. Moreover, this kind of abstraction, unlike the postulate of the liberal subject, does not carry any presumed historical narrative with it. True, Mansbridge's examples tend over time to produce more rather than less inclusion. But this is an artifact of the dynamic in question—the logic of formal justice, in which nondiscrimination is the default position. Another dynamic—say, Pettit's example of sentencing trends—leads *away* from what ordinary liberal, democratic, or consequentialist reasoning would produce.

This leads me to perhaps the most important break that provisional theory makes with Kantian political philosophy. Kant, when he writes about the principle of provisional right, presumes that the dynamics of the public sphere will lead to moral and political progress. He knows what constitutes this progress: movement toward the realization of the republican ideals of freedom, equality, and independence.[42] Provisional theory does not try to identify conclusive political goals but instead tries to investigate the conditions under which a plural political agency is possible. Provisionally legitimate hypothetical goods, such as democracy, are taken from the contexts in question. As we shall see by chapter 5, however, the dynamics that provisional theory identifies do not naturally lead to outcomes identifiable as "progress."

2

provisionalism and democratic theory

Democratic theory is a particularly good place for a book on provisionalism to begin; provisional theory's insistence that theorists themselves ought not to attempt to reach particular policy outcomes that transcend temporal, geographical, and policy context is at least antipaternalist if not essentially democratic.[1] The task for provisional democratic theory will be to investigate the conditions of possibility for the principle of affected interest, that most abstract of democratic precepts. The principle of affected interest—roughly, that one ought to have a say in the policies that affect one—is of course not the only possible gloss of democratic principle. I have selected it because it captures democracy's egalitarianism without presupposing a system in which a powerful, unified central state translates some general will into policy. Democracy throws the general problem of paternalism for provisional theory into sharp relief.

DELIBERATIVE DEMOCRATIC THEORY

A few years ago, Bruce Ackerman and James Fishkin proposed that the United States spend $2.3 billion of taxpayers' money once every four years to promote Deliberation Day, or DDay for short. DDay would be an exercise in reasoned decision-making among ordinary voters on an unprecedented scale. Two weeks before a national presidential election, citizens would gather in public schools and conference rooms across the country to listen to candidate appeals and to deliberate among themselves. Each participant would be paid $150 "for the day's work of citizenship."[2] The expected results of a commitment of public resources at the multibillion-dollar level included both enhanced democratic practice and improved policy outcomes.

Reviewers glossed the proposal generally as "highly imaginative" and criticized its details, including the price (high), the expected benefits (inflated), and the process (vulnerable to manipulation, potentially disempowering, and missing critical elements of accountability).[3] Easy as it is to make light of visionary proposals like Deliberation Day, I shall nonetheless argue that Ackerman, Fishkin, and some other deliberative democrats have identified something extremely important. I do not think that they have discovered the ideal model for increasing public deliberation, even in present-day rich democracies. However, democrats ought to endorse their basic project—to discover institutions that would remedy democratic deficits while encouraging practices of reason-giving in political decision-making.

Baseline and Preference Aggregation Problems

Deliberative democrats focus on two basic flaws in the aggregative conception of democracy.[4] First, aggregative theory tacitly privileges the status quo in politics and society by isolating each democratic decision (the "baseline" problem); tacit decisions promoting the present-day order of things thus falsely appear to involve no political action at all.[5] The legal theorist Cass R. Sunstein calls this the problem of "status quo neutrality."[6] In *The Partial Constitution,* Sunstein argues that much of the tension in present-day constitutional jurisprudence derives from an outmoded, pre–New Deal understanding of status quo neutrality. Judges mistakenly assign natural status to current distributions or circumstances that are in fact the products of law itself. This leads, argues Sunstein, to a series of untenable legal distinctions; what counts, for example, as the difference between state action and inaction really distinguishes between state action to change the status quo and state action to uphold the status quo.[7] In cases of sex discrimination, affirmative action, property rights, and even freedom of speech, Sunstein shows us judges relying on a tacit and empirically insupportable view of a natural, prepolitical baseline.

Sunstein's complaint about mistaken views of status quo neutrality leads to an argument familiar to provisional theory—namely, that application of conclusive principles across contexts can undermine the original principles themselves. In the case of racial discrimination, Sunstein quotes Dewey approvingly: "Even when the words remain the same, they mean something very different when they are uttered by a minority struggling against repressive measures and when expressed by a group that has attained power and then uses ideas that were once weapons of emancipation as instruments for keeping the power and wealth they have obtained. Ideas that at one time are means of producing social change assume another guise when they are used as means of preventing change."[8] I shall return to the problem of status quo neutrality in chapter 3, on property rights. For the present context, what matters about Sunstein's analysis is that he shows us how the misidentification of some aspects of government as prepolitical allows essentially conservative defenses of the status quo to go unchallenged, even in a democratic system.

Perhaps Sunstein's strongest example in this regard is the case of campaign finance regulation. Sunstein compares the Supreme Court's famous determination in *Buckley v. Valeo* (424 U.S. 1 [1976]; 75–436)— that restricting the use of private wealth to buy political speech amounts to an unjust limit on the free expression of the wealthy—to its now-defunct but equally famous predecessor in *Lochner* (198 U.S. 45 [1905]; 292) (which prevented most government regulation of working conditions for more than a quarter century). In both cases, the Court viewed the status quo in the distribution of wealth as prepolitical and natural, despite the state's essential role in maintaining the conditions under which markets exist: "The existing distribution of wealth is seen as a given, and failure to act—defined as reliance on markets—is treated as no decision at all. Neutrality *is* inaction. . . . This is so despite the fact that that markets are conspicuously a regulatory system, and reliance on markets for elections is a regulatory choice. *Buckley,* like *Lochner,* grew out of an understanding that for constitutional purposes, the existing distribution of wealth must be taken as simply 'there.'"[9]

Deliberative democrats seek to expand the sphere of deliberative decision-making beyond the traditional liberal limits, to include a broader scope for moral questions and also, importantly, deliberative institutions that force the system to evaluate not only quotidian policy questions but the baseline as well. From this point of view, a move from deliberation in which the status quo is taken as given to deliberation in which the status quo is the object of democratic scrutiny counts as progress. For example, Gutmann and Thompson discuss a decision about the provision of health care for the poor in Oregon.[10] As the process began, panels engaged in a ranking of the value of various health care procedures provided by the state. Though they did take public views into account when evaluating each procedure against the others, these ordinary aggregative institutions did not allow for consideration of any change in the overall *level* of health care resources provided by the state, until the process was opened up to public deliberation. Though the process was imperfect, deliberation contributed to an outcome in which democratic decisions were not merely aggregated according to a given structure that favors the status quo by ignoring the baseline. Instead, arguments were made in public about the distribution of resources, the level of public commitment to health care for the poor, and the political process itself. In this case, the addition of deliberative institutions to the democratic mix led not only to public consideration of the issue as presented by the political establishment but also to more substantive discussion and eventual change. It was not possible under deliberative conditions to misperceive the baseline status quo (level of funding) as neutral.

The second main flaw in the aggregative conceptions of democracy as criticized by deliberative democrats is that aggregative conceptions tend to treat easily observable expressions of public opinion as transparent indicators of the public will (the "preference aggregation" problem). If there is any unity among the various strands of deliberative democratic theory, it is to be found on this point. Fishman and Ackerman, for example, complain that ordinary electoral and opinion survey procedures fall far short of the accurate reflections of genuine public opinion that democratic legitimacy requires.[11] Problems with agenda setting, issue framing, and access to the public sphere are well documented in the conventional as well as the deliberative democratic literatures. Though some versions of aggregative theory would correct for marginal problems like misinformation, the basic difference remains: while aggregative democrats take preferences as given, seeking only fair methods of combining them into workable outcomes, deliberative democrats consider not just preferences but also their justifications.[12]

In short, deliberative democrats argue that aggregative democrats make heroic assumptions about two kinds of citizen capacity: the capacity to address substantial political concerns in the public sphere (the baseline problem), on the one hand, and the capacity to have their views ac-

counted for by democratic institutions, on the other (the preference aggregation problem). In response to these baseline and preference aggregation problems, deliberative democrats usually recommend supplementing
the processes of preference aggregation with some kind of public reason.
Sometimes the reasoning is provided by the theorists themselves; they
may, for example, offer rules for legitimate political argument. As I explain below, sometimes reason affects the democratic process through
procedures of reason-giving, either by representatives of government (as
in Gutmann and Thompson's example of environmental impact reports
by a government agency to the public) or by the citizens themselves (as
in Karpowitz and Mansbridge's description of the Princeton Future
process).[13]

Deliberative democracy's critics raise questions about deliberative
democracy's own heroic assumptions. These problems include deliberative democracy's unduly narrow conception of public reason (Sanders),
exaggerated expectations for consensus (Shapiro), and an insufficiently
inclusive idea of public deliberation (Young).[14] Persistent complaints
about unacknowledged, antidemocratic paternalism also continue to be
raised, particularly when deliberative democrats call for preelection education of the public by experts (Fishkin) or when deliberative democratic
theory prescribes specific policy outcomes that, it is claimed, public reason will necessarily reach (Gutmann and Thompson).[15] It would be reasonable to wonder whether a theory that seeks to temper aggregative decisions with reason can ever be sufficiently inclusive and responsive to
warrant the adjective 'democratic.' However, I argue that—when properly understood as the practice of reason-giving in the public sphere—an
application of reason can indeed cure aggregative democracy's diagnosed
problems without suffering from painful deliberative side effects.

Deliberative Practices of Reason-giving

We ought to look to what I call "discursive dynamics" for practices of reason-giving that might be effective in a given political context, for the results of a particular set of reason-giving arguments that constrain what
may be argued in a given context, and for evidence about the conditions
under which reason-giving practices may be particularly effective.[16] Discursive dynamics have been studied under various headings: the history
of political and social concepts (Koselleck, Richter), the languages of

political thought (Pocock, Skinner), discourses (Foucault), the public sphere (Kant, Habermas), and everyday talk (Mansbridge), among others.[17] There are interesting differences among these schools, but I shall leave those differences for others to address.[18] For my purposes here, discursive dynamics refer to changes in the arguments made in the public sphere, to the shifting patterns of discursive constraint facing political actors, and to conceptual and institutional conditions that affect what it is possible to argue in the public sphere. If reason-giving practices are to supplement aggregative democratic institutions, they must avoid both heroic presumptions about citizen capacity and the kind of paternalism that accompanies conclusive theorizing about properly political decisions.

Democratic theory ought to look for practices of reason-giving in the discursive dynamics of the public sphere, where citizens make and evaluate arguments about political life over the medium and long term. Provisional theorists focused on discursive dynamics for deliberative democracy will not themselves be able to provide conclusive answers to vexing policy problems, and this is as it should be. No set of experts will be able to match the inventiveness or the legitimacy of the public sphere over the long term. Instead, study of discursive dynamics should lead theorists to suggest means of enhancing discursive dynamics in the endless variety of contexts provided by the constantly shifting political environment. There is not going to be any permanent, much less universal, solution to these problems, least of all from the top down. The best that theorists can do is focus on the conditions of possibility of enhanced citizen capacity to make and realize political arguments as these vary from context to context, learning from the past by endeavoring to explain it while applying knowledge to normative arguments in the present.

Over the past fifteen years or so, deliberative democratic political theorists have been arguing against an apparent consensus among democratic theorists to restrict the scope of democratic decision-making for the sake of mutual toleration and political stability. Part of the continuing legacy of the English social contract tradition has been the (at least partial) exclusion of divisive moral and religious questions from the purview of the state. Faced with the misery, absurdity, and downright wastefulness of much of the English civil wars, contract theorists like Hobbes and Locke sought—in their very different ways, of course—to prevent religious and moral enthusiasts from wielding the state as a weapon against their social enemies. The sober conclusion that no good can result from allowing the state to become a prize in apparently permanent moral and religious conflicts provides the background for a number of hoary, if contestable, liberal democratic principles familiar at least in the context of U.S. politics, such as the separation of church and state, the sanctity of the home, and the adoption of an official position of state neutrality. Against this established view, then, deliberative democrats argue that moral questions ought not to be excluded from political life. Moreover, the deliberative democrats claim, restricting the scope of democratic decision-making by removing morally divisive questions from the purview of the state amounts to an undemocratic and even arbitrary usurpation of the people's authority by the scholarly and political establishment.[19] These claims are similar to those reviewed in chapter 1's discussion of provisional theory's presumption in favor of expansion rather than reduction of political possibilities.

The solution to this problem offered by the deliberative democrats does not, however, return all power directly to the people. Instead, they offer a *new* defense of limits to majoritarianism, this time on the basis of common desires for political justice, rather than on the basis of a determination of the just outcome by contract theorists and their successors. This is the key move made by some deliberative theorists, especially by Gutmann and Thompson, and one that it too often overlooked. It puts them in the *provisional* rather than the conclusive or absolutist camp of scholars of politics.[20] Gutmann and Thompson call their theory a "second-order," rather than a "first-order," theory. They intend to distinguish their views from what Rawls would call a comprehensive doctrine. Both the traditional liberal solution of scope limitations and the new deliberative theory reject straight aggregative democracy, but while the traditional liberal view comes to definite conclusions about the limits set by reason on democratic decision-making, the deliberative view concludes only that *reason-giving in general* must constrain democratic politics.

In a recent book on the topic, Gutmann and Thompson illustrate this view with the example of the decision on the part of the United States to topple Saddam Hussein's government in Iraq. Arguing for deliberation against pure aggregative democracy, Gutmann and Thompson write that "no one seriously suggested that the decision to go to war should be determined by logrolling."[21] In other words, the baseline and aggregative shortcomings of conventional democratic institutions lead deliberative democrats to suggest that reason-giving practices supplement them. More generally, deliberative theorists argue that democracy itself is incomplete without the incorporation of reason-giving practices. Deliberative democrats mean to distinguish their limits on democratic decision-making from traditional elitist worries about the unruly mob. Rather than paternalistically determining what rational justice would demand of democracy and democratic citizens, deliberative democrats argue that aggregative democracy untempered by reason-giving practices fails on its own terms (that is, fails to be sufficiently democratic). Iris Marion Young, for example, reminds her readers that people traditionally have expected democratic outcomes to be just according to commonly agreed reasons.[22] Gutmann and Thompson offer a series of standards for deliberative democratic practice based on the claim that the demands of democratic citizenship entail democratized access to both the public sphere and the means of identifying arguments in the first place.[23]

Reason-giving as a political practice, argue Gutmann and Thompson, contributes essentially to democratic justice. In a series of books and articles, they argue (1) that classical scope limitations on state involvement in moral questions are illegitimate and undemocratic, (2) that pure majoritarianism likewise fails the test of democratic legitimacy, and (3) that the classical liberals are right that reason must temper majoritarian democracy but wrong to prejudge the conclusions reached by reasoners in public. How, then, do the deliberative democrats propose to enjoy the benefits of public reason without paying the undemocratic costs in terms of paternalism? They make the provisional move, retreating from determining particular policy outcomes as a conclusive theory would and concentrating instead on the preconditions of deliberative democracy itself. This does not amount to mere proceduralism, as Gutmann and Thompson have recently argued, because the conditions that enable just deliberation, though they vary by context, are themselves substantive.[24]

Practices of reason-giving are the nonpaternalist constraints that will give deliberative democracy its just character, according to Gutmann and Thompson. Deliberative democrats must presume that in the process of giving reasons for political action, agents will be moved to act otherwise than in their narrowly defined interests, as an aggregative conception of democracy would expect.[25] Gutmann and Thompson provide a number of examples of the type of constraint they have in mind. For example, the process of providing environmental impact reports for proposed changes in policy or development projects should, in itself, constrain actors from proposing actions that violate standards like fairness and reciprocity. In an inclusive deliberative context, actors should be constrained from using what in an aggregative context would be excessive political power for self-interested purposes. The very practice of having to argue for a policy constrains what anyone may propose. As we have already seen, Gutmann and Thompson provide the example of the debate on health care provision for the poor in Oregon, where mere public exposition of the sorts of trade-offs made necessary by inadequate public funding led to increased funding by the legislature.[26] As Gutmann and Thompson note with regard to the Oregon health care case, even a modified version of aggregative democracy with a built-in apparatus for limited reason-giving will fail to offer genuinely democratic outcomes most of the time. In the state's first attempt to resolve its health care crisis, first experts and then citizens were engaged in an effort to determine the worth of various medical procedures so that they could be ranked in terms of their costs and benefits. The resulting proposal provoked public outrage, since rote application of the model produced plainly irrational results, ranking tooth capping, for example, higher than appendectomy.[27] Though Gutmann and Thompson recognize the deliberative shortcomings of the whole series of procedures applied by the state of Oregon with regard to its health care crisis—especially the virtual exclusion of the voices of those most affected by the program, the poor—they nonetheless argue that the expansion of the decision-making procedure from modified aggregative democracy to a combination of aggregation and deliberation resulted in a better outcome. Legislators were forced by the process to recognize the results of their underfunding of the public health system. While they were able to speak the language of fiscal conservatism generally, they were not able to argue specifically against, say, appendectomies for the needy.[28] The procedure of public reason-giving improved the democratic process by including more of those affected by public health care and by encouraging participants to see themselves as members of a broader community, while the outcome was the realization of a morally substantive goal: increased funding of medical care for Oregon's poor. As Gutmann and

Thompson argue, even the rationally modified aggregative procedure originally in place in Oregon could not reach the issue of substance in the case; it could only propose alternative schemes of distribution for a level of funding taken as given. Until the process was opened to more public deliberation, policy-makers could not address "the most serious flaw in the proposed policy [which] was not the ranking of treatments per se, but the unfairness of rationing under these circumstances."[29]

The model of public reason-giving offered by deliberative democratic theory is attractive in many ways: the intuitions are good, in that prejudged outcomes for reason in politics are not democratically acceptable, and thus the move to second-order provisional theory allows the deliberative democrats to replace concrete rational suggestions with a process that includes public reasoning on a mass basis.[30] However, the model operates on an implausible scale, with deliberative democrats expecting, for example, that public opinion will quickly change when confronted with adequate information or with the representatives of losers in a proposed policy change. Better models would use much longer time scales (years or decades), consider larger publics (societies, not individuals), and differentiate among policy areas. I argue below that much more appropriate models of the application of public reason to the democratic process are provided by intellectual historians and discourse theorists, including Reinhard Koselleck and the *Geschichtliche Grundbegriffe* school, Jane Mansbridge with her theory of "everyday talk," and other students of discursive dynamics.

A critical if underemphasized premise of deliberative democratic theory is the *empirical hypothesis* that the very practice of justification operates as a constraint on political action. It is presumed that the requirement of reason-giving precludes some political actions for which reciprocally acceptable reasons simply cannot be given.[31] But if provisional democratic theory rests on an empirical premise, we ought to investigate the conditions under which the premise holds true. Promoting the possibility of public reason's effectiveness becomes a normative imperative, encompassing both the construction and promotion of appropriate institutions.

It is one thing to claim that public reason ought to matter, and quite another to show that it has, does, and can effect concrete political change.

Kant struggled with this issue while trying to find an empirical "sign" that public morality was real and not merely the product of his own moral imagination.[32] For Kant, the problem was to separate interested from disinterested behavior. If he could find an example of disinterested expressions of moral-political argument, then his case for the concrete power of moral reason in practice would be supported with real-world evidence. As is well known, Kant did find such an example, in the Prussian sympathizers with the French Revolution, who spoke out in favor of republican principles despite the significant personal danger they faced in doing so.[33] One added benefit of Kant's model of the moral authority of disinterested expression in the public sphere arose from its own critical flaw: the uncertain connection between arguments and policy outcomes. True, in retrospect it is nearly impossible to determine what combination of arguments and interests made the ultimate difference in any particular policy change. But this very uncertainty insulates Kantian participants in the public sphere from the taint of interest. Since they cannot know whether their arguments would have any concrete effect, argues Kant, their only incentives to make their cases are moral ones: commitment to expressing what they see as the true state of affairs. A related advantage of the Kantian model is that the connection between individuals' social standing and individuals' arguments is supposed to be severed, since arguments in the public sphere ought to be judged according to their own merits, and not by the status of their authors.

Thus the search for a model of nonpaternalist and yet constraint-providing practices of reason-giving in public is hardly unprecedented. Kant, however, provided only "hints" and "signs." We need to investigate the medium-term political dynamics of relatively functional public spheres as locations for the identification of practices of reason-giving in democratic discourse. If we are to improve on aggregative democracy without defending rationalistic paternalism, we must give a coherent, empirically plausible, historically demonstrable account of reason in the public sphere. We should seek to describe the discursive dynamics not of "Reason" but of reason-giving practices, considering many individual events of reason-giving and argumentation aggregated over a fairly long term (years or decades) *that change what it is possible to argue in particular political contexts.*

CONCEPTUAL HISTORY, EVERYDAY ACTIVISM,
AND DEMOCRATIC THEORY

In the previous section of this chapter, I argued that deliberative democrats have some of the right goals in mind, including making institutions more genuinely democratic and improving the outcomes reached by those institutions. I also made the case for the authoritative inclusion of practices of reason-giving in democratic politics, incorporating consideration of the baseline of decision-making and taking democracy beyond mere aggregation of presumed interest.[34] Though the history of attempts to qualify democratic institutions and outcomes with reason is fraught with antidemocratic sentiment and outright paternalism, I argued that focusing on reason-giving practices rather than reason itself allows us to avoid these dangers. I now confront the difficult problem of *how* reason-giving practices ought in fact to be integrated within democratic governance.

Of course, many before me have wrestled with this problem. Most deliberative democrats expect reason-giving to affect practice over too short a time span, and on too narrow a level of analysis.[35] Ackerman and Fishkin represent one extreme end of this spectrum, at least with regard to time: their proposal allows for two days of popular deliberation conducted once every four years (though they do insist that the democratic system as a whole would respond to DDay institutions in ways that would have longer-term reason-enhancing effects). Gutmann and Thompson offer a range of institutional suggestions, most of which involve time spans of less than a year. Moreover, their suggested limits on potentially reasonable arguments in the public sphere would apply rational standards even before public deliberation gets under way. But even discourse-sensitive theorists like Young and Mansbridge offer relatively short-term, institutionally vague suggestions. Young diagnoses the exclusion of a significant portion of the citizenry from democratic deliberation by subtle but powerful forces such as prevailing rhetorical norms.[36] Mansbridge identifies activist groups as a source of innovative political concepts that sometimes restructure political possibilities as the concepts move into the mainstream.[37] In a recent article with Katherine Flaster, Mansbridge argues that even citizens who do not participate in ordinary and easy to observe social movement activities like demonstrations can have significant effects through their ordinary construction of political concepts.[38]

These are important but scattered hints about democratically legitimate functions and sources of reason-giving in politics. Reason-giving
can and does affect democratic processes and outcomes, but not on the
scale anticipated by deliberative theorists. The most attractive institutional location and timescale for reason-giving in democratic politics is
the public sphere and its discursive dynamics.[39] Expecting reason to constrain political will on a short-term, one-on-one basis is both unrealistic
and undemocratic; Sidney Lumet's jury film *Twelve Angry Men* is a poor
model even for a deliberative democratic theory.

The discursive dynamic view is both more empirically accurate and
less paternalistic, looking not at what reason demands universally but at
what it is possible to argue in a given political and social context. As the
linguistic constraints determined by the interplay of concepts, institutions, and power shift over time, so do the horizons of possibility faced by
political actors. Mansbridge's everyday talk model provides an attractive
illustration of this dynamic: "In social movements, new ideas—and new
terms, such as 'male chauvinism' or 'homophobia'—enter everyday talk
through an interaction between political activists and non-activists. Activists craft, from ideals or ideas solidly based in the existing culture,
ideals or ideas that begin to stretch that base."[40] Political possibilities
change as vocabularies shift. For example, a world without a word for homophobia is a world in which the public may not have considered the
moral status of prevailing antigay attitudes. These longer-term discursive
practices of reason-giving provide dynamic sources of moral argument
based on the agency and plurality of actual citizens rather than the authority of tradition or the mind of the theorist.

I would like to suggest that contemporary democratic theory has
overlooked a significant resource in this regard: the study of the history of
political and social concepts.[41] More than fifty years of work has been
done in this field, producing a body of analysis of discursive political dynamics in dozens of areas, covering hundreds, occasionally even thou-
sands, of years.[42] Historians of political and social concepts have provided the relatively raw data of conceptual histories across a broad variety
of important topics; it is up to political theorists to ask the kinds of questions these data can answer. Under what circumstances has slavery been
defended as legitimate? What is the range of possible types of political
membership available to beings such as ourselves? What conditions have

contributed to or hindered practices of political accountability? How tightly have arguments for citizen self-rule and political exclusiveness been linked? What kinds of institutions tend to accelerate conceptual change generally? What practices tend instead to foreclose more political possibilities than they reveal? Of course, inquiry into the empirical record of arguments made cannot provide an exhaustive list of answers to such questions as these. However, we can learn two kinds of interesting things: first, what kinds of normative arguments tend to be offerable under particular conditions; and second, how discursive dynamics tend to operate in relation to political, societal, and linguistic institutions.

Just as political scientists collaborate to construct data sets covering as many observations over as long a period of time and as broad an area of space as possible, in order to provide the raw data needed to test hypotheses about politics, political theorists and historians of ideas can collaborate on these kinds of projects. Often the collectors of political scientific data have very little information about how the data will be used; sometimes old data are reworked to serve entirely new purposes. In what follows, I argue that democratic theorists interested in discursive dynamics would do well to treat the results of the decades of research by the history of concepts school as a particularly rich data set to be mined for provisionally normative arguments and discursive dynamics; the same ought to hold for other sources of information about discursive dynamics. Even snapshots of a particular moment in the development of public discourse on a concept can be of use here, since all of the public discourse up to the moment of the snapshot contributed to the single set of constraints on possible arguments available in a particular context. Even survey research, suitably conducted so as to minimize paternalism, suggestion, false dichotomies, and the rest of survey research's well-known shortcomings, has something to contribute to this endeavor. There are, to repeat, two main reasons for provisional theory to examine discursive dynamics: first, to remedy democratic theory's baseline and preference aggregation problems while avoiding deliberative democratic theory's paternalism and its heroic assumptions about citizen capacity; and second, more generally, to identify patterns of institutions that promote rather than constrain discursive dynamics themselves. Toward these ends, I now turn to two studies of discursive dynamics: Reinhard Koselleck's history of the concept of emancipation and Jane Mansbridge and her colleagues' ongoing studies of everyday activism.

Koselleck on 'Emancipation'

I shall not attempt to summarize the accomplishments of the history of concepts school here.[43] Instead, I shall concentrate my efforts on one aspect of that literature: Koselleck's work on the concept of emancipation. Briefly, the second half of the twentieth century in Germany saw the publication of an enormous new work of collaborative history of concepts: the *Geschichtliche Grundbegriffe* (GG for short).[44] Werner Conze, Otto Brunner, Reinhard Koselleck, and a team of scholarly experts together produced a multivolume set of almost book-length articles describing the development of more than a hundred key concepts from social and political life. The GG is far more than a dictionary or philological work, however. Instead, in it scholars combine a focus on social and political history with attention to the history of concepts, analyzing the dynamic development of political concepts in relation to the social and political institutions which they describe and by which they were influenced. Moreover, GG articles begin with the idea that modernity entails both the acceleration and the increased influence of discursive dynamics.[45] Many of the concepts described go through intense transition during the so-called *Sattelzeit* period of about a hundred years beginning around 1750, with relatively little change either before or since.[46] A basic premise of this research is that the history of concepts has operated according to a different dynamic since the Enlightenment: now concepts are not merely collected from reality but are expected to drive and respond to a constantly changing political environment. New political terms create expectations about change rather than simply reflecting contemporary practices.[47] In fact, "the lower their content in terms of experience, the greater the expectations they created—this would be a short formula for the new type of political and historical contexts."[48] Koselleck concludes: "Political and social concepts become the navigational instruments of the changing movement of history. They do not only indicate or record given facts. They themselves become factors in the formation of consciousness and the control of behavior."[49]

By showing how various concepts shift their meanings over time,

Koselleck illustrates the dynamics of differing styles of political argument. In fact, as certain terms acquire new political meaning, old strategies of legitimation become, as it were, linguistically impossible. In a discussion of the establishment of French revolutionary political language in the context of emancipation generally, Koselleck argues, "In France, the platform of revolutionary language, victorious after 1789, rapidly and effectively rendered the privileges of the estates incapable of legitimation."[50] He traces the development of the concept of emancipation from its roots in the Roman practice of fathers releasing their sons from the household up to the as yet unrealized implications of present-day emancipatory practices.[51] Significantly, the concept undergoes its most important transformation during the transition to modernity. Whereas classical usage envisioned emancipation as an act performable by a master on some subservient person (a son, a slave, a servant, or a serf), as early as the fifteenth century a few writers were using the concept reflexively. Emancipation became something the dominated party could achieve unilaterally: "The following thesis may be ventured: with the introduction of the reflexive verb 'to emancipate oneself' (sich emanzipieren), a profound shift of mentality was, for the first time, foreshadowed and then brought about. While initially it was a word used by the cognoscenti, the poets and philosophers, who sought to liberate themselves from all pregivens and dependency, the new active word usage was expanded to increasingly refer to groups, institutions, and entire peoples. . . . Contained within the reflexive word usage was eo ipso a thrust against the estates system."[52]

After the conceptual change has become established, then, political actors find themselves operating in a changed space of linguistic constraint. They are always constrained, of course, but the constraints operate differently in different contexts. Once what Koselleck calls the "natural substratum" of the concept of emancipation—the idea that each generation naturally emancipates itself in the process of replacing the previous one—realizes itself in the reflexive verb 'to emancipate oneself', it becomes much harder to justify institutions that rest on the permanent minority of at least some human beings.[53]

Sometimes Koselleck's discussion of conceptual change in the case of 'emancipation' sounds like traditional history of concepts, free of the constraining contexts of social and political institutions. For example, he argues that once each of the concepts associated with the political enlightenment—not only emancipation but also reason, nature, and free will, for example—gained legitimacy, they reinforced each other.[54] Similarly, the political doctrine of emancipation seems much more inevitable to Koselleck once the traditions of Stoic and Christian innerworldliness have gone into decline.[55] Koselleck, however, repeatedly insists upon the importance of social and political conditions to conceptual change, and of concepts in turn to social and political conditions. He identifies the social classes and groups associated with particular arguments for emancipation, noting that the concept sometimes moved rather smoothly from the realm of the intelligentsia into common parlance, while at other times the groups using the term were far less successful. Koselleck's discussion of the "backlashes" suffered by African Americans, nineteenth-century British Catholics, and European Jews makes clear that even after a society grants legal authority to the concept of emancipation, "actual history has so far never linearly followed such a clear-cut program."[56] Koselleck insists that "social and economic conditions always come into play alongside arguments."[57]

Koselleck's account of British Catholics' fight for political rights is both illuminating and frustrating for my purposes in this chapter: "If one follows the history of the ratification of legal emancipation acts, one *first* observes that they are retarded again and again by backlashes. When the Catholics gained the right to run in elections in 1829 and thereby broke the political monopoly of the Anglican state religion, the British parliament, in the same act, raised the property qualification for suffrage from forty shillings to ten pounds. Because of this, the Catholics lost about 60 percent of the seats that they were expected to win. What had become absolutely necessary to concede on political grounds became largely undermined again by conditions of economic power."[58]

Koselleck is illustrating the constraining effect conceptual change has on what is politically possible. Restricted by developments in what it is possible to argue about legitimate restrictions on political freedom, the parliament cannot prevent a new, more inclusive legal posture from taking hold. Note that Koselleck emphasizes that conceptual change is driven by interested political groups (not philosophers or other scholars), and that social and political power differentials are affected by the change and exercise influence on the form it takes.

However, the example as narrated stands in frustrating tension with

Koselleck's earlier declaration that history is never linear. Koselleck's image of a series of backlashes on the way to the realization of emancipation's potential strikes one as frankly teleological. But Koselleck's subsequent remarks on emancipation's "four situative aporias" transforms the discursive dynamics of the concept of emancipation into a much more ambiguous, and also much more politically realistic, picture.[59] As Koselleck puts it, the discursive dynamics of emancipation in the realms of politics, society, religion, and economics do not run together but tend to block each other variably and unpredictably across contexts. "A legalization of emancipatory demands generates new problems that hinder their realization."[60] Particularly troubling for Koselleck here is that the individualistic thrust of emancipatory rights tends to undermine the "multitude of concrete units of action"; in other words, the inevitably communal and social context in which individuals realize their freedom. None of this, however, negates the original power of the reflexive concept of emancipation itself, which Koselleck finally suggests must be conceived as a "constant challenge."[61]

Mansbridge on Everyday Activists

In a series of works, Jane Mansbridge has described an ideal-typical pattern for the development and dispersion of political concepts.[62] Working between social movement studies and political philosophy, Mansbridge identifies conceptual innovations that emerge from protected enclaves of committed activists into the broader public sphere, where they make new kinds of political argument possible. Such concepts as 'homophobia' and 'male chauvinist' have successfully made this journey; other concepts, such as 'patriarchy' and 'white chauvinism,' have not.[63] The discursive dynamics of interaction among committed activists in enclaves and ordinary people deciding whether to apply concepts from the activist world represent one kind of reason-giving that should interest provisional theorists of democracy.

Mansbridge reports the results of survey research and focus groups on women's use of terms pioneered by feminist activists; she notes that ordinary women use the term 'male chauvinist' to defeat traditional justifications for exclusion.[64] Confronted with the defenders of practices that would unjustifiably limit their political possibilities, these "everyday activists" defeat the exclusionary argument by tarring it with the brush of chauvinism, then using the "logic of formal justice" to reach an egalitarian conclusion. Though the concept of chauvinism was developed in feminist and socialist enclaves, and survived what Mansbridge describes as a Darwinian process of variation in enclaves and selection in the public sphere, no special talent is needed to wield it successfully against everyday domination. In fact, argues Mansbridge, a term's selection will depend on how well it serves that purpose for the everyday activists who make it part of our political vocabulary. Though Mansbridge emphasizes the importance of political and social conditions for successful movements against domination, she argues that everyday activists tend to use "acts of persuasion more than acts of power" in their efforts to achieve equality.[65] The everyday activists do the real work of social movement just by listening and talking and thinking about new concepts: "Without much conscious reflection [they] adopt some ideas and discard others. This intellectual and emotional work of considering and sifting joins their front-line work of direct action in the home and workplace to make everyday activists in many cases the heart of a social movement."[66]

Discursive dynamics are important both inside and outside the social movements that Mansbridge studies. Discursive dynamics can develop under conditions much less demanding than those listed by Mansbridge as key to social movement success. Of particular interest here, however, is Mansbridge's emphasis on the development of oppositional concepts within protected enclaves: "Counter-hegemonic ideas are most likely to appear when subordinates in a system of domination can engage in interactions of high intensity, in settings with barriers that keep the outside out and the inside in, with incentives for experimentation and change, and with a lowered fear of punishment. Such 'safe spaces' usually produce both creativity and commitment."[67] Mansbridge does not romanticize enclaves; she recognizes that small group settings, while providing safe spaces for concept-building, also can have unpleasant group dynamics or serve as hothouses for pernicious ideologies.

Cass Sunstein also emphasizes the double nature of social enclaves as both spaces for discursive development and insulated arenas of group dysfunction. In *Why Societies Need Dissent*, Sunstein focuses on the negative dynamics of group decision-making. He identifies three kinds of problems suffered by groups (conformity, cascades, and group polarization), all of which lead to poor decisions that can be avoided if dissent is encouraged. Even so, Sunstein emphasizes that protected enclaves are a necessary element of an open society's public life: "It is desirable to create spaces for enclave deliberation, without insulating enclave members from those with opposing views and without insulating those outside of the enclave from the views of those within it."[68] For both Mansbridge and Sunstein, protected enclaves offer an important source of conceptual innovation to society.

Incidentally, Mansbridge's and Sunstein's recognition of the double nature of enclave deliberation dovetails nicely with provisional theory's insistence on the important of context. Theorists cannot come to any conclusive determination about the value of protected societal subgroups, even in a limited context such as Mansbridge's social movements or Sunstein's open society. Provisional theory evaluates institutions hypothetically, not categorically. In these cases, enclaves are simultaneously safe spaces for conceptual innovation and hothouses for the denial of individual human rights; both the place where innovation happens and the place where radically retrograde ideas can flourish. There are no conclusive answers to the status of groups and their rights claims.[69]

Mansbridge divides the discursive developmental process into two stages: variation, in which many concepts are developed by activists in enclaves; and selection, in which everyday activists, "translators" like intellectuals and journalists, and ordinary people make the countless decisions that determine whether a concept eventually constrains what may be argued in a given context. "The logic of formal justice, then, does political work through persuasion entwined with but analytically separable from acts of power defined as the threat of sanction or the use of force. Those acts of persuasion emanate . . . , in large part, from everyday activists, who take the variation in ideas that ordinary activists produce, select from those ideas, and use them to help create the change in everyday life that undermines the legitimacy of one normative order and replaces it with another."[70] Social and political institutions matter a great deal in Mansbridge's model, and she emphasizes the occasionally favorable historical conditions enjoyed by the women's movement in her work. However, for Mansbridge, "Although philosophical ideas never stand alone, uninfluenced by the material structure lying under them, they can have an independent force. Social scientists, comfortable with material, psychological, and even symbolic associations, often hesitate to acknowledge the causal force of philosophical logic. The logic of formal justice, I suggest, has an independent force parallel to the force of the logic '2 + 2 = 4.'"[71]

Mansbridge recognizes that powerful representatives of interested parties will try to promote or denigrate ideals that provide material advantages and disadvantages, but she argues that "material loss and gain do not fully explain adherence to or rejection of an idea. People are governed in part by their ideals, and they often want to act consistently."[72]

FROM CONCEPTUAL HISTORY AND EVERYDAY ACTIVISM TO DISCURSIVE DYNAMICS

What should a deliberative theorist conclude from this look into Koselleck's history of concepts approach and Mansbridge's work on everyday activism? This chapter's investigation has covered just one very narrow aspect of the discursive universe, since Mansbridge's and Koselleck's examples both involve emancipatory projects in the modern Western tradition. Even so, the work at hand suggests several broader conclusions. First, Koselleck and many other scholars from Kant to Mansbridge identify an ideal-typical path of conceptual innovation from what Mansbridge calls "enclaves of protected discourse and action" through co-optation by interested parties in political battles to norm-changing, widely accepted principles.[73] Since the conditions of conceptual innovation vary so greatly with their contexts, it is difficult to draw any generalizable conclusions about them; indeed, this is one of the reasons I hope scholars will heed Melvin Richter's call for "reanalysis" of the work done by the history of concepts school. However, whether the initial protected enclave is a Kantian literate public sphere or a Mansbridge-style identity community, or something else appropriate to its context, we can reasonably infer that the protection of such enclaves in general serves to promote conceptual innovation. Beyond the usual and not at all trivial protections of freedom of expression, we may encourage the proliferation of potentially disinterested communication (in the sense of freedom from immediate financial incentives, rather than in any strong liberal sense that would hinder the community identity that both Mansbridge and Young identify as an important source of conceptual innovation). Kant's favored mode of reason-giving, free expression of moral principle in the public sphere, depended on a particular set of contextually specific institutions in order to protect this enclave of discourse. The inhabitants of the "republic of letters," including the famous Prussian sympathizers for the French Revolution Kant describes in *Conflict of the Faculties,* make use of a network of coffeehouses, literary journals, pamphleteers, and even (Kant hoped) protection of intellectual property rights, without which their reason-giving in public would not be possible.[74] The particular set of institutions that protects enclaves of discourse varies by context; we can say generally, however, that provisional promotion of agency and plurality would be served by institutions that protect such *enclaves.*

A second possible generalization from these examples would be that actual political leverage on the part of diverse groups of citizens is essential for the second ideal-typical step in conceptual innovation—co-optation by participants in political conflicts of immediate interest. In Koselleck's example of the granting of political rights to British Catholics, conceptual change constrained political actors from resorting to outmoded arguments for exclusion, but this only set the stage for a series of conflicts in the aggregative and deliberative spheres. The specific institutional forms such political leverage takes cannot be theoretically specified outside relatively narrow contexts. In Kant's work, written as it was in the context of enlightened absolutism, the essential institutional safeguard of political leverage was the right of citizens to bring grievances before the throne.[75] Other contexts have different requirements. Robert Reich has argued that citizens in the contemporary United States have to achieve quite a high level of competence (the "symbolic analyst" level) before they can hope to exercise political leverage.[76] Similar arguments may be found in Jacob Hacker and Paul Pierson's and Theda Skocpol's recent work.[77] Regardless of the context in question, however, discursive dynamics direct the theorist's attention to institutions that increase *citizen capacity.*

Finally, Mansbridge's model of concept selection and Koselleck's description of the development of a reflexive concept of emancipation suggest that a context of institutional competition for legitimate authority, particularly situations in which political institutions' contestable purviews overlap, promotes conceptual innovation. Contexts in which conceptual innovation is dangerous are not necessarily deadly to the process. Kant, for example, celebrates the Prussian sympathizers with French emancipatory politics just because they participated in this discourse at substantial personal risk. A more serious threat to conceptual innovation than oppression, this inquiry suggests, is institutional monopoly. A single outlet for discursive dynamics, even a benevolent one, is likely to stifle rather than encourage conceptual innovation.[78] This preliminary lesson from the history of concepts literature is supported by deliberative democracy's insistence on provisional rather than conclusive theorizing, since the continued existence of *competing institutions* will tend to multiply rather than foreclose political possibilities.

Deliberative theorists may not approve of the kinds of conceptual innovation that these three generalizations—protected enclaves, citizen capacity, and overlapping authority—might promote in any given context. Conceptual innovation does not follow any deterministic path to some necessary set of political principles. This result does, however, reflect the essentially democratic values of respecting insiders' wisdom, inclusion, and opposition.[79] A theory that promotes these goals will not present conclusive solutions to political problems, but it should support a democratic theory capable of overcoming the traditional shortcomings of aggregative democracy.

TWO EXAMPLES FROM DEMOCRATIC PRACTICE

In this section I present two examples of proposals to improve on traditional aggregative outcomes, one based on mainstream deliberative principles, and the other from Ian Shapiro's democratic theory. In both instances, innovation is motivated by dissatisfaction with conventional outcomes in the present-day United States; both innovations are attempts to devise institutions that will supplement current aggregative procedures in order to bring the process in line with democratic values.

In a 2005 book chapter, Christopher Karpowitz and Jane Mansbridge describe the results of a well-meant exercise in deliberative democratic decision-making at the local level called Princeton Future.[80] In this case, local authorities faced a decision about providing parking, housing, and commercial and public space around a new public library. Rather than leave a question about downtown development to established aggregative institutions, community leaders arranged for a series of neighborhood meetings conducted according to explicitly deliberative democratic principles. The meetings were held in homes and churches, led by trained coordinators, and consisted mainly of discussion about citizens' visions for Princeton's development. Citizen comments were transcribed, and an effort was made to include previously excluded voices in the process. The leaders of Princeton Future submitted a development plan based on the consensus they extracted from these meetings to another round of citizen comments, and then to the borough council, which submitted it to a developer. After a series of negotiations with the developer, the Princeton Future leaders ultimately threw their support behind a modified plan (with less public space and more parking than originally called for). The venue for decision-making shifted to the aggregative space of the borough council meeting. After hearing hours of citizen testimony reflecting not consensus but deep, interest-based conflict, the borough council voted nonetheless to support the development proposal.[81]

This outcome should disappoint deliberative democrats. Particularly striking is the change in the tone of public input, from civic-minded inclusion in the early neighborhood meetings to angry expressions of opposition in the final borough council meeting. There and in the weeks leading up to the meeting, residents called not only the development decision but also the deliberative process into question. Karpowitz and Mansbridge quote one participant as follows: "We have a right to vote! Princeton Future did not allow for real give-and-take! Why won't you let the people vote?"[82] Karpowitz and Mansbridge emphasize that the Princeton Future process, aimed as it was at achieving consensus, necessarily failed to address the deep conflicts at issue. As they say, "Much seemed to hang on parking and taxes."[83] These conflicts were not resolved at the deliberative level, and they reemerged with a vengeance at the aggregative level. Confronted with the failure of this exercise in deliberation, Karpowitz and Mansbridge do not conclude that deliberative democracy is a dead end. Instead, they argue for what they call "dynamic updating" of the range of interests under discussion as a necessary part of any successful deliberative institution. Conflict cannot be wished away, and dynamic updating (a "process of discovery in which group members try to analyze the state of interests as they see them") is Karpowitz and Mansbridge's deliberative response to that fact of democratic life.[84] From a provisional point of view, dynamic updating would indeed provide one institutional mode of attacking the baseline problem, if not a perfect deliberative solution.

If we view the Princeton Future effort from the point of view of deliberative democracy's attempted amelioration of aggregative democracy's endemic flaws, the picture looks more bleak.[85] The obstacles to deliberative success in this case spring directly from the process's failure to address either baseline or preference aggregation problems. Karpowitz and Mansbridge indirectly gesture toward this issue in a graph they use to draw a contrast between the processes of deliberative meetings and council meetings.[86] On the horizontal axis, they arrange the processes from highly unitary (that is, consensus oriented) to highly adversarial, with the deliberative process being much more consensus oriented than the more adversarial council meeting. On the vertical axis, however, Karpowitz and Mansbridge distinguish between high and low levels of citizen control of the decision-making process. *Both* processes are ranked "low" on this scale. While "dynamic updating" within deliberative processes might keep them from eliding important conflictual decisions, it cannot increase the leverage exercised by citizens over the policy-making itself. Gutmann and Thompson's Oregon health care example exhibits this same pattern: a combination of deliberative and aggregative institutions allows a previously overlooked, interest-based conflict over resources to be addressed, but without affecting the aggregative baseline or the leverage ordinary citizens exert politically. In the Princeton Future case, deeper conflicts about patterns of residency (reflected in the parking/walking space trade-off) were never on the table; the agenda for deliberation did not reach the source of the conflict, which would have required it to challenge the status quo in power relations. Neither was the level of accountability enjoyed by the citizens changed by the process; the moment of greatest accountability takes place only after the decision is made, when borough council members stand for reelection. The project did aim to increase citizen capacity, but only from a relatively paternalistic point of view: the project's leadership hoped to "educate citizens, making them better decision-makers."[87]

The deliberative democrats associated with Princeton Future began with relatively specific ideas about what the eventual deliberatively legitimate outcome of the process might look like. Though they anticipated representative responses to underlying social injustices (such as including traditionally underrepresented groups in special sessions that partially satisfy our "enclave" condition), they did not expect those underlying issues to move onto the agenda, as they seemed about to do in the last borough council meeting. There was never any question about whether the basic proposal of library, parking, and commercial and residential development was an appropriate starting point for deliberation. Most of the anticipated citizen contributions were on questions of detail or degree (how much parking), or raised merely in terms of a sort of self-realization by expressive members of the community.

In sharp contrast to this relatively conclusive set of eventual outcomes in the Princeton Future deliberation, Ian Shapiro's proposal for a deliberative process to resolve conflicts over school vouchers leaves multifarious political possibilities open.[88] Shapiro begins his discussion of school voucher programs in the present-day United States with a refusal to foreclose any particular policy outcome. As is well known, school voucher programs provide public money in the form of vouchers distributed to individual parents to pay for private school for their children. Most of the voucher programs in operation at this writing operate on a small scale, usually in response to a perceived failure to provide basic education by the public schools. Proponents of vouchers sometimes argue that because some public schools fail to provide adequate education, those students should be offered alternative schooling regardless of ability to pay. Other provoucher arguments include the claim that competition for students will lead to higher educational quality for public and private schools. Some school voucher program funds go mainly to parochial school alternatives to failing public schools, while others target their vouchers differently. Opponents of voucher programs also make several types of argument. Some argue that this kind of public support for private, often parochial, education violates the constitutional separation of church and state. Others claim that the voucher programs, though defended in terms of economic justice, are essentially an inegalitarian attack on public education generally. Another common complaint about voucher programs is that it weakens the public schools without transferring any of their state-mandated burdens as schools of last resort, sources of special education, and the like, to the private sector.

Scholarly commentators have taken positions on many different sides of the debate around school vouchers, though the majority appear to oppose voucher programs in general. Shapiro, however, begins by refusing to proscribe voucher programs, or indeed to support any particular policy option. Instead, he proposes a deliberative process by which voucher supporters might legitimate their claims: "We might . . . replace proscription of voucher schemes in education with a solution in which parents of those who do not opt out of the public schools are given delay, appeal, or perhaps even veto rights, enabling them to insist on guarantees that promised benefits for their children's education do in fact eventuate. Those proposing voucher schemes would have to engage in deliberation with them, take account of their concerns, and persuade them that these concerns would be dealt with."[89]

Rather than making the conclusive determination that voucher schemes violate democratic principles, Shapiro imagines a deliberative mode in which citizens could decide for themselves. He does not, however, trust conventional aggregative democratic institutions to resolve the problem. Instead, Shapiro insists that reason-giving practices—in this case, justification by the would-be conceptual innovators that the scheme satisfies all affected interests—supplement existing democratic means. He further insists upon increased citizen leverage over these decisions, in the form of context-sensitive rights of "delay, appeal, or even veto," and on overlapping institutions for the vindication of the rights at stake. Rather than rely on a single institution (the courts, perhaps) to make a final determination of the justice of the voucher proposal, Shapiro argues that the degree of deliberative rights granted "would still require an independent judgment as to how seriously threatened the children's basic interests in fact were, but not an exogenous adjudication of the merits of the voucher scheme."[90]

Unlike the other deliberative projects discussed in this chapter, Shapiro's voucher scheme makes discursive dynamics an integral and ongoing part of the aggregation of interests in a democratic system. The usual pattern is to find democratic deficits in the aggregative conception, add a deliberative moment aimed at improving the reasonableness of the preferences expressed, perhaps applying deliberative standards of argument aimed at insuring that the process takes baseline as well as ordinarily generated political questions into account, and then revert to the aggregative democratic process. The deliberatively improved outcome is supposed to arise from an expected increase in rationality of the "inputs" (either more reasonable expressed preferences or a limit among policy options to those deemed rationally defensible). Shapiro departs from this pattern. The outcome is left undetermined: "Rather than have the government try to evaluate the merits of innovative funding schemes . . . it would use its power to make those who advocate them persuade those whose basic interests are most plausibly at stake."[91] The discursive dynamics that lead to conceptual innovation are encouraged by a process that increases the leverage exercised by citizens with affected interests, promotes insiders' wisdom rather than paternalistic determinate outcomes, and provides multiple institutional interests in the process in order to prevent any player from parlaying temporary advantage into discourse-suppressing dominance. Scholarly advocates of deliberative democracy may not like the outcomes of such deliberations, as they may result in more of the possibly unjust voucher schemes, or even in solutions as yet unimagined by theorists themselves. But this is of course the great strength of relying on discursive dynamics rather than conclusive theorizing: democratic decision-making remains in the hands of citizens themselves.

DISCURSIVE DYNAMICS AND PROVISIONAL DEMOCRATIC THEORY

I am not the first person to call for increased attention to be paid by political theorists to the history of concepts literature, and to discursive dynamics in general. Melvin Richter calls for an English-language research effort analogous to the GG.[92] Beyond the formal research effort that would result in an English-language encyclopedia of the history of political and social concepts, there has been a substantial volume of important work in the field of conceptual history generally and in discursive dynamics in particular.[93] Others have called for connecting the literature on the history of concepts to the understanding of particular traditions (Martin), modern crisis (Koselleck), the subversive elements of normative arguments (Palonen), or ecology (Ball).[94] For my part, it seems to me that attention to the long-run dynamics of political and moral discourse allows us to suggest patterns that might promote agency and plurality. Rather than hoping for short-run enlightenment to be brought about by deliberation and then translated into policy through ordinary aggregative institutions, deliberative democrats ought to promote institutions that require the application of discursive dynamics as they already exist to policy, and that promote the continued possibility of discursive dynamic political change.[95]

As I have mentioned, some suggestions for appropriate institutions in context have been already been made. In addition to Shapiro's call for deliberative schemes in the case of voucher initiatives, Gutmann and Thompson call for the expansion of the environmental impact report statement to a broad array of policy areas. Such an institution requires political actors to engage arguments made in the public sphere before, during, and after the ordinary processes of democratic decision-making. No policy for which discursively acceptable reasons cannot be given would, under this institutional regime, even reach the democratic arena. The arbiter of "discursively acceptable reasons," however, is not a political theorist or any other paternalist authority, but the democratic public sphere itself. Kant considered raising the philosophical faculty to the level of deliberative arbiter in his political work but ended up placing more emphasis on the long-run workings of the public sphere.[96] For would-be antipaternalists, this is the right choice.

Gutmann and Thompson continue, however, to rely on traditional aggregative institutions, especially to insure that decisions in conflict-ridden areas are eventually reached. As they say of the Oregon health care case, "Deliberative politics almost always has to be supplemented by other decision procedures—in the Oregon case by a recommendation of a commission and a vote by the legislature."[97] Deliberative procedures are essentially provisional, while democratic decision-making has to impose solutions to conflicts, at least in the short run (though a key element of decision-making that renders it democratic is its reversibility; see chapter 5). The criticisms of aggregative democracy as uncritical of the status quo and as naively accepting of expressed preferences that I mentioned at the outset of this chapter remain in force, even when aggregative institutions are supplemented with deliberative democratic ones. Gutmann and Thompson insist that democratic deliberation applies to the dynamic institutional settlement as well as to the policy process, and indeed this is part of an appropriate answer. However, my comparison of some different proposals in democratic deliberation should demonstrate that without adjustments in the expected timescale and in provisions of citizen capacity in both the deliberative and the aggregative sphere, deliberative democracy cannot live up to its promise.

Princeton Future, the Oregon health care debate, Deliberation Day, and most of the other recent experiments in democratic deliberation are strongest in their efforts to achieve more legitimate expression of genuine citizen preferences. Survey research, referenda, elections, and other traditional means of describing the "primary material for democratic decision-making" in the aggregative sense suffer from pathologies resulting in one or another characteristic distortion of the public will.[98] Many recent complaints about democratic theory, from critics as different as William Riker and Anne Norton, center around this basic fault of aggregative theory: it takes expressed preferences as transparent indicators of public will. Deliberative experiments are rightly attempting to resolve this problem. Unfortunately, thus far they have not succeeded. Even if DDay or citizen juries were to be instituted universally, the evidence from experiments thus far suggests that baseline problems and some problems of preference aggregation would remain.

Study of the history of political and social concepts, however, points us to a better approach. As in Koselleck's account of the career of the concept of emancipation, we should not expect the landscape of conceptual constraint to shift without some change in citizens' real political capacities. The language of emancipation helped move the British parliament to grant increased political rights to Catholics, rights which were effectively blocked by the exercise of political power until another generation of battles on behalf of emancipation was fought and won. My preliminary analysis of the discursive dynamics around the concept of emancipation suggests that protected enclaves, increased citizen capacity, and overlapping institutions all contribute to healthy discursive conditions.

Provisional democratic theory, while sympathetic to the deliberative goal of incorporating reason-giving practices into democratic politics, remains suspicious of any potentially paternalistic reform of conventional democratic procedure. While democratic values express themselves differently in each context, we would expect that only rarely would agency and plurality be subverted by an excess of popular participation. Rather than asking what the popular will ought to be, or what it might be under perfect circumstances, provisional democratic theory seeks to integrate the conditions of democratic agency and plurality into political practice itself. Institutions that tend to protect enclaves, enhance citizen capacity, and promote overlapping authority are provisionally likely candidates. Like Shapiro's voucher proposal, they may not lead immediately to policies that political theorists might find attractive. However, they are likely to provide bulwarks against domination and exclusion, which would in turn promote the conditions of future agency and plurality.

3

provisionality and property

Provisionalism should allow us to respect the ubiquitous role played by moral discourse in politics without mistakenly reifying particular principles. We should be able to recognize the power of ethical arguments when and where they matter, and to locate the conditions under which different kinds of arguments are more and less possible. In this chapter, I demonstrate this sort of provisionalist enterprise with regard to the crucial case of property rights.

Discussion of property rights among philosophers and political theorists tends to fall into one of two categories: either property rights are taken as self-evident natural rights and their consequences examined from that perspective, or property rights are exposed as the product of interested narratives and treated as illusory. Membership in one or the other category affects analysts' views of the relationship between property rights and the state. Advocates of natural property rights take the conventional contractarian view that the state exists to defend rights to life and property, and therefore that these rights take priority over other collective interests the state might represent. Opponents of natural property rights normally take the opposite position, namely, that the general will represented by the state is the condition of the vindication of any individual rights.

Provisionalism rejects both of these perspectives. Like all political principles, arguments for property rights are to be understood as context-sensitive claims for authority in a dynamic political environment. A conclusive claim about natural rights to property, then, can neither be vindicated nor be disproved across time, place, or policy area. Instead, the theorist must inquire hypothetically about the conditions of a principle's potential vindication in context. Taking the basic political values of agency and plurality for granted hypothetically, one can investigate whether an authoritative principle of property rights promotes or hinders their realization under a variety of particular conditions.

My provisionalist argument regarding property rights begins with Kant; Kant's principle of provisional right receives its most thorough treatment in connection with property rights and contract theory.[1] For Kant and for would-be modern contractarians, I show, property rights have no conclusive authority. However, Kant makes a number of strong arguments for the provisional recognition of property rights in context. One need not, I argue, claim a universal natural right to property in order to recognize the agency-promoting effects of such a principle in practice under a wide variety of important conditions.

In a way, the argument here boils down not to utilitarianism proper but to a kind of abstracted consequentialism: rights talk is never conclusively true, but it is often provisionally useful. That is, users of rights discourse in some contexts are better able to promote the conditions of agency and plurality than they would be without it. Consider my example from chapter 1 of the Inuit complaint against the United States for injuries due to global warming. In this instance there is little indigenous tradition of rights talk in the Western sense; it is reasonable to presume that some of the suppositions involved in a liberal rights regime would be found convincing to an audience composed of members of the Circumpolar Conference, while other suppositions would be dismissed. These considerations have not stopped Sheila Watt-Cloutier from claiming injury under the principles of human rights recognized by the Human Rights Commission of the Organization of American States. She is not cynically manipulating a foreign system in the service of interest; rather, she is making a perfectly legitimate political argument within the constraints of available discourse. By adopting the language of human rights, Watt-Cloutier accepts a number of serious constraints on her future argumentative stratagems; she does not, however, commit herself to the universal validity of the principles to whose authority she is appealing, she commits herself only to their application in this particular complex set of circumstances (a multinational group with limited sovereignty and few material resources seeks to redress injuries by a dominant group that recognizes the language of rights).

In this chapter, I begin with Kant's account of the provisional right to property. From a Kantian point of view, I criticize present-day contractarians who would reify seventeenth-century justifications of property rights, making property a universal natural right rather than a conditional right. One can hold contractarian values, under provisionalism, without asserting any strong natural right to property. Remembering Kant's strong advocacy of the provisional respect for property, however, I turn to the conditions under which respect for individual property rights might serve agency and plurality. Based on the results of chapter 2, I imagine conditions under which respect for property rights serves agency and plurality by protecting enclaves, encouraging overlapping authority, and increasing citizen leverage.

I then turn to a tough case for conventional rights discourse: the problem of "property grabbing" in parts of late twentieth and early twenty-first century Kenya. I describe an ongoing conflict between the international human rights perspective, which views the seizure of family property upon the death of a male head of household by his relatives as a violation of women's and children's basic rights of property and inheritance, and the customary law perspective, which recognizes no such rights. As we shall see, even the narrow slice of reality presented in this chapter, which excludes non-Kenyan and most other historical elements of property grabbing, is extremely complicated in its details. These details turn out to be highly significant, as the simple dichotomy between global human rights and local custom fails to do justice to the empirical situation of multiple histories and overlapping sources of authority. To anticipate the conclusions of this case study, I end up arguing that even though no conclusive defense of property rights can be given, strong provisional arguments for respecting property can be made across quite a stunning variety of contexts. This is so, I argue, because of some of the basic political dynamics that provisional analysis can reveal. Reified conditions of property holding, converted to conclusive policies and applied without attention to context, tend to limit political possibilities. On the other hand, property rights discourse, wielded provisionally in the service of agency and plurality, can be a powerful weapon against domination.

KANTIAN CONTRACTARIANISM AND THE PROVISIONAL
RIGHT TO PROPERTY

Contemporary contractarians tend to fall into the first category of scholars I described earlier in this chapter, those who take a natural property
right as given. In defending conventional social contract theory in the
present day, they face a difficult commonsense question: How can political authority derive from contract theory's frankly hypothetical, ahistorical description of prepolitical human agents agreeing to leave the state of
nature and submit to government? Frustration with contract theory's
failure to answer this question has led some theorists to dismiss it as "fic-
tion" or to attempt to go "beyond the social contract" with an alternative
approach.[2] I, however, argue that these criticisms reach only the minimalist type of social contract theory, not the provisional contractarianism
advocated by Kant and his successors.[3]

Both normative and empirical scholars of politics have mistakenly
identified social contract theory with minimalist contractarianism.[4] Students of democratic politics often presume that minimalist values such as
a prepolitical right to property represent uncontroversial contractarian
principles. Social and political theorists, making the same presumption
about the status of the minimalist view, argue against its uncritical acceptance. Students of democratic politics tend to presume contractarian
values because they are widely held and popular in practice; critics of
contractarian thought argue that these same values are ahistorical and
incoherent. Paradoxically, both sides are right. The contractarian values
undergirding present-day democracy are indeed broadly accepted, but
they are not the values defended by contemporary minimalist contractarians. Political theorists have rightly criticized minimalist views of property "as just one more installment in a tradition inherited from Locke of
mystifying anachronism."[5] In identifying contract theory generally with
the minimalist version of it, scholars of politics mistakenly focus on the
conditions of consent, rather than the *principle* itself. Moreover, since the
conditions of genuine consent change over time and space, the values
commonly associated with contractarianism in the literature have grown
increasingly irrelevant to arguments about democratic governance today.

By adhering to a seventeenth-century model of civil society, in which
individuals independently endowed with property and with the capacity

to exercise political judgment contract together to found the state, minimalist social contract theory fails to realize the fundamental contractarian value that legitimate rule is by the consent of the governed.[6] As Kant recognizes in his work on provisional right, vindicating such a principle in the dynamic political world requires an ever-changing set of institutions aimed at adjusting political reality in the direction of its ideals. It does not make sense, then, to identify contractarianism proper with certain seventeenth-century views on the necessary preconditions of genuine consent. The social contract idea remains the basis of contemporary democratic politics; particular theories of property rights have continuing relevance only insofar as they promote contractarian freedom under prevailing social circumstances.

I shall argue that Kant's revisionist contractarianism improves upon conventional minimalist social contract theory by giving a dynamic account of property rights while retaining contract theory's attractive commitments to agency and plurality. Kant's account of the provisional right to property addresses the traditional complaint about contract theory's unempirical commitment to an imaginary "baseline" status quo.[7] Moreover, Kant's approach to thinking about legitimate institutions as a series of provisional efforts to improve imperfect political reality while maintaining the conditions of the possibility of progress provides a model for politics that is both more realistic and closer to contractarian essential principles than the minimalist view. Our provisional view departs from Kant's teleological presumptions about progress, while retaining his moral yardstick for political principles in context: paraphrasing Kant, we shall seek the conditions of possible political vindications of agency and plurality.

Minimalist Contractarianism

A provisional understanding of contract theory demonstrates that minimalist bias toward a baseline status quo is not an essential element of the contractarian argument (any more than it is essential to democratic theory, as I discussed in chapter 2). Kantian provisionalism denies what minimalist contractarians like David Gauthier assert, that prepolitical circumstances take normative priority over political will. The logic of contract theory, with its central ideal that legitimate government rests on the consent of the governed, does not entail any single, conclusive system of property rights. Seventeenth-century English landholders brought very different capabilities to the political table than twenty-first-century wage laborers do, and a minimalist contractarianism vindicating the autonomy of the former may end up denying the freedom of the latter. Sophisticated contract theory has always been hypothetical rather than historical, asking about the legitimation of current government rather than justifying it according to any real agreement among distant ancestors.[8] But some contexts require more hypothetical distance than others. In the context of the English civil wars, talk of choosing to suspend the exercise of some natural rights in return for common security was at least plausible; the choice between life with or without a state was also relatively close to the reality of periods of lawlessness and frequent, violent, changes of regime. In the rich democracies these days, the hypothetical choice to submit to state sovereignty rather than remain a free agent with full exercise of one's natural rights seems far less plausible. Wealth and other resources, even developed natural talents, that a supposed free agent might bring to the contractarian bargaining table all depend in one way or another on the stability and environment guaranteed by the state.

Must we conclude that since all social goods are made possible by the order guaranteed by the state, collective priorities as assigned by the sovereign trump all other concerns? Certainly not.[9] Instead of reasoning from the hypothetical example of the transition from the state of nature, which has never been more than a highly useful mode of illustration for the logic of contractarianism, we ought to reason from the social contract's most basic commitment: legitimate rule is by consent. Rule by consent is a provisional principle, and the conditions of its even partial satisfaction vary according to the political context. In present-day rich democracies, the conditions of citizen self-rule are more demanding than ever. Today's minimalist contractarians recognize this fact, but they draw the wrong conclusion. Gauthier argues, for example, that only relatively enabled citizens capable of exchanging benefits with their fellows (and this criterion excludes the severely disabled, among others) ought to be parties to the social contract that legitimates government.[10] But modern citizens do not assemble a package of enabling conditions under prepolitical circumstances. Instead, the development of citizen capacity occurs in a dynamic institutional setting in which state and nonstate actors respond to broad sets of incentives set by the marketplace, government regulation, and historical conditions. The distribution of citizen capacities in any given context is the product of political negotiations as well as social and economic conditions, not to mention countless decisions made by individuals with differing levels of interest in self-development.[11] Since citizen capacity is an essential condition of contractarian consent, contractarian theory cannot simply presume that agents bring such capabilities to the political arena under all possible social circumstances.

Recognizing that the imperatives of the state-of-nature hypothesis conflict with those of the demand for government by consent, Gauthier chooses the former: "A nonarbitrary society must improve on the natural outcome for everyone."[12] Gauthier's declaration of principle emphasizes the minimalist presumption in favor of the status quo in property rights, as well as a counterfactual baseline state of nature. But note that despite Gauthier's explicit decision to accord priority to property rights, the more fundamental value presumed in this sentence is that of "nonarbitrary society." Gauthier recognizes that the human aspiration to transcend arbitrariness is what I would call a provisional goal; of course every social condition contains arbitrary, unjust, morally irrelevant elements. However, like all social contract theorists, Gauthier is ultimately committed to an ideal of human freedom. Perfect freedom is impossible, but freedom as an ideal is not only possible but also necessary for Gauthier and for contractarian thought of all stripes. Gauthier rightly prioritizes freedom, but wrongly identifies it with the state-of-nature hypothesis rather than the more fundamental ideal of government by consent.

For Gauthier, a free citizen is someone of whom one can say that it is in his rational interest to be a member of the state that has authority over him (this is the exit-from-the-state-of-nature test, which I call the "minimalist test"). Gauthier knows that real citizens are not offered such a choice, but he argues that legitimate government must be one that ideal citizens would freely choose to join. He uses a rich definition of freedom that includes a Kantian dimension of moral autonomy, explicitly rejecting what he calls "Hobbesian or anarchistic interaction, in which each may pursue his greatest benefit without concern for the effects of this pursuit on others."[13] Gauthier's choice of the minimalist, join-it-or-leave-it test, however, cannot do justice to his notion of freedom in any but the simplest of counterfactual contexts. In fact, the demands of the kind of political freedom that would make government by consent at least a provisional reality require modern contractarians to reject the conclusions that minimalists draw from the state-of-nature hypothesis, including especially their account of property rights.

Provisional Property Rights

Recall that for Kant, provisional right is the right that applies in real-world civil societies (6:257; 410). An early version of this view appears in *Toward Perpetual Peace,* where, as we have seen, Kant argues for a standard that takes the consequences of policy changes into account. In determining whether a policy ought to be tolerated, such a view considers not only the policy's moral status (conformity with the moral law) but also the likelihood of its contributing toward the establishment of peace and justice more generally (8:343–47; 317–321). Similarly, in his discussion of property in the section on private right in the *Rechtslehre,* Kant distinguishes between provisional and conclusive rights, and in the process distinguishes himself from his predecessors in social contract theory. "*Conclusive* acquisition takes place only in the civil condition," whereas provisional acquisition takes place "under the idea" of civil right (6:264; 416). Provisional possession for Kant is possession in the absence of a rightful civil condition. All existing societies fall into this category: their people are not in a state of nature, but they do not enjoy a just legal system as sketched in Kant's image of the ideal republic. Thus property rights in these intermediate societies, which include all real ones, are always provisional.

Private right, for Kant, is "the sum of laws that do not need to be promulgated." That is, private right exists without actual legislation; a people need not even be constituted as such before private right comes into play. By this, however, Kant does not mean to agree with minimalist contract theorists that private right prevails in a state of nature. The contrary is the case: though private right comes into force without explicit legislation on the part of any body, by its very nature it implies the existence of a state of civil order (6:210; 368–369; 6:256–257; 409–411). Katrin Flikschuh, in a brilliant analysis of a much-misunderstood passage, explains the differences between Locke and Kant on property and the state of nature: "In fact, Kant faults the Lockean view on two counts: first, in thinking that property rights denote a direct relation between subject and object; and, second, in assuming that a unilateral act of empirical acquisition (such as the act of investing one's labour in the object) can establish a rightful claim."[14] Kant insists that there can be no rights to things as such; rights for Kant are one kind of relation among persons: "Speaking strictly and literally, there is . . . no (direct) right to a thing" (6:261; 414). All such relations, if they are to honor the only natural right, which is to autonomy (6:237; 393), must be based not on a unilateral but a general will (and unilateral here of course includes any number of wills less than the whole); by their very existence property rights presume the republican state, at least provisionally.

While for Locke property rights are established as soon as one's labor has been mixed with natural resources, for Kant the necessity of property's possibility implies a condition in which mutual obligations to respect each other's autonomy prevails.[15] These rights of persons against each other are one practical application of Kant's universal principle of right: "Any action is right if it can coexist with everyone's freedom in accordance with a universal law, or if on its maxim the freedom of choice of each can coexist with everyone's freedom in accordance with a universal law" (6:230; 387). Kant claims to have deduced the possibility of property rights from this principle conclusively, a claim that has not withstood the test of time.[16] However, what matters for my purposes here is that Kantian property rights are, first, based on relations among persons rather than between persons and things, and, second, divided between provisional and conclusive rights.

For Kant, the only natural right is the right to autonomy (6:237; 393). Why, then, would he begin his account of political obligation with the contractarian story of the prepolitical establishment of at least provisional rights to private property? The answer must lie in the physical conditions of pragmatic autonomy, though of course an argument from abstract principle such as that given in the main text of the *Rechtslehre* cannot begin from such "anthropological" premises. As Robert Paul Wolff has argued regarding this passage, human beings must appropriate objects from nature in order to sustain themselves.[17] If, the argument goes, autonomy is to be practicable, some independent access to our means of sustenance is necessary for us. Some form of private property, then, must be possible for potentially autonomous agents.

Note that in this case private property is justified as a condition of possible human agency. Minimalist contractarians, by contrast, take private property as a part of what contracting agents bring to the prepolitical bargaining table.[18] Property on this minimalist account is a constitutive element of personhood. Not so for Kant. Even though elsewhere he makes a robust pragmatic case for respecting property rights through political transitions, he does not make the case for any fundamental right to property. Kant's direct argument on the subject, the failed deduction, only deduces the necessity of the possibility of property rights. Instead, for Kant property rights ought to be respected provisionally because such respect serves other, more fundamental interests, including especially an interest in political stability.

In the minimalist contractarian story, independent rational agents form a society and authorize a government in order to protect their lives and property. Government by consent in this account *follows from* the conditions of the exit from the state of nature (what Gauthier calls departures from the natural outcome). Kant's contract theory reverses these values. Agents must enter into mutually enforceable and mutually agreed-upon contracts in order to vindicate their natural right of autonomy, that is, of being free from determination by another's choice. No agreement, even one to respect property, can be prior to this fundamental agreement for Kant. However, since even outside established society and rule of law human beings will need to appropriate objects in order to survive, Kant grants provisionally rightful status to property held in the absence of the just state. Thus for Kant the conditions under which agents would rationally exchange their natural freedom for the security of government are relatively unimportant; what matters are the conditions under which government by consent is at least provisionally possible (and these conditions may well include some form of property rights). Provisional property rights thus *follow from* Kant's natural right of autonomy and its principle that legitimate government is by consent.

Kant introduces the problem of property rights thus: "It is possible to have something external as one's own only in a rightful condition, under an authority giving laws publicly, that is, in a civil condition" (6:255; 409). Kant has already argued that ownership of property must be possible; now he sets out the distinction between natural and positive rights, arguing that the only natural right is to one's freedom (in the sense of autonomy outlined earlier: freedom from others making choices for one) (6:237–238; 393–394). Kant argues that for property and personal autonomy to coexist, no one should have to acknowledge anyone else's property without guarantees that his own property will be acknowledged in exchange. To do so would be to violate the only natural right, since the one unilaterally acknowledging others' property will have to rely on the others' presumed good will for the security of his own property (and will thus enter a condition of heteronomy) (6:255–256; 409–410; 6:307; 452). Since for Kant only a "collective general (common) and powerful will" can provide the guarantees necessary for this property rights regime to exist, a "unilateral will" (any will less than general) cannot command anyone's obedience without infringing on autonomy. Potentially interacting persons, then, must submit themselves to a common source of authority for the validation of their reciprocal natural right (6:256; 409–410).

Unlike minimalist contractarians, Kant holds that property rights do not precede the advent of the state. He admits the necessary possibility of private property generally but argues that the assertion of property rights under heteronomous conditions amounts to an illegitimate, unilateral fiat. Rather than denying the possibility of just property holding outside (an unreachable) state of republican perfection, however, Kant introduces the concept of provisionality: "In a state of nature something external can actually be mine or yours but only *provisionally.* . . . Possession in anticipation of and preparation for the civil condition, which can be based only on a law of common will, possession which therefore accords with the *possibility* of such a condition, is *provisionally rightful* possession, whereas possession found in an *actual* civil condition would be *conclusive* possession" (6:256–257; 410).

For Kant, an actual civil condition requires the general will to be realized; in the *Rechtslehre,* "Theory and Practice," and elsewhere, Kant sketches the demanding conditions required of any polity wishing to conform to ideal republican standards. All existing states fall short of these ideals, though Kant argues that by their very claims to provide order they implicitly recognize the standards' normative authority. Since all existing states fall between prepolitical chaos and ideal republican governance, provisional right is the rule that applies to them (6:264; 416).

Thus Kant's contractarianism places first priority on the demand for autonomous consent and only grants secondary status to private property as a condition of civil society's acceptance of government. Kant does call for the status quo in property rights to be respected during political transition, but not in the name of any original legitimacy. Instead, he refers to a general societal interest in reformist rather than revolutionary transitions. In a significant departure from conventional contract theory, Kant denies the legitimacy of violent revolution, arguing from the principle of provisional right to the effect that quick rather than gradual transitions actually undermine rather than promote the possibility of eventual good government. The problem of revocable contracts is a thorny one for contractarians, particularly for Hobbes, but Kant sets it aside almost too easily. That he can do so demonstrates that the language of the exit from the state of nature is less important to Kant than the principles underlying the social contract in the first place.

Kant's argument for respecting the status quo in private property thus rests on the empirical hypothesis that the moral interest at stake (everyone's interest in living under some stable order, even one only on the way to justice) would be best served by a policy of provisional respect. *The claim is in principle falsifiable* and subject to different answers at different times and places.[19] A Kantian contractarianism takes no conclusive stand on property rights; instead, property is accorded provisional respect as circumstances demand.

CIRCUMSTANCES UNDER WHICH PROPERTY RIGHTS DISCOURSE PROMOTES AGENCY AND PLURALITY

It is simple enough to come up with examples of the reification of property rights that have had pernicious effects for agency and plurality. United States Supreme Court doctrine before the New Deal, for example, prevented the state from remedying some of the inegalitarian and collectively unproductive circumstances to which it had itself contributed. A return to *Lochner*-era reasoning about property right in the present day could have dire consequences for such collective goods as breathable air and drinkable water.[20] However, the ease with which these examples multiply should not lead us to make conclusive arguments against property rights in general, either. Provisional theory leads us to expect the validity of property rights discourse to vary according to the historical, geographical, and policy context in question. Kant, for example, though he regarded respect for property as a provisional rather than a conclusive principle, argued for strong respect for property rights over the course of political transition. The instability that would result from a general uncertainty regarding property rights would undermine the stability on which the vindication of right as such depends. As we saw in the last section, this is an empirical hypothesis; it may or may not be true under different circumstances that respect for property rights promotes the conditions of agency and plurality. Under many circumstances, strong property rights could increase citizen leverage, promote protected enclaves, and encourage overlapping institutions. (We cannot say for certain that these three patterns of politics necessarily promote agency and plurality, but we saw in chapter 2 that they are promising options.) Kant's intuitions about the conditions of autonomous citizenship, for example, which I discuss in more detail in chapter 4, lead him to argue that only those with access to significant property rights could enjoy the social independence that he sees as the basis of "civil personality." In other words, without independent control over the means of one's economic survival, a citizen would be unable to make substantively autonomous decisions as a member of the sovereign people in a republic. Kant recognizes that real citizens are always in fact interdependent, but he argues that a certain minimum of economic autonomy provides a baseline for civil personality. These considerations constitute one of many possible arguments for the provisional respect for property rights in context, not as conclusive rights that spring from the very nature of human existence but as conditional goods that promote agency and plurality under particular circumstances.

Thus it is plausible that under many circumstances, respect for property rights increases citizen *agency*, both against the state and against nongovernmental potential sources of domination. When a citizen can marshal resources for the vindication of her rights without having to appeal to some other authority, we can say that her personal agency has been enhanced. This dynamic becomes clearer if one considers cases in which property rights are not respected that lead to reduced citizen leverage. If one relies on political authority for direct access to the means of survival, that authority is likely to be able to exact obedience. Take the example of states requiring ration cards for the purpose of purchasing basic foodstuffs: these tend to be democracies in wartime or authoritarian states, which are essentially in a state of war all of the time. A shift from ration cards to a free market in food, so long as military defeat or massive shortages do not dominate the political context, would almost certainly mean enhancement of citizen leverage and personal agency, at least in relation to the state. As I discuss in the next chapter, Kant recognized this when he argued that free market rather than personalistic economic relations were a condition of political agency.

Respect for property may also provide a condition of possibility for civic *plurality* in many contexts. In Kenya, for example, a group of women have successfully defended their right to inhabit a female-only village ("Umoja," or "unity") safe from harassment and threats from local men; within this rare experiment, feminist leaders like founder Rebecca Lolosoli are able to encourage discourses of empowerment and consciousness-raising for local women, along the lines described in chapter 2's account of protected enclaves. [21] Without ownership of this safe space and their independent means of survival (they run an information center for tourists, among other enterprises), the women of Umoja village would be unable to sustain their relatively radical group identity. To take a different example, in South Korea recent court rulings have enabled traditionally excluded women to gain access to clan property, allowing them to pluralize the formerly all-male domain of clan ritual and economic activity. [22] To consider a final example, in the quasi-pluralist world of present-day politics in the United States the commitment of individually held property to the cause of a marginal point of view frequently makes the difference between obscurity and success in the public sphere. [23]

For Kant, provisional respect for property rights undergirds the stability that is a condition of gradual transition toward the just state. Thus, while Kant refuses to recognize property rights categorically, we can say that for him provisional property rights are a condition of expanded political possibilities. These few examples give us some justification in saying, in a Kantian tone, that though property rights are not conclusive, there are many contexts in which we can say that, provisionally, property rights promote agency and plurality.

Thus far I have been discussing the various results with regard to agency and plurality of respect for property generally. But what about the kind of individualistic, liberal, conventionally Western property rights regimes that present-day international institutions tend to encourage? Provisionalism is generally suspicious of attempts to transfer political institutions across contexts, since such efforts usually mistake the particular conditions of principles' vindication in context for the general principles themselves. The history of efforts by the United States and other rich democracies at the end of the twentieth century to mold postcommunist societies into copies of themselves is not a pretty one; by the turn of the century, most scholars and policy-makers realized that simple provision of Western institutions to postcommunist societies would have few of the intended consequences. The miserable record of American "nation-building" in Haiti, Somalia, Iraq, and Afghanistan contrasts painfully with the successes of postwar Japan and Germany, reminding us that changing contexts provide different conditions for the vindication of similar principles like democracy and development. This line of thought might lead us to dismiss attempts to inculcate such particular practices as individualistic property rights regimes into societies where they have not developed through local public discourse.

Though there are indeed good reasons to be suspicious of the attempt, I shall argue that dismissiveness is also an inappropriate attitude, for one obvious reason: in the present-day context of globalization, both of trade and, more important, of ideas and information, contexts are more interconnected, affecting each other more directly than they used to do. Tracing the patterns of moral-political constraint on public discourse is even more complicated in an era of global information transmission than it was before. Demonstration effects may come from neighbors, hearsay about more distant fellow citizens, vague and inaccurate yet powerful impressions transmitted by popular media, and any number of other sources. In short, while we should not forget the intricate and particular conditions underlying any application of the principle of a human right to property, neither should we expect property rights discourse to remain the isolated inheritance of a few geographically isolated and materially privileged groups.

Instead, general considerations in favor of provisional respect for property rights may well prevail under a large number of very different circumstances. Even though, as we saw earlier in this chapter, conclusive concepts of property rights tend to undermine the conditions for agency and plurality, explicitly provisional respect for property rights need not have the same pernicious effects. Furthermore, given the global influence that bearers of a particular version of individualistic property rights regimes wield today, adoption of this rather than another more local version may be more discursively attractive than it might have been in a more isolated context. As I discuss in the next section of this chapter, the Kenyan adoption of Western discourses of property and human rights has certainly had some counterproductive and sometimes unintended consequences, but it is by no means the least attractive option for those wishing to promote agency and plurality in that context. Although the conclusive discourse of property rights itself, especially when made by Western agencies, can ring self-serving and even plainly false, its judicious and provisional use in a context of Western dominance might be the best choice available.

THE CASE OF WOMEN'S PROPERTY RIGHTS IN KENYA

Like other avid newspaper readers, I became interested in the case of Kenyan property grabbing after reading heart-rending anecdotes about widows and orphans subjected to cruel torment at the hands of their own relatives. Though the stories came from across southern and eastern Africa, the basic narrative rarely changed. A married woman has lost her husband to AIDS; though she and her husband worked together to support the family, upon his death members of his clan swoop down and confiscate the family's belongings, leaving the woman with the clothes on her back and no means of supporting her children. In some cases, the woman has refused to be "inherited" by her deceased husband's brother or other close relative; in others, clan members take the opportunity of a woman's period of mourning to invade her property, driving her off the homestead and back, perhaps, to her natal home. The first story I read on the topic described a woman who had run a bicycle repair shop with her husband; after his death, relatives claimed all of the shop's stock and equipment as clan property, leaving the woman with no means of survival or support for her children.[24]

The practice of disinheriting wives unless they remarry within the clan, where it was prevalent, seemed to be getting more attention because the AIDS pandemic was producing unprecedented numbers of widows, particularly young ones with small children. International human rights groups as well as local nongovernmental organizations were calling for action to stop these outrageous violations of women's property rights. There were already any number of other crises affecting small farmers, pastoralists, and others in southern and eastern Africa—including chronic poverty, market barriers and even the near collapse of markets for many of their products, ineffective government, land and food shortages, persistent plagues like malaria, not to mention the accelerating disaster of HIV/AIDS. Thus this additional, apparently preventable injustice affecting women's property rights provided a compelling cause for Western activism. The global rights organization Human Rights Watch (HRW) issued a series of letters documenting Kenya's lack of compliance with its international obligations regarding women's property rights, culminating in a report issued in 2003. In the run-up to Kenya's failed constitutional referendum of November 2005, HRW released a letter to the Human Rights Committee of the United Nations directly proposing specific constitutional reforms.[25]

When I first became aware of the problem of property grabbing, it seemed to me to be a relatively straightforward conflict between modern, international human rights regimes and the individualistic property rights that go with them, on the one hand, and customary, local practices and the clan-based property rights that they protect, on the other. Perhaps, I theorized, there is a necessary trade-off in this case: protection of the culturally unique indigenous property regime might depend on denial of at least some of the internationally recognized human rights of local women. This certainly seemed to be the view taken by Janet Walsh, author of the very widely cited HRW report "Double Standards: Women's Property Rights in Kenya."[26] In an interview, Walsh said that her organization "believes in upholding customs that are beneficial," but also that "it is important that the customs that undermine women's rights be reformed . . . as an obligation under human rights law."[27] Walsh's report includes so many specific and sweeping policy recommendations aiming to establish in present-day Kenya the practices and protections enjoyed by citizens of rich democracies that I wondered whether the overall message was less "stop violating rights" than "modernize, now." More seriously, I noted that the HRW report does not raise the possibility that institutionalizing the conditions of the vindication of women's property rights in Kenya might have serious unintended consequences for other aspects of Kenyan economic and political life. Of course, these ancillary consequences are ambiguous. Most of the scholarly work on women's property rights in Kenya emphasizes the association between tenure insecurity and persistent underdevelopment.[28] On the other hand, as Ayelet Shachar has argued, there are often resources with which women may oppose injustice available within their identity communities, such that a sacrifice of cultural identity in the name of equal rights should not be necessary.[29] The question of unintended consequences remained an open one. At any rate, it seemed to me at first that HRW and other well-meaning opponents of women's rights violations in Kenya were overlooking the potential costs in terms of economic and cultural self-determination that would have to be paid in order to institute these kinds of rights from without.

As it happened, however, the actual conflict was not nearly this simple. The clan-based economy that supposedly rested on women's subordination as regards property turned out (a) to have been inaccurately codified (to the detriment of women's interests) under the collaboration of interested local elders and colonial authorities, (b) to vary not only by microlocation and over time but even according to individual perspective, and most significantly for our purposes, (c) not to be viable over the medium term anyway, since it was declining due to pressures independent of women's rights.[30] I had thought that the price of the vindication of women's rights to property in this case would be the destruction of a clan-based, nonliberal economic regime incompatible with dominant international norms. As so often happens, reality turned theory's predictions on their heads, since no viable alternative to individual property rights regimes as imposed by international institutions *was* in fact dependent on women's subordination. As we shall see, the real conflict was not a struggle between two contending modes of economic life but competition among various groups for control of property and the life that goes with it; each of the players in these conflicts used arguments that served a particular interest while being constrained in a shifting context of acceptability that included customary, rights-based, and other kinds of principle. Economic conditions in Kenya at the turn of the twenty-first century may not have conformed to market ideals (they lacked, among other things, adequate titling and registration of property, and fluid markets in land), but they were moving away from clan-based tenure toward some barely predictable hybrid of formal and informal rights.[31]

As I have already argued in this chapter, provisional theory cannot provide a conclusive set of principles regarding property rights in general. Kant defended provisional property rights not for their own sake but insofar as they promoted other important goals, including the stability that Kant believed to be the essential underpinning of any civic right, and the social autonomy that Kant believed active citizenship required. In the case of property grabbing in present-day Kenya, the empirical conditions that allow provisional theory to make judgments about whether particular principles promote agency and plurality are changing so rapidly and unpredictably that it is quite difficult to say anything about a policy's likely results. What provisional theory can do in this case, however, is identify thinking that is likely to be in error, and suggest intermediate policy goals that are more likely than others to succeed.

The Human Rights Watch Report on Women's Property Rights Violations

The 2003 HRW report "Double Standards: Women's Property Rights Violations in Kenya"[32] and the associated HRW campaign garnered worldwide attention for the problems facing women in Kenya and elsewhere in the region. News stories featured women who had been chased off their land by greedy in-laws after the deaths of their husbands from AIDS, and usually included lurid details of coercive and dangerous customs such as the "ritual cleansing" of widows by their having unprotected sex with a social outcast. Kenyan officialdom, relatively responsive to international pressure in the years immediately following the election of Mwai Kibaki, moved to address domestic and international demands by offering some of the requested reforms as part of a draft constitutional revision. Whether the proposed revisions were sufficient is now a moot point, since the referendum failed; 57 percent of the voters made the "orange," or "no," choice, while only 43 percent of the voters selected the "banana" to support the new draft constitution.[33] Despite its reputation at the time as an unusually successful new democracy, Kenya in 2003 was facing widespread hunger, poverty, chronic corruption, underdevelopment, the HIV/AIDS pandemic, relatively high economic inequality, and rising violence, even in rural areas.[34] Against this bewildering backdrop of frustration and persistent misery, the HRW campaign found an easily identifiable target of moral criticism: violations of women's rights to property.

"Double Standards" does not pretend to be a scholarly study, though it is sometimes cited as if it were such. The researchers conducted 130 interviews in Kenya in October and November 2002, speaking to members of different ethnic groups, to victims of property rights violations, and to

Kenyan and international officials and civic leaders. As the authors of another study sponsored by the Food and Agriculture Organization of the United Nations point out, the HRW researchers reported people's impressions of the problem rather than confining themselves to reports from those who had direct experience; also, the HRW report does not cover those who are not affected, and thus it provides little guidance as to the magnitude of the problem.[35] "Double Standards," however, successfully raised the profile of women's property violations as a human rights problem with which the international community should be concerned. In addition to dramatizing the problem with a series of narratives, the report provides clear arguments against current practices on the basis of internationally recognized human rights principles. In the months following the release of the report, major U.S. newspapers covered the story, and other human rights organizations joined the call to end practices such as "wife inheritance" (that is, the forced marriage of a widow to a close relative of her deceased husband).[36] Two years later, in a response to Kenya's second periodic report on compliance with the International Covenant on Civil and Political Rights, the United Nations Human Rights Committee specifically raised the problems of land insecurity for women, the practice of wife inheritance, and continuing inequality and discrimination against women as regards property and inheritance.[37]

In its report, HRW argues that women's property rights are subject to widespread violation in Kenya, and that in addition to these direct injustices, women's property rights violations have other pernicious effects for the general welfare, including contributing to chronic underdevelopment and perpetuating the HIV/AIDS crisis. The report describes a variety of unjust practices across many different cultural and physical contexts, all of which are rooted attitudes that treat women as minors incapable of handling property. These attitudes, as reported by HRW, range from stark descriptions of wives as property to more subtle evocations of male responsibility for their female relatives. Many of the respondents describe a loosening of customary practices in which women had traditional expectations of usage rights to land and livestock, if not rights of disposal, and also expectations that customary practices would see to their basic needs and those of their families. However, in the HRW examples, traditional arguments about women's status tend to be made in order to expropriate vulnerable women's property without taking on traditional duties, as might be expected. For example, a victim might report that traditionally women do not anticipate inheriting any property from their fathers, because their husbands' families are expected to provide them with land. In the event of a husband's early death, a woman might be obliged to undergo some sort of ritual cleansing and then be "inherited" by a male relative of her dead husband; as reported, this tradition was intended to provide for the dead man's family without weakening the clan holdings. Though they were justified with reference to customary arguments, the practices reported by victims in the HRW reports tended to harm the interests of wives, widows, and children, even their very modestly represented interests as clan dependents. The report is full of such stories, in which traditional discourses are used to justify nontraditional or semitraditional practices: of women whose in-laws claim that customary wedding practices were not followed, in order to justify grabbing a widow's family property; of brothers-in-law seizing property and even children from widows with the argument that women do not inherit, and without making provision for the family; of widows agreeing to be "inherited" only to be chased off their land soon afterward; and many other stories. Some victims interviewed by HRW do not agree that they have rights that have been violated; many make the standard argument that women do not inherit because they will be given land by their husbands' families, though their own situations and some (the HRW report does not say how many) examples of property grabbing belie this. Other victims question current practices, though they may not feel that they can oppose them openly.

Both the stolid traditionalists and the tentative radicals among the HRW interviewees agree that current conditions have weakened the customary system; the traditionalists complain about children out of wedlock and immorality undermining the traditional tenure system, while the radicals note that those with money and connections seem to be able to use the mixed system to vindicate their interests without regard for customary mores. The report documents the enormous barriers facing any woman seeking to defend her property rights, beginning with the social stigma associated with any woman's complaint, proceeding through unsympathetic or corrupt local officials, to the high cost, slow pace, and contradictory principles of the formal legal system.[38] In sum, the report argues, "When women in Kenya are forced out of their homes, stripped of their belongings, and coerced into risky sexual behaviors in order to keep their property simply because they are women, and when the government does little to prevent and redress this, they are not just experiencing 'culture.' They are experiencing human rights violations."[39]

Though the report generally makes a simple distinction between sexist "culture" and principled human rights, it does recognize that innovations in the colonial and postcolonial periods damaged customary practice's existing, if paternalistic, protections for women and children. The process of granting individualized land titles to traditionally held lands, for example, formalized men's rights of disposal while ignoring women's traditional usage rights. Overall, however, the HRW report makes a straightforward case for modernization in the name of women's property rights. Among its recommendations are the repeal of Kenya's traditional deference to customary (and, where applicable, Islamic) law where such deference is discriminatory.[40] (Kenya has in fact committed itself in several instances to the vindication of the rights of women: it is a signatory of the International Covenant on Civil and Political Rights, and its own laws call for gender equality. Along with this commitment to human rights and gender equality, however, the Kenyan system enshrines respect for customary law; in many of the areas affected by property grabbing against widows, modern law in Kenya defers to local custom.) [41] Other HRW recommendations include: revision of Kenya's constitutional and statutory law where it discriminates, including especially enforcing a presumption of joint title;[42] registration of all marriages; criminalizing spousal rape; an end to dowry requirements as part of marriage where they exist; prosecuting harmful practices like ritual cleansing and forced wife inheritance; and finally a laundry list of useful institutions for the vindication of women's rights in general, including women's sections in ministries, a network of battered women's shelters, and so forth.[43]

The HRW report's assessment of the situation regarding women's property rights in Kenya, though narrated outside the bounds of scholarly restraint and defended with mostly anecdotal evidence, is confirmed by a number of other, more rigorous studies.[44] Although property grabbing was probably a less pervasive problem that one might conclude from the HRW report, it certainly has been a problem in parts of Kenya. Moreover, women's general insecurity in their property, and the discriminatory conditions underlying that insecurity, are universally acknowledged in the scholarly and advocacy literatures.[45] The efforts of advocacy groups like Human Rights Watch and Amnesty International can be enormously helpful in applying widely felt moral principles to public policy.[46]

What, then, is troubling about the HRW report? Provisional theory leads us to suspicion of the following aspects of the report: its application of conclusive principles across contexts; its reification of context-dependent conditions of principles' vindication, such that the conditions are stated as principles themselves; the paternalism the report shows toward the Kenyan victims of these practices; and finally, the very narrow focus that allows HRW to make such strong and successful campaigns against particular rights violations breaks down in the policy stage, where these social, political, and economic contexts are inextricably linked. The result is that the HRW report, though, as I have said, correct in the main and admirable in achieving publicity and leverage against rights violators, nevertheless repeats the errors of its colonial-era predecessors by imposing a set of one-size-fits-all policy solutions from a resolutely supralocal perspective.

Provisional and Conclusive Arguments for Women's Property Rights in Kenya

The conflicts over land documented in the property-grabbing cases are the products of a complex history that a simple culture-versus-modernity stance cannot capture. Moreover, the policies that enable women in some contexts to use property rights to vindicate their agency and plurality will be different from policies that enable them in others. Rather than seeking to identify, as the HRW report does, *which* specific institutions are missing from the Kenyan setting, we should ask *how* different institutions tended to operate in these different contexts.

Though traditional land tenure in Kenya varied by region and by type of land use (agricultural, pastoralist, or commercial/urban), it did not conform to the conventional contractarian notion of property right described earlier in this chapter. Different rights of usage were assigned to different people in relation to the land and livestock.[47] For example, in traditional Maasai culture, men were said, even by women, to "own" all the cattle, but women were accorded the right to milk those cattle that were considered "theirs."[48] In smallholding agricultural areas, women were only rarely considered landowners, but they often had strong claims of usage and access to particular plots according to their relationships as wives of clan members, as mothers holding land in trust for their sons, or sometimes as unmarried daughters.[49] The men's rights to property were also constrained by communal ties; their right to dispose of their property was highly restricted and often directly regulated by traditional authorities.[50]

If these traditional landholding patterns had remained intact throughout the colonial and postcolonial period, then my initial argument about the vindication of women's rights coming at the price of an indigenous way of economic life might have been defensible. However, actions of the colonial and postcolonial governments, as well as interactions between locals and the global market, have weakened these traditional forms of landholding so greatly that they survive only piecemeal, most merely resonating as still-authoritative arguments without having much impact on reality. For example, one of the men interviewed by HRW argues that women must always leave their land after a divorce, since they are dwelling on "ancestral land." Remembering, perhaps (the HRW report doesn't say), that since colonial-era settlers moved Kenyans off of the majority of their "ancestral land" in order to give it to European farmers, hardly anyone can be said to inhabit such land, the man added that even if Kenyans don't live on ancestral land, regardless of whose land it really is, the woman ought to be the one to leave.[51] Traditional discursive stratagems, then, have outlived their bases in social practice.

A series of Kenyan regimes has engaged in policies aimed at a transition from informal clan holdings to formal individualized land tenure. One consequence of these registration efforts has been to make women's customary secondary rights to property legally invisible.[52] Even though the formal land registration system is incomplete, and lags behind the informal economy as people avoid the costs associated with registration, the Western norm of individualized landholding is nonetheless very widely recognized.[53] Women seeking to vindicate their property rights attempt to get or to hang on to titles; in-laws and others seeking to prevent women's security in land tenure deliberately seize, withhold, or destroy title documents and registration numbers. In places where collective landholding is in place, either in relatively traditional form like pastoralists' ranches or in alternative cooperative ventures like Umoja women's village, those with the authority to allocate land for individual use exercise extraordinary power.[54]

Consider, then, the policy of requiring individual registration of land parcels so as to grant absolute title to property owners (while providing states with the cadastral maps and individualized records they need for taxation and other purposes).[55] Viewed over the long term, the history of land titling in Kenya provides a sort of provisionalist case study in cross-context policy-making. At least officially, land registration grants conventional, conclusive rights to the titleholder; under the Registered Land Act, Section 27a: "The registration of a person as the proprietor of land shall vest in that person the absolute ownership of that land together with all rights and privileges belonging or appurtenant thereto."[56] The statutory regime exists alongside the officially recognized traditional systems of property holding, none of whose norms are consistent with this kind of conclusive and unified right to property; across rural Kenya, Land Control Boards, elders, chiefs, and other authorities limit the ability of title-holders to dispose of their property without the consent of others (family members, clan members, or other interested parties). This contradiction does not undermine the importance of the formal regime of land titling. One study concludes that, "notwithstanding the common perception that the statutory tenure system is superfluous in an area where customary tenure norms are so strong, it is clear that the functioning of the state's land administration system is in fact of enormous importance. . . . Unfortunately, the importance of the system is mainly honoured in the breach; people recognise the importance of the formal systems, but struggle to access them or complain that they have been corrupted to their disadvantage."[57]

The aims of the colonial and postcolonial titling efforts included encouraging rural productivity, developing a market orientation among local producers, and making agricultural and pastoral society more transparent and accessible to state authorities. Periodic, scattered registration drives have had some success, but they have inexorably deviated from what minimal accuracy they achieved at first, once informal subdivisions and transfers begin to take place without official notice. Rural Kenya is certainly moving toward individualized land tenure, but the values that the individualized property regime is realizing in the Kenyan context are different from those that colonial and postcolonial administrators expected. For example, increased subdivision, formal and informal, rather than the hoped-for larger, economically viable plot sizes, has been the pattern. To take another example, though in some cases access to land titles has allowed small farmers to get the credit they need for expensive, productivity-enhancing inputs like fertilizers and farm equipment, as Western property rights advocates would expect, the barriers to land sales remain enormous. Informal barriers like the prospect of destitution should one lose all of one's land, customary barriers like community members' unwillingness to allow sales deemed inappropriate, and formal barriers like high transaction costs have made the market in land far less fluid than expected.[58] One study by political scientist Esther Mwangi emphasizes the perverse incentives provided by a system that includes individualized land tenure distributed with little oversight or accountability by political authorities: "The move to private, individualized land holdings, that have been so important in the economic development of the West is fraught with problems that could undermine the potential economic gains that had been hoped for."[59]

Interestingly, the HRW report argues for just the kind of single system of registration and enforcement that, in its colonial and immediate postcolonial incarnations, deprived Kenyan women of defensible secondary rights to their property. Though it is far from perfect, the Kenyan system of multiple and overlapping authorities has served as a residual buffer protecting rural and pastoral women from the stark results of conventional contractarian property rights.[60] Given that titles are overwhelmingly held by men, those women who are able to enforce their rights to consent to any sale, or to vindicate their customary usage rights, are better off than they would be in a modern and internally coherent legal system that would offer no channels of use besides registered ownership.[61] In fact, were it enforced in a nondiscriminatory way, the current Kenyan mixed system, in which titles are held but transfers and usage are often adjudicated at the community level might well survive provisionalist scrutiny. The mixed system, ideally, could function as an enabler of citizen leverage (neither the state nor your neighbors can exert undue influence over you if you have independent access to property) while serving the collective interest in stability (though would-be dominant parties cannot expropriate your property, you have to justify your potentially unproductive or unfair use of it to the community). One might describe an idealized version of Kenyan Land Control Boards, which are often sexist and corrupt, but which do sometimes vindicate women's rights by refusing to allow sale of family property without consent, for example, as a sort of deliberative institution. Just as we saw in the case of Ian Shapiro's proposal for deciding about school vouchers (in chapter 2), such Land Control Boards would recognize a potentially legitimate interest but require the would-be exerciser of that interest to satisfy all affected parties before pursuing it. It appears that HRW is acknowledging this dynamic when it recommends requiring family consent for land transfers, in principled contradiction to its other recommendations tending toward individualized, formally titled ownership with specific policies for property division in cases of death or divorce.[62]

Provisional analysis suggests that the focus, by rights groups and other opponents of women's property rights violations, on the central state as the defender of rights may be misplaced. There is nothing wrong in principle with supporting progressive constitutional reform, to be sure. However, in proposing reforms that strengthen the central state, such as formal registration of all marriages, constitutional reform, and networks of offices to enforce constitutional norms, HRW is seeking paternalistic protection from above for women victims, rather than seeking to empower them to vindicate their rights themselves. The history of central reforms in Kenya should give pause to anyone expecting that the next reform will benefit women. The results of national land distribution did not, as was hoped, provide much benefit to ordinary Kenyans but instead contributed to Kenya's rank as one of the most inegalitarian societies in Africa.[63] Of course, women would benefit from access to the resources that could be made available by a possibly progressive central state. But we should be cautious about expecting a new bearer of paternalistic authority to be any more effective or any more benign than the last one.[64] The basic problem with the HRW perspective is that it reifies a particular set of conditions of agency and plurality, associating modernization efforts and absolute tenure with the vindication of right. The question from the perspective of HRW should not be: How can we persuade the giver of political rights to favor us this time? Rather, it should be: What changes will make the vindication of our desired rights more likely? Provisional theory suggests that citizens empowered to vindicate their rights under multiple possible institutional auspices are more likely to succeed than those to whom abstract rights are granted and guaranteed by a paternalistic central authority alone.

The land registration process has, up to now, mostly failed to vindicate women's formal property rights, all the while depriving them of legal recognition of their traditional secondary rights. Titles, when they matter, are held by men; adjudication processes outside formal titles occasionally vindicate women's rights, but arbitrarily, and without providing the benefits that security in land tenure can offer.[65] Customary law no longer reliably provides local paternalistic protection, while formal legal remedies are systematically discriminatory and also mostly unavailable. Provisional theory asks, What conditions are likely to promote agency and plurality in this context? Will defense of overlapping authority, protected enclaves, and citizen leverage work to redress the domination and denial of difference that affect Kenyan women today? What value does a discourse of a human right to property have for women who seem to have suffered great injustice, but most of whom do not recognize anything like a women's right to secure tenure in property?

These provisionalist questions can help us suggest conditions for the vindication of principles in context, but they cannot often lead us to the concrete policies themselves. The question of overlapping institutions is a good case in point. The present-day Kenyan system is a perfect example of overlapping institutions in practice. The formal, relatively modern, central constitution relies on internationally recognized principles of government (and would have done so even better had the reforms of 2005 passed). However, the constitution makes provision for many different legal systems to hold sway in their cultural spheres of influence, if they are not "repugnant to any written law."[66] Kenyans seeking political redress may choose among formal and informal, central and local, customary and modern sources of authority. This undoubted context of overlapping authority has certainly not led to the widespread vindication of women's property rights at this writing. Even so, provisional theory asks not whether overlapping institutions produce a particularly attractive policy outcome (that is for citizens to decide) but whether overlapping institutions have provided favorable conditions for political possibilities that vindicate agency and plurality. Whether this will promote women's property rights will depend over the longer term on whether arguments can be made in these competing locations that move the whole system closer to

women's equality. A reduction in the number of available arenas of argumentative contestation would mean fewer possible places for innovation
to succeed, and thus a greater chance that a few failures would constrict
political possibility.[67] Therefore, even though informal, often patriarchal
local authorities seem to represent a bulwark against women's progress
from the HRW perspective, and even though a central state susceptible to
the "boomerang effects" of international advocacy groups would seem
the most likely candidate for progressive reform, provisionalist analysis
suggests that these customary forums should be maintained in their diversity if women's agency and plurality are to have the greatest chance of
vindication. One African feminist editorial writer, for example, argues
that even though customary law is often patriarchal, it is also dynamic;
she adds that criminalizing it would be counterproductive since it would
likely just drive it underground.[68] The HRW report's modernizing and
centralizing suggestions could have the unintended consequence of reducing the number of possible arenas for women's success. Since no
political institution can be expected to remain static, no victory at the
national level, however helpful, can be considered conclusive. The maintenance of multiple venues for the vindication of right ought to enhance
the conditions of possibility for agency and plurality for Kenyan women.

In fact, part of the reason for the failure of the government's constitutional reforms was popular suspicion of their centralizing tendencies.
Inegalitarian policies, with their reduction of the numbers of those
with the means of active political participation (agency) and the concomitant reduction in the range of views expressed (plurality), also tend
to constrain rather than enhance political possibility. Class and ethnicity
based suspicions around the constitutional reform would have been well
grounded in history. Unfortunately, the events of 2007 (in which political
and opportunistic violence followed an election widely perceived to have
been rigged) seem to bear these suspicions out.

Individualized property rights, though their distribution has been
characterized by serious injustice, also provide some protection against
future attempts at domination. In the case of one group with a long history of grievances against the central government, the Maasai pastoralists, opportunities to hold absolute titles are sometimes seen "as a defen-
sive strategy against appropriation by the state, and from politically
privileged individuals both within and without the Maasai commu-

nity."[69] The ability to defend private property has also, as previously re-marked, been essential to the women of Umoja village, whose unusual ex-periment in protecting women from violence depends on their security in land tenure. In these and other protected enclaves, Kenya's nascent women's movement can develop the discourses, strategies, and human resources necessary to accomplish the very hard work of effecting social change.

T. H. Marshall, in his account of the development of rights in Great Britain, and Reinhard Koselleck, whose work on emancipation I dis-cussed in chapter 2, both rightly emphasize that the development of new political discourses must be accompanied by social organization and hard-fought political battles.[70] Though the context here is different, the dynamic is similar. We cannot expect legal change on its own to effect substantial change in women's experience of property rights. For that, a home-grown Kenyan women's movement, communicating with but not relying on international rights groups, will be necessary. Such a move-ment already exists, though it is relatively small; protection of the enclaves where women can safely pursue their social movement is a vital condition of the possibility of political change. There is hardly any mention of the women's movement in the HRW report, which treats women as victims rather than potentially empowered citizens. However, some of the HRW report's recommendations, though they seem simply to import Western institutions, actually would make significant contributions in the Kenyan context; laws making it possible for women to support their families without submission to male relatives, for example, would serve this pur-pose.

The rural and pastoral people of Kenya are facing the same kinds of problems faced by all farmers and herders making a transition from tra-ditional to individualized landholding in a market economy. Any student of development history will recognize the social pressures accompanying the commercialization of agriculture, including both excessive subdivi-sion and brutal consolidation of plots;[71] displacement of rural people to the cities (ironically, both as the result of excessive subdivision, since mar-ket labor is required to supplement too small a farm income, and as the result of plot consolidation); new sources of instability resulting from de-pendence on a volatile market for goods; and physical changes to the land itself due to exposure to market forces. The question, then, is not one of a conflict between tradition and modernity. Kenyan property practices are neither wholly traditional nor entirely modern; there is no viable clan-based alternative economic system that might defy Western, individualized land tenure norms. Instead, there is now a collection of practices and ad hoc arrangements, many of which are only slightly constrained by the rule of law.[72] Some of the practices opposed by HRW, such as "wife inheritance" and "ritual cleansing," are indeed traditional, though any economic justifications that existed for them are diminishing. Others, such as property grabbing by in-laws or disposal of common property without consent, are actually innovative responses to present-day conditions defended by a creative mix of customary and modern arguments.

Taking the long view in this case leads us to understand process of transition in Kenyan land tenure a little better. Old systems of protections for the vulnerable are being swept away; no reliable new system in which they should be able to vindicate their own rights is in place. The personal histories in the HRW report reminded me of Theodore Dreiser's novels and Karl Polanyi's historical sociology: they depict the terrible effects of transitional social forces on individually vulnerable people. But this long view, if it is to be accurate, must take into account the role that principled political and moral arguments will play in effecting the changes that will either vindicate or bury women's property rights in some future order. Despite the fact that rights discourse is accorded little popular legitimacy in rural Kenya, the provisional theorist ought to inquire whether its adoption is likely to promote or to constrain the kinds of political possibility that will promote agency and plurality. The Kenyans themselves will invent the institutions and practices that eventually realize some mix of these possibilities.

4

citizenship and provisional right

In this chapter, I argue that a provisionalist point of view supports the revision of currently prevailing views of citizenship away from the idea of citizenship as status and toward the idea of citizenship as standing. I draw an analogy between the judicial processes for establishing a person's standing to enforce legal rights (the person must have a sufficient and protectable interest in the case) and a possible policy-based alternative to traditional geographically, culturally, or genetically based citizenship. Though they constitute an interesting empirical set of observations for a provisional theory of citizenship, nonnational voting rights cases do not overcome the basic dilemmas associated with territoriality and political rights. Pragmatic considerations may require provisional respect for territoriality, but the ultimate source of democratic legitimacy for contemporary political institutions must be the principle of affected interest rather than any updated republicanism or other naturalized source of identity.

The argument proceeds in three steps. First, I read a few key passages from Kant's political writings that together present a puzzle about citizenship in the context of provisional right. For Kant, citizenship rights are not absolute but context-based institutions that serve to promote the conditions of human freedom. Next, I examine contemporary discourses around citizenship; these analyses reveal the necessary incoherence of conclusive arguments about citizenship, and the realism and moral weight of provisional citizenship discourse. Finally, I argue for a system in which citizens' capacities for self-rule are determined by the citizens' stake in the policy itself, rather than in morally arbitrary geographic or other membership groups. Half a century ago, T. H. Marshall demonstrated one path the development of citizenship rights could take, with his historical analysis of the case of Great Britain; Marshall made clear that as each new form of citizenship rights policy becomes reality, it makes other forms of citizenship possible. Similarly, provisionalism looks at citizenship rights in terms of what political possibilities they open or foreclose. For example, as Kant argues, a citizen's right to rule of law and the stability that accompanies it grounds the possibility of the realization of other rights. Other theorists have argued for the disaggregation of citizenship rights to accommodate identity politics or the reality of global interdependence. Provisional theory, however, sees citizenship rights not as principles in themselves to be justified and variously realized but instead as the conditional means of promoting political principles like agency and plurality. Viewing them in this light, one does not ask: Which is the appropriate group denominating the exercise of citizenship rights? Rather, one asks: How in a given context may the rights and duties of citizenship promote agency and plurality? I argue that these contexts vary not only over time and space but over policy area as well, and that citizenship policy ought to respond to that variation.

The possibility of distributing rights of decision based on standing rather than geography is not only less utopian than it sounds, it also represents a solution to the tensions inherent in conclusive theories of citizenship. Prevailing conclusive arguments about citizenship are caught between two unattractive alternatives: either they are based on moral principles that empirical conditions inevitably degrade, or they espouse a historicist realism that undermines any principled claim citizenship might make. Provisional arguments about citizenship, by contrast, allow us to recognize compelling moral arguments without ignoring the real politics of membership.

KANT ON CITIZENSHIP

There are three key passages in Kant's political writings on citizenship: the distinction between active and passive citizenship (from the *Metaphysics of Morals;* 6:314–315; 457–459); the argument from the *globus terraqueus* (6:352–355; 489–492); and the case for cosmopolitan right (in *Toward Perpetual Peace,* 8:357–360; 328–331; also in the *Metaphysics of Morals*).

Kant's view of the importance of political stability as an enabling condition for political right in general is also relevant here. While there is very little disagreement among commentators about the relevance of these three passages, there is deep disagreement about how to read them.[1] I shall not survey the literature on Kant's cosmopolitanism here; nor shall I attempt a full-fledged interpretation of Kant's views on citizenship, cosmopolitan or otherwise. Rather, I would like to introduce the problem of citizenship and provisionality with a look at what Kant had to say on the matter.

In the *Rechtslehre,* Kant famously and wrongly sets out a distinction between active and passive citizens, consigning a large portion of society to mere civil rights while limiting positive political participation to a minority.[2] I am not interested in defending this position. What matters about it for my purposes, however, is that Kant's awkward distinction reveals his awareness of a critical problem in making his version of contract theory coherent. As I argued in chapter 3, Kantian contractarianism prioritizes the basic principle of government by consent over any set of presumed natural rights to property carried over from prepolitical existence. Such a theory places great demands on citizens as autonomous self-legislators. Making good on the ideal of autonomous consent is no easy task. Minimalist contract theorists such as Gauthier seek to limit reciprocal political obligation to those "enabled" to exchange fruitfully with their fellows (this follows from their emphasis on the conditions of a hypothetical exit from nature). Other students of politics have described citizenship as an ongoing series of battles for rights (Marshall), or have sought to limit democratic citizenship to those societies predisposed to it (Huntington) or developed enough to handle it (Mill).[3] Kant, then, is certainly not alone in seeking to address the problem of the high demands of contractarian citizenship through exclusion. However, the democratic implications of his moral presumptions and the dynamic nature of his provisional theory of politics make it much harder for Kant than for other theorists coherently to maintain exclusion as his solution to this problem. As I shall demonstrate, the resulting tensions in Kant's writing on citizenship point in the direction of a Kantian contractarianism that rejects exclusion and thus more fully embraces its commitment to the bedrock principle of citizen consent.

At *Rechtslehre* 6:314–315 (457–459), Kant makes his notorious distinction between active and passive citizenship, arguing that full citizens must be free, equal, and independent. In order to satisfy the criterion of independence, citizens must have what he calls "civil personality." He illustrates his distinction with a series of contrasts between citizens able to support themselves and those who are somehow dependent on others for their livelihoods, including among others women, apprentices, domestic servants, and day laborers. This distinction has been widely and rightly criticized as illiberal and undemocratic. However, in order to understand how provisional contractarians address the problem of citizen capacity (what Robert Sugden and other minimalists call the problem of "reciprocity"), we need to grasp the reasons motivating Kant's view.

Kant's distinction between active and passive citizenship occurs in the empirical remark that follows his description of the third key attribute of the citizen considered as legislator in an ideal republic: civil independence.[4] Kant explains in the general argument preceding the remark that this civil independence of the citizen means "owing his existence and preservation to his own rights and powers as a member of the commonwealth, not to the choice of another among the people. From his independence follows his civil personality, his attribute of not needing to be represented by another where his rights are concerned" (6:314; 458). Kant knows that he is outlining an ideal standard that can never be met in practice. Real citizens are enmeshed in webs of interdependent relationships, just as real states are begun when someone seizes supreme power and establishes order (6:372; 505–506; see also 6:323; 465). What matters is that citizens, considered as legislators, must be accorded the respect that would accompany such a feat of civil independence; they must be treated as if they are independent civil personalities. Perfect liberty, equality, and independence are not to be had even among self-legislating human beings. Nevertheless, their converse qualities of servitude, inequality, and dependence threaten the authority of the citizen-legislators. Rather than concluding that would-be free people must either undergo deep social and psychological transformation in preparation for self-rule or accept tyranny as their lot, Kant makes an argument from provisional right. Promote the possibility of progress toward ideal citizen-legislators with the counterfactual presumption of their liberty, equality, and independence, Kant implies, and one will have powerful arguments to wield when servitude, inequality, and dependence threaten the legislators of the republic.

Now all this is very nice in theory, but in practice Kant actually followed this general, *a priori* passage with an empirical discussion of just which citizens might actually qualify as legitimate possessors of civil personality. He argues that "an apprentice . . . a domestic servant . . . a minor [in natural or, even more, in civil minority] . . . all women, and, in general, anyone whose preservation in existence (his being fed and protected) depends not on his management of his own business but on arrangements made by another (except the state). All these people lack civil personality" (6:314; 458). In perhaps his most telling example, Kant contrasts the Indian and the European styles of blacksmith work: the Indian blacksmith carries his tools to his customers, and thus lacks, for Kant, independence, while the European blacksmith works in his shop and sells his goods on the market, and thus possesses, for Kant, the requisite civil personality. With the benefit of many years' hindsight, we are able to say to Kant that embeddedness in market rather than premodern personalistic economic relations is no guarantee of civil personality.

But what was Kant trying to achieve with his blatantly "anthropological" point about the social roots of civic standing? He argues that freedom, equality, and independence are the qualities that will lead to the best achievable political judgment on the part of human legislators.[5] With his distinction among members of society and their qualifications for full civil personality, Kant is trying to establish authoritative political judgment by the only available means: the partial, limited human beings that he famously compares to "crooked timber." Critics of Kant who complain about his unrealistic expectations for abstraction and universalization on the part of ordinary reasoners should consider this part of Kant's political work. Here he seeks to approximate authoritative political judgment by excluding what he considers to be the *social* sources of corrupt judgment: servitude, inequality, and dependence.

Kant recognizes the demands of morality regarding citizenship, but he does not believe that the institutions available are up to the task of providing even provisionally independent citizenship to all members of society. He admits that "the concept of a passive citizen seems to contradict the concept of a citizen as such" (6:314; 458). However, Kant's commitment to providing a dynamic theory of politics in the provisional mode prevents him from simply condemning his unworthy contemporaries or from revising the strictures of the moral law in the direction of realism.

Instead, Kant insists on the primacy of the moral law in generating political legitimacy, at the same time imagining transitional institutions that would be the best socially possible approximation of the moral law's criteria while promoting the possibility of getting closer to those goals. With regard to citizenship qualifications, Kant tries to identify those among his contemporaries most likely to behave as if they enjoyed fully independent civil personality. Recall that Kant is writing from the northeastern hinterlands of eighteenth-century Prussia; when he compares Indian with European handworkers, he is encouraging his fellow citizens of Königsberg to identify with the European model, not describing an accomplished economic transition. Kant's views on the connection between civil personality and market rather than personalized economic relations were typical of enlightened thinking of his era. However, his case for the provisional exclusion of passive citizens from a role in legislation contains none of the usual arguments; he does not fear mob rule, essentialize second-class status, or seek to empower a natural aristocracy. Kant's worry about participation by those in positions of dependence has to do instead with the institutional barriers against free, equal, and independent judgment faced by such people. Far ahead of his time, Kant recognizes the "private roots of public action."[6] True, there are echoes here of the classical democratic conception of the demos as a collection of independent heads of household, with their status as tyrants in their domestic spheres guaranteeing independence in their public roles as citizen legislators. But, as is often the case, Kant is right on the cusp of a modern conception of politics. Unlike either Rousseau or Jefferson, Kant did not expect a reordering of society to undergird the autonomy required of modern citizen legislators. This autonomy would have to remain an authoritative if unreachable *ideal* toward which citizens strive and by which they judge each other.

An advantage of Kant's provisionalism as opposed to Rousseauian and Jeffersonian radicalism is that in Kant's system, citizen self-rule does not presuppose but proceeds concurrently with progressive societal transformation. For pragmatic purposes, Kant could not imagine universal citizen self-rule applied to his society. The gap between the idea of autonomy and the reality of near-feudal economic and social relations was too wide. But rather than build a closed society of self-legislators on the foundation of permanent exclusion, and furthermore given that no really ex-

isting citizen meets the criteria for full civic personality in practice anyway, Kant suggests two means for approximating the ideal of universal
civic autonomy. First, he requires genuine social mobility: "Anyone can
work his way up from this passive condition to an active one" (6:315;
459). Second, he requires that citizen legislation be justified in the name
of the interests of all, not just of those who are provisionally granted the
exercise of a civil personality for which they only partly qualify: "Whatever sort of positive laws the citizens might vote for, these laws must still
not be contrary to the natural laws of freedom and of the equality of
everyone in the people corresponding to this freedom" (6:315; 459). Elsewhere in the *Rechtslehre* Kant argues that positive law must enact what
the general will of the people could hypothetically approve. From a pragmatic point of view, having to justify political action in public according
to a particular set of conditions limits the range of possible action available even to a would-be tyrant. If a provisional republic excludes from active membership some subgroup of its citizens, it will have to demonstrate how excluded citizens can expect to gain full civil personality, and it
will have to argue for provisionally enacted legislation in the interests of
all rather than some subgroup of those citizens.

Kant's admittedly undemocratic distinction between active and passive citizenship demonstrates his awareness of the difficult problem of
the gap between contractarian demands on citizen capacity and the reality of widespread citizen incapacity. Provisional contractarianism emphasizes the promotion of the possibility of a just political system (moving through conceivable if not actual consent, toward self-rule). Kant's
theory respects the voluntary ideal of contractarian citizenship, but not
by unrealistically expecting domination-free interaction in the present
world. Instead, a modern-day provisionalist contract theory would propose a series of context-sensitive, continually evolving institutional responses to the gap between the ideal and the practice of autonomous citizenship. Just as minimalist contractarians rely on public institutions like
markets and banks to make good on their claims for the transhistorical
value of private property, so Kantian contractarians would rely on public
institutions to help them meet the substantive demands of citizenship
(6:326; 6:315). Freedom is at the heart of both strains of contract theory,
but the Kantian strain recognizes that the state is not the only, or even the
primary, source of domination in most citizens' lives. With such a Kant-

ian revision of the traditional theory, minimalist assumptions about property rights and citizen capacity may now be seen as context-dependent efforts to realize the provisional conditions of the contractarian ideal of government by consent.

Thus we see that for Kant citizenship rights are not conclusive but are granted provisionally to serve the goal of autonomous self-rule. Were citizenship for Kant a reflection of membership, he could not have made it contingent on the achievement of the social preconditions of civil personality. Instead, citizenship is conditionally granted to those who, in Kant's admittedly exclusionary judgment, will best serve as independent self-legislators. In this section on active and passive citizenship, Kant has addressed the qualities citizens must bring to self-rule, but not the basis for identifying the appropriate object of rule. Kant does not, in fact, devote much thought to national identity, civil wars, or the determination of appropriate borders.[7] One reason for this is that Kant has a robust theory of universal interdependence: the concept of the globus terraqueus.[8]

Kant begins his discussion of cosmopolitan right in the *Metaphysics of Morals* with a reminder of the distinction between morality and politics. Peaceful international relations, he writes, are not based on ethics but have "to do with rights" (6:352; 489; again, Kant does not mean that morality does not matter for politics, only that moral arguments in politics come from the public sphere composed of the citizens themselves, rather than determining political principles directly). Political principles of right are derived from the necessary conditions of human interaction. In this case, "nature has enclosed them all together within determinate limits (by the spherical shape of the place they live in, a *globus terraqueus*" (6:352; 489). With this Latin term, Kant glosses the physical constraints—residence on a sphere of earth and water—that require each of us to enter into lawful relations with all the other inhabitants, because each of us potentially interacts with every other one. Another way to put it is that none can escape the globus terraqueus, and thus the exit option that is essential to minimalist contractarians like Robert Nozick is not available in Kant's more realistic theory.

Later in this chapter I pursue this idea of Kant's in connection with the democratic principle of affected interest, in order to argue that necessarily interacting citizens should be able to have a say in the policies that affect them, insofar as this institution does not undermine the conditions of possibility of future agency and plurality. Kant, however, is less interested in democratic self-rule than in liberal restraint, so he applies the idea of the globus terraqueus to the question of the possibility of rightful colonial and imperial conquest.[9] There is nothing in principle to deny people the right to try to establish relations with others everywhere, Kant argues, but this cosmopolitan right does not confer any "right to make a settlement on the land of another nation" (6:353; 489; emphasis removed). We do have the duty to attempt to establish the conditions of worldwide peaceful relations (6:354–355; 491), but we have no right at all to conquer other nations, even those who seem to us backward or whose way of life strikes us as uncivilized. Kant specifically recognizes that different societies have different ways of settlement (some are "shepherds or hunters . . . who depend for their sustenance on great open regions"), which must be respected. He rails against the "specious reasons to justify the use of force" common in his time; "all these supposedly good intentions cannot wash away the stain of injustice in the means used for them" (6:353; 490). Kant's explicit mention of the "American Indian nations" in this regard is particularly relevant; only after dozens of independently viable ways of life had been destroyed to make way for settlement did arguments respecting those differences become common in the American public sphere.[10] Kant's discussion of the this topic in *Toward Perpetual Peace* glosses the same argument with precision: leaders of the European colonial powers (particularly the Dutch in this case) "make much ado of their piety and, while they drink wrongfulness like water, want to be known as the elect in orthodoxy" (8:359; 330).

Compared with the robust treatment Kant gives the other two levels of right in *Perpetual Peace*, this discussion of cosmopolitan right seems, at first, little more than a scolding of the Dutch traders for overstepping the limits of hospitality. Kant proposes no institutions to guarantee respect for cosmopolitan right, even though here, as in *Metaphysics of Morals,* he begins by reminding us that cosmopolitan right is a matter not of ethics but of political right. The implicit conclusion would be that institutions for its enforcement are required, but Kant draws no such conclusion. Instead, he complains about international injustice, reminds us that globalization has "now gone so far that a violation of right on *one* place of the earth is felt in *all,*" and insists that this code, though "unwritten," binds us all (6:360; 330–331). Implementation of cosmopolitan right is a "condition" of progress toward peace, and yet Kant suggests no concrete means to achieve it.

This is not the place for sustained consideration of Kant's motives in writing about cosmopolitan right.[11] One possible interpretation is this: Kant insists in many places that all three levels of right—citizen/citizen, state/state, and human being/state—are conditions of future peaceful coexistence. Just as he is willing to permit temporary violation of right by, say, personalistic rulers, so long as their rule promotes the conditions of future rightfulness, it could be that Kant is willing to leave the details of future institutions for guaranteeing cosmopolitan right to future generations. Not unlike Klosko's provisionalist Plato (see chapter 1), Kant may be recognizing that dynamic political conditions require institution-building responses from citizens themselves, rather than from castle-in-the-air-building theorists.

We can say at any rate that while Kant limited his discussion of cosmopolitan right to hospitality, given that the violations of cosmopolitan right he saw before him could be criticized adequately under that rubric, in the present day we need not limit ourselves as Kant did. Provisional requirements to realize the conditions of agency and plurality combine with Kantian recognition of cosmopolitan interdependence to suggest revision to common conclusive understandings of citizenship rights.

CONTEMPORARY CITIZENSHIP DISCOURSE IN THE CONCLUSIVE AND PROVISIONAL MODES

In her book *The Claims of Culture,* Seyla Benhabib rightly complains that normative discussion about citizenship usually takes place "in a sociological vacuum."[12] John Rawls's famous presumption of a stable society with nonporous borders is just an extreme example of this tendency to imagine citizenship in its moral dimensions by abstracting from its spatial and temporal context.[13] Not only have philosophers been unwilling to view citizenship in context, public discourse about citizenship also remains mired in the conceptual categories of the early days of national integration. I argued in chapter 3 that the reification of seventeenth-century conditions of political agency misleads contemporary minimalist contractarians into taking property rights as a conclusive principle of political right rather than as a context-dependent condition of the exercise of agency. Here I shall argue that contemporary citizenship discourse makes a similar mistake, by taking the conditions of agency and plurality in the context of the eighteenth- and nineteenth-century national state for permanent principles of democratic citizenship. The conditions of citizenship rights were always provisional, and tensions arose between the national origins and the democratic aspirations of citizens even before the twentieth century. As Benhabib remarks, "While democracy is a form of life which rests upon active consent and participation, citizenship is distributed according to passive criteria of belonging, like birth upon a piece of land and socialization in that country or membership in an ethnic group."[14] The present-day gap between ostensibly conclusive principles and very different actual practices of citizenship makes it nearly impossible for public discourse to produce coherent moral arguments on the subject.

From a provisional point of view, citizenship is about the *conditions* of agency and plurality rather than conclusive membership. A heartening, if deceptively simple, case in point is provided by the Canadian members of the Sikh community who aspire to become members of the Royal Canadian Mounted Police, or "Mounties."[15] Abstracting from the details of their respective rituals, one can say generally that Sikh religious practice requires men to wear turbans, while RCMP tradition requires Mounties to wear Western-style Stetson headgear. In the early 1980s, a rote application of the rule that "Mounties wear Stetsons" was employed to exclude devout Sikhs from RCMP service. The opportunity to serve one's country as a member of the police force or armed services is an essential part of modern-day citizenship practice, which is both positive in the sense of conferring participation rights and negative in the sense of providing protection against interference.[16] As first the courts and later mainstream Canadian public discourse came to recognize, Stetson-wearing is a mere particular condition for the exercise of an aspect of participatory citizenship in some contexts; in the context of a plural religious and ethnic community of Canadians, Stetson-wearing as a reified rule became exclusionary rather than empowering. Ultimately, Canadians proved receptive to the provisional idea that particular conditions merely enable the realization of political principles. They modified their rule, and it became possible to include members of religions whose practices prevented them from wearing Stetson hats. In 2006, Baltej Singh Dhillon celebrated his fifteenth anniversary as a turban-wearing member of the Royal Canadian Mounted Police.[17]

Most examples of contemporary citizenship discourse are less satisfactory, from a provisionalist point of view. The gap between ostensibly conclusive moral argument and practical reality, in addition to making it hard to produce coherent argument, has a corrosive effect on public moral-political discourse in general. Take, for example, recent arguments made regarding access to voting rights in the United States. In the state of Georgia, legislators are battling the judiciary for the right to require picture identification, such as a driver's license, in order to vote; when the courts struck down Georgia's first attempt to require such identification as an unconstitutional poll tax, the legislature returned to the drawing board with a fee-free version of paper obstacles to voting.[18] Despite wide recognition that the cited problem of vote fraud would not be addressed by requiring new identification, and despite the association of this sort of tactic with attempts to exclude members of minority groups from the electorate, public officials continue to argue for the requirement as a fraud prevention measure.[19] The argument that voters should "show some sort of responsibility" also undergirds exclusionary laws in the many states that set up barriers for felons seeking to regain the franchise.[20]

For Kant, as we have seen, citizenship is not a marker of conclusive membership but a condition of autonomous self-rule. In a democratic context, a Kantian provisional judge of citizenship would not ask: Is this person a member of our group (a Stetson-wearing, fee-paying, literate, member, say)? It would properly ask: Is this person able with some degree of autonomy to have a say in the policies that affect him? Group membership is very often a provisionally useful proxy for determining the community of affected interest, and thus provisional theory does not declare group membership to be simply imaginary or otherwise illegitimate. Moreover, it would be unjustifiably paternalistic to presume that freely choosing self-determiners would never choose a form of government that constructed boundaries according to group membership. Just as Kant is unwilling to deny provisional respect to the property rights that undergirded transitional stability, so provisional theory today would not deny that conventional citizenship markers are often the best available determiner of the community empowered to decide. Crucially, however, provisional theory does not mistake arbitrary claims of membership, which are mere conditions of provisional self-rule, and often very distant ones at that, for conclusive principles of political right.

Territorial communities are therefore no more fundamental in principle than other communities of interest. For example, as eighteenth-century revolutionaries noticed, community of interest among various members of European royal houses often seemed deeper than the community of interest between ruler and ruled of a single nation. To take an example from the present day, Robert Dahl, George Edwards, and other critics of the U.S. Electoral College have pointed out that by distributing electoral votes according to territorial states instead of by the population as a whole, the American presidency can be won without winning the popular vote.[21] Edwards notes that the Electoral College and its disproportionate distribution of votes persists despite the fact that any new proposal to grant extra weight to the vote of citizens of certain states would have little chance of success in today's political environment.[22] One wonders in principle what difference there is between giving residents of some states extra leverage in the presidential elections and giving members of nonterritorial groups (white people? rich people? those whose ancestors have been citizens for generations? college professors?) enhanced political power. Given empirical uncertainty about depth of commitment in each case, the burden of proof is on the normative supporters of territoriality to show why it rather than other, potentially more freely chosen, aspects of personhood should form the basis of political empowerment. Territory is strong when reinforced by other cleavages, such as class or belief system. In many cases, however, territory is used invidiously as a normatively acceptable proxy for class, generation, belief, or racial conflict. To underline provisionalism's refusal to take territory as a conclusive, citizenship-determining category, let us briefly investigate a few examples.

Race and Citizenship in the Contemporary United States

Clarissa Rile Hayward has argued that students of politics, for all our attention to difference, have failed to recognize the critical role played by state entities in inscribing and reproducing categories of difference in society. More concretely, she demonstrates the seemingly pervasive if often unwitting or at least unacknowledged role of state actors in drawing boundaries among members of different racial groups in the United States: "Even as state actors worked, and continue to work, to localize collective problems in African-American ghettos, they helped reduce, often minimize, contact across the lines of identity/difference that they mapped. They erected physical boundaries to contact with racialized others, such as highways and high-rise housing projects. They erected legal boundaries as well. . . . [S]tate actors have not only helped produce and maintain racialized difference. They further have transformed that difference from mere strangeness to foreignness."[23] Moving beyond Benedict Anderson's famous discovery of the political construction of "imagined communities," then, Hayward demonstrates the active if sometimes unwitting complicity of government in *constructing* territorial boundaries that it regards as *natural.*

Hayward cites the work of the legal theorists Richard Thompson Ford, Gerald Frug, and Lani Guinier and of the political theorists Iris Marion Young and Susan Bickford, all of whom challenge the reified status of political boundaries as undemocratic, as sources of solutions for the problem of state-enacted racialization of politics. She notes that institutional innovations such as cumulative voting systems can provide incentives for politicians to cater to interests outside narrowly constructed boundaries. Most important for the purposes of this chapter, Hayward shows that, far from functioning as a policy-neutral and essentially natural marker of political identity, political borders (even very local submunicipal borders!) have in themselves profound and substantive effects. She praises Ford and Frug for recognizing that "people are affected by decisions taken not only within, but also across the borders of the municipalities in which they reside."[24]

Ford, in his 1994 law review article "The Boundaries of Race: Political Geography in Legal Analysis," employs a formal model to demonstrate that even without presuming active racism, preexisting racialized geography would reinforce itself quasi-naturally. Like Hayward, he shows that racialized boundaries are not the "natural" products of economic or social forces but the aggregate result of decades if not centuries of state actions tending to reinforce segregation. He criticizes more recent state-led attempts at racial separation, reserving particular critique for movements toward private governments like homeowners associations: "Privatization may be seen as the ultimate boundary manipulation."[25] Finally, Ford makes several institutional suggestions for redressing the unacknowledged but pernicious effects of racialized geography in the United States: "I propose semi-autonomous local governments with permeable boundaries. Under this proposal, local governments would retain authority over land-use planning and over the administration of most services currently conceived as local, but boundaries would be rendered permeable in two ways. First, local *elections would not be limited on the basis of residence,* but instead would be open to all members of a metropolitan region or even to all citizens of a state. All local elections would be held on the same day and voters would receive a number of votes equal to the number of open seats, which they could cast in any election they wished. Hence voters would effectively draw their own jurisdictional boundaries."[26] In addition, Ford proposes centralized revenue collection, boundary changes at ten-year intervals, and application of democratic control to all quasi-governmental agencies.

As Ford and Hayward reveal in their respective studies, conclusive arguments about territorial citizenship and its qualifications turn out to be reified conditions for the exclusion of some from the benefits of autonomous self-rule. When the legal scholar Lani Guinier, recognizing this same pattern, proposed the introduction of proportional representation in the United States as an institutional remedy, she was vilified by some as un-American. Those who thought so, however, were mistaking an arbitrary institutional tradition of first-past-the-post electoral systems for a conclusive element of civic identity. In fact, as we shall see in the next section, the United States and other rich democracies are full of experiments, and even some established practices, not only of different electoral systems but even of noncitizen voting.

Noncitizen Voting in the United States and Europe

We are less involved because really all we can do is watch as they set policy for our children. . . . I feel like we don't have our chance to say what's on our minds. If I could vote, I would pay more attention.

—Ednor Altidor, Haitian immigrant with three children in the Cambridge, Massachusetts, public school system, quoted in "Noncitizens Seek Right to Vote in Local Elections," by Jordana Hart, *Boston Globe,* September 17, 2000

From a provisionally democratic point of view, citizenship is meant to enable people like Ednor Altidor to have a say in the policies that affect them. Most Americans would be surprised to learn that in many places, some even in the United States, people do not have to enjoy national citizenship to exercise at least some autonomous self-rule. Provisional theory recognizes that for many people, citizenship signifies membership in a conclusive (and exclusive) group. This point of view is as acceptable in the public sphere of discursive dynamics as any other view. The fact that many people value arbitrary geographical, ethnic, and other kinds of membership and believe that these memberships are linked to the enjoyment of rights of self-rule is a significant part of the political context in which any determination of political right must operate. However, from a provisional point of view, these ideas about conclusive membership are reified conditions of self-rule inherited from the age of national consolidation and even earlier. It is one thing to rally your fellow Frenchmen (who had only recently learned to call themselves French, in fact) to the barricades against the foreign forces of absolutist rule.[27] It is quite another to declare that someone living in, say, the Czech Republic, whose ancestors lived within the territorial borders of a larger Germany, has a greater claim to autonomous self-rule than a child of foreign guest workers born within the boundaries of the present German state.[28] These claims are affected by their political contexts, and thus they do condition what is politically possible. But they do not express any transcendent relationship.

In fact, a number of cities in the present-day United States have granted noncitizens the right to vote in school board and other local elections. The cities of Cambridge and Amherst in Massachusetts, and of Takoma Park in Maryland, and even large cities like New York and Chicago, have movements supporting the inclusion of noncitizens in the decisions that affect them. Those who argue against noncitizen voting in the name of tradition are reading their history selectively, since alien suffrage existed in the United States from the founding through most of the 1920s.[29] A more common argument against the enfranchisement of noncitizens is that it dilutes the meaning of citizenship. The best argument in favor of this view is given by David Miller, who has argued that nationalism is defensible because the strong ties it engenders are capable of supporting the kind of redistribution that justice requires.[30] Provisionally, Miller can indeed make this case, if in fact in each context there is no alternative means to achieving this redistributive end, and if in fact the nationalist sentiment encouraged by states does not undermine as many desirable qualities as it engenders. These are empirical questions, however. No conclusive case can be made for nationalism or for geographically arbitrary qualifications for self-rule.

Noncitizen voting has existed on a local level in Europe since the 1970s and is now common in European Union countries. Europeans today enjoy citizenship on a variety of levels, according to their birth country, their application for particular statuses like residency, and their place of residence. Some countries allow noncitizens indirect representation on consultative councils (with all the consociational difficulties this brings with it). Others allow them direct voting rights in municipal elections. Transnational rights are enjoyed on a much broader level by citizens of EU countries, whereas non-EU nationals are relatively disenfranchised.[31] Although Europe has recently suffered a period of increased ethnic tension, including riots in France, assassinations and threats in Holland, and anti-immigrant sentiment rising across the Continent, these problems have not been linked to the partial enfranchisement of nonnationals.

The near-invisibility and relative insignificance of noncitizen voting practices should not surprise us, since while granting municipal representation is indeed a step in a provisionally defensible direction, noncitizen voting on the basis of residency only broadens the arbitrary designation that leads to self-rule a little bit. Noncitizen voting encourages agency insofar as individuals have more say in their city's business and promotes plurality insofar as it does not make assimilation a condition of self-rule. However, the principle of affected interest has not been the ground of most of these improvements. Instead, public discourse on the issue has centered mainly on "who" the Europeans "are," essentially. Meanwhile the national and international level decisions that affect the interests of noncitizens quite significantly remain inaccessible to them.

Provisional Theory and Citizenship Rights:
Toward Citizenship as Standing

Taking agency and plurality seriously in a democratic context, as we have seen, requires recognition of the principle of affected interest. Civil, political, and social freedoms may be undergoing separation according to status in Europe. But the logic, as opposed to the European practice, of citizen autonomy militates against any such separation. Different bundles of rights may be needed in different contexts in order to promote agency and plurality as much as is locally possible (recall that for provisional theory, rights are not categorical but hypothetical imperatives). In the context of present-day American pluralism, for example, access to the means of influence may require quite a substantive package of civic, political, and social guarantees, while in the mid-twentieth century, arguably, federated mass-membership organizations served the same purpose for some Americans with considerably fewer individual resources but with access to organizational power. Rather than allow stronger or weaker agency according to territorial and job-market status, a commitment to agency under conditions of plurality would distribute the right to take part in decision-making on the basis of affected interest. Just as litigants in a court case are allowed to participate on the basis of their interests in the matter, autonomous citizens ought to have access to participation in the political decisions that affect them and their interests.

For Kant, as I have argued, the conditions of life on the globus terraqueus mean that it is in principle possible for me to interact in politically relevant ways with anyone else on earth. As Kant recognized implicitly when he underplayed the radical implications of this cosmopolitan condition for public right in both *Perpetual Peace* and the *Metaphysics of Morals,* there is a deep tension between the contractarian idea of collective self-determination as a founding of a people and a state, on the one hand, and another contractarian idea that any two potentially interacting persons ought to submit to a common authority for the regulation of the political interaction. Richard Thompson Ford, Lani Guinier, Will Kymlicka, Clarissa Rile Hayward, and also some deliberative democrats have all in their very different ways examined the empirical, historical, and contingent "we" demarcating the borders of the democratic polity and found it to be much more substantive than is often presumed. Far from being a mere neutral placeholder, the territorial borders of democratic polities function antidemocratically. If we are to move beyond classic conceptions of the demos toward the provisional citizen approaching autonomous self-rule, we shall have to face this tension squarely.

MOVING BEYOND TERRITORIAL CITIZENSHIP

It is a surprising fact about contemporary political theory that although very few arguments are offered in defense of present-day bounded territories, almost no one is willing to oppose them. From a wide variety of scholarly perspectives, two conclusions are reached: first, that hard boundaries are morally indefensible, and second, that they are politically inevitable. This is all the more surprising given that national state sovereignty and the boundaries that define it are relatively young political practices. As Will Kymlicka puts it, "Territorial boundaries are a source of embarrassment for liberals of all types, and particularly for liberal egalitarians."[32]

The main problem with hard boundaries is that they distribute packages of exclusive privileges on the morally arbitrary basis of territorial location. "Hard boundaries," as Loren Lomasky calls them, are arbitrary, restrict both the freedoms of those inside and those outside them, impose unchosen duties of citizenship on those within them, and impose unchosen duties of respect for the rights they distribute to insiders on outsiders who have no political say in the matter.[33]

The arguments usually offered in defense of boundaries turn out either to be merely traditional or to present problems that hard boundaries can indeed resolve, but that other institutions might resolve just as well. Kymlicka summarizes the difficulty with this first type of argument: "In the real world, the locations of boundaries have almost always been determined by factors which we now recognize as illegitimate—conquest, colonization, the ceding of territories from one imperial power to another without the consent of the local population, and so on. We know, in short, the existing boundaries are largely the product of historical injustice." Even worse, according to Kymlicka, the refusal of liberals to discuss borders and secession amounts to tacit support for the "very conservative view that existing boundaries and restrictive membership rules are sacrosanct."[34]

Other arguments for hard boundaries are at least initially more compelling. As I have already mentioned, David Miller's contention that national boundaries enable the redistributive policies demanded by justice is the most important of these. While a classical liberal could dismiss the argument for welfare-state policies out of hand (as Lomasky does), provisional theory must recognize that in some contexts agency and plurality are enhanced by just the kind of redistribution for which Miller calls.[35] However, one wonders why considerations of justice done toward the least well-off *within* shared national borders ought to trump the demands of the probably even worse off noncitizens who are thereby excluded. As many scholars have established, hard borders impose heavy costs on those excluded from the richer countries.[36] By what moral logic should the residents of poorer countries be required to bear the burdens of redistributive policies within the richer national borders? Moreover, even if we consider only the interests of those within an arbitrary set of hard boundaries, it is by no means clear that maintenance of those boundaries is a precondition of internally redistributive policies.

Kymlicka offers a different defense of national boundaries, on the basis of "the foundational liberal commitment to individual freedom can be extended to generate a commitment to the ongoing viability and flourishing of national cultures."[37] He recognizes their arbitrariness and their moral costs, and agrees that public denial of these facts has a corrosive effect on public discourse, but he nevertheless supports the maintenance of national boundaries in the service of cultural survival. While opposing illiberal nationalisms that would, for example, restrict citizens' exit options and deny the public sphere a role in changing cultural norms, Kymlicka supports what he calls a "liberal nationalism" that buys egalitarian and democratic advantages with exclusionary coin. "Democratic politics is in the vernacular," writes Kymlicka.[38] He means that without a national state that excludes outsiders and promotes local linguistic and other types of culture, ordinary individuals will not be empowered democratically or have their civil rights protected. Kymlicka associates bilingualism with elite politics and speculates that reasoners in the Rawlsian original position, faced with the choice between freedom of movement and protection of domestic culture, would choose the latter.[39] As for the costs that hard national boundaries impose on those excluded from them, Kymlicka joins the long list of scholars who suppose that a redistributive tax on richer countries can redress global injustice without disturbing the system of exclusive territorial memberships.[40]

It is possible, however, to oppose the practice of hard boundaries demarcating packages of citizenship rights without advocating an international free-for-all. Lomasky, for example, argues that "soft" boundaries analogous to those among the fifty American states would offer the right combination of stability in government and freedom for both insiders and outsiders. Though he does not use provisional language, Lomasky's standards are similar: "Fulfillment of [borders'] primary function requires that they be construed so as to facilitate maintenance of civility within and defense against predation from without. If borders are strategically indefensible or subsume perpetually hostile groups unwilling to live at peace with each other, their functionality is compromised, perhaps fatally."[41] He adds that the degree of "hardness" at the border should be determined by its protection of these functionalities. The advantage of this approach is that Lomasky is able to articulate and respond to the injustices that arise from the imposition of arbitrary territorial boundaries, without sacrificing the important goods that depend on some demarcation of the subjects and objects of political will. In the present day, national governments provide the most important forum for the vindication of individual rights, for example. One need not support the use of boundaries as a means of defending traditional cultures in order to see that potentially empowered citizens need some route to redress against injuries. Perhaps the most interesting extant proposal for provisional recognition of international borders is that of Ayelet Shachar and Ran Hirschl, to which I now turn.

Citizenship as Inherited Property

Shachar and Hirschl compare contemporary citizenship practices, considered as an intergenerational transfer of exclusive rights within a territory, and the medieval practice of entailed inheritance of estates. Entailment kept property consolidated within great landed families, while current international boundaries and practices keep the valuable package of rights called citizenship within a particular group of people and their descendants. Shachar and Hirschl use this apt comparison to criticize contemporary citizenship practices as essentially feudal in both justification and result: rights gained by the accident of birth allow a morally arbitrary group of individuals access to disproportionate wealth at the expense of everyone else. After considering several alternative scenarios for the amelioration of the injustice of inherited citizenship, Shachar and Hirschl argue for a global "birthright privilege levy" transferring wealth from those unjustly advantaged to those unjustly disadvantaged by accidents of the location of their birth.

As Shachar and Hirschl demonstrate, the contemporary discourse on citizenship tends to make the intergenerational transfer of wealth-conferring rights seem natural. "To frame citizenship in terms of inherited property and acknowledge birthright entitlement as a human construct not impervious to change is to expose the extant system of distribution to critical assessment" (255). They note rightly that the life chances enhanced by good luck in the lottery of birthright citizenship contribute not only to general well-being but also to substantive political autonomy. Shachar and Hirschl estimate that about half the world's people are effectively without the basic freedoms necessary for autonomous citizenship, adding that the inequalities traceable to transfers of citizenship are much greater than inequalities traceable to ordinary property inheritance (258–259). This fact has been neglected in the literature, Shachar and Hirschl note with surprise. Moreover, the conventional arguments about citizenship focus overwhelmingly on identity and community ties protected by hard boundaries, when by far the most significant function of such boundaries is their "crucial role in preserving restricted access to the community's accumulated wealth and power" (269). Shachar and Hirschl comment: "This is a blind spot, if not the 'black hole,' of citizenship theory" (274). In response, they call for substantial reform, ameliorating the injustices of the intergenerational transfer of citizenship rights without losing the civic benefits of bounded citizenship itself. Shachar and Hirschl recommend a tax solution, the "birthright privilege levy" that transfers wealth from the most to the least privileged citizens. In addition to redressing unjust inequality, the birthright levy "does not require significant sacrifices or alterations to the level of benefits that citizens in the well-off polities have come to expect" (281).[42]

Shachar and Hirschl are not the first to compare today's hard boundaries with yesterday's feudalism, but their specific analysis of inherited citizenship and entailed property is original and fascinating. Two main difficulties, however, are connected with their project. First, Shachar and Hirschl arbitrarily identify birthright citizenship with inheritance transfer; though their general critique of the consequences of birthright citizenship is supported by other less arbitrary considerations, the analogy with entailment is weak. Second, their proposed solution dodges the consequences of both the analogy with entailed property and of the other arguments against birthright citizenship. Rather than disturb the "level of benefits that citizens in the well-off polities have come to expect" (281), Shachar and Hirschl retreat to a mild version of the very common proposal for a north-south transfer of global wealth. Fortunately, however, the argument is susceptible to provisional improvement. Shachar and Hirschl argue rightly against treating inherited citizenship as natural; as we shall see, one can also cease treating the exclusive packages of rights distributed territorially as natural, without consigning the present system to counterproductive disorder.

Regarding the first problem, Shachar and Hirschl's argument depends on the premise that citizenship rights are in fact transferred from one generation to another by a mechanism analogous to inherited property. Even on the most generous reading, this is strictly true only in that small fraction of countries with strong *jus sanguinis* policies (in which citizenship is conferred from parents—sometimes only fathers—to children). Many countries have a mix of *jus sanguinis* (right of blood) and *jus soli* (right of soil) policies; by granting jus soli rights, polities avoid the problem of the presence of unenfranchised residents over multiple generations, while some jus sanguinis policies allow war victims or other returnees to claim rights according to ethnic heritage.

With regard to this first problem about the characterization of citizenship as an intergenerational transfer, Shachar and Hirschl could ask us to ignore empirical complexities for the moment, and to take the pure jus sanguinis perspective on citizenship for the sake of argument. Granting such a request, however, would only move the problem back a step: Why should we consider citizenship rights as something inherited rather than as something normally granted to an individual upon entry into the world? Neither pure perspective adequately describes the empirical landscape, either historically or in the present day. Therefore, we, along with Shachar and Hirshl, are forced to select a simplified model that provides the most normatively significant details for analysis. Both the simple jus sanguinis and the simple jus soli models describe the acquisition of a package of exclusive rights by children through accidents of birth. (Of course, some citizenship policies allow would-be citizens to earn such rights in a nonarbitrary way through their own efforts, but since entry by individual effort is nowhere the dominant means of gaining citizenship, we may safely exclude it from consideration here.) Both models result in what Russell Hardin calls "maldistribution" of relevant resources.[43] However, only under the first (jus sanguinis) set of assumptions do these unjust consequences arise from a practice analogous to inheritance of prop-

erty. Under the jus soli model, which is just as intuitively appealing a sim-
plification as its alternative, the entailment analogy disappears.

Like most other political theorists writing about citizenship these
days, Shachar and Hirschl pursue two distinct goals: first, to criticize existing practices, and second, to propose alternative policies that might be
more likely to survive critical scrutiny. Though we have just seen that
Shachar and Hirschl's critical attack on citizenship as inherited property
hits a much narrower target than they intend, even so, this article's original criticism plus the other arguments against current citizenship practices made by a wide variety of political theorists, some of whom I have
reviewed in this chapter, together give us powerful reasons to doubt the
legitimacy of contemporary citizenship policy. Not only can the policy be
compared with the feudal practice of entailment, but, as we have seen in
the other views, current hard-boundary policies violate outsiders' rights
to a say in the policies that affect them, as well as insiders' rights to associ-
ate freely with whomever they wish. The critique of citizenship practices
from within a great variety of ethical worldviews is devastating; the most
powerful argument remaining in favor of hard boundaries is a simple
realist argument about the likelihood of their persistence.[44]

More troubling, then, than the limited reach of Shachar and Hirschl's
analogy with entailment is the limited imagination they apply to their
proposed remediation of the injustice associated with contemporary citizenship practices. "Unlike advocates of global citizenship who seek to
redistribute membership itself, we wish to mitigate the *inequality of starting points* that attaches to the present system of birthright laws," write
Shachar and Hirschl.[45] They conceive of their task by analogy with the
traditional North American debate between policies promoting equality
of outcome and policies promoting equality of opportunity, placing
themselves in the latter category. But while it is admirable to seek to
broaden opportunity with minimal reliance on paternalistic central
power, the contrast between distribution for outcome and distribution
for opportunity distracts us from the failure of either proposal to attack
the root cause of the injustice itself, which is the distribution of exclusive
packages of rights according to territorial group membership.

Here Shachar and Hirschl's analogy to inherited property goes even
further than they admit. Elimination of the historical practice of entail-

ment did solve some problems for the British public, reducing, for example, the concentration of land in the hands of those with little incentive to productivity. However, reform against entailment did not end inequality in property holding. Instead, it strengthened the system of inherited property rights and allowed it to go on generating new kinds of inequality for years to come. Shachar and Hirschl do rightly distinguish between traditional property views and "new property" views, with the latter treating property more as a provisional means to solve social problems than as a conclusive right. Even so, they endorse both citizenship and property rights as conclusive principles of political right: "Our critical account of birthright citizenship is not targeted . . . against the political ideal and institution of citizenship. Full membership in a self-governing *and bounded* polity involves invaluable properties for the right holder, especially for the less advantaged: it guarantees for even the most vulnerable within a given society the fundamental security of an inalienable right to membership" (275, emphasis added).

Shachar and Hirschl raise a series of important objections to "outright abolition of bounded citizenship," and I address them toward the end of this chapter. For the moment, however, let us examine Shachar and Hirschl's attempt at amelioration. As we have already seen, they recommend a "birthright privilege levy," or a tax that would flow from those born in rich countries to those born in poor ones, while maintaining the current system of exclusive packages of rights to territorial group members. The burden of the tax falls only upon a small number of the richest residents of the more privileged countries. Most residents of the better-off countries would experience no change in their ordinary lives, except perhaps (though Shachar and Hirschl do not say so) a reduction in the guilt some of them feel when contemplating the injustices of global inequality. This aspect of Shachar and Hirschl's plan makes it relatively likely to be implemented, certainly. However, the price of realism in this case is too high: continuation, even strengthening, of the underlying system of exclusive rights distributed territorially is what Shachar and Hirschl foresee. As in the example of entailed property rights, whose reform contributed to the productivity that drove British commerce to its eighteenth- and nineteenth-century triumphs, such a timid reform of citizenship rights would only deepen the roots of the current system. Some wealth would be transferred from unjust rich to deserving poor, but—as

Shachar and Hirschl have already argued in their defense of revisionist "new property" doctrines—wealth is morally significant here only insofar as it undergirds substantive autonomy, the ability of people to make meaningfully free choices. Under a strengthened system of exclusive bounded citizenships, most people would still be excluded from having a say in the policies that affect them. They might be somewhat richer, and were those riches to be significant and somehow to avoid the usual problems with resource-based or otherwise unduly direct cash flows, perhaps their new wealth would encourage fledgling democracies to survive the challenges of transition better than they otherwise would. Beyond those speculative and politically superficial benefits, however, the proposed birthright levy is less a solution to global inequality than a form of absolution for the privileged but occasionally guilt-ridden few.

"I need not think, if I can only pay; others will readily undertake the irksome business for me," writes Kant in his early essay "An Answer to the Question: What Is Enlightenment?" (8:35; 17) (1784). But the problems with bounded citizenship are only indirectly financial, and the moral reasons for financial transfers from the best-off to the worst-off transcend arguments about citizenship.[46] Presuming, as I have already mentioned, that counterproductive consequences of such a payment can be anticipated or remediated, there are many strong reasons to support a global tax on the rich in support of the poor. Left libertarians argue that violations of the original community of resources leave today's majority with injuries for which they deserve to be compensated. Rawlsians argue that the difference principle enjoins even global transfers for the benefit of the least well-off. Consequentialists argue for transfer of marginally less utile surplus to be transferred from the best-off to those in need, sometimes advocating a simple formula such as Peter Singer's 1-percent ideal.[47] Many more convincing arguments could be found for the idea of a global transfer from rich to poor. However, even if we presume that a global north-to-south transfer through a birthright privilege levy is a good idea, we cannot conclude that it resolves any of the inherent difficulties associated with bounded citizenship laws. Shachar and Hirschl's proposed solution leaves the source of ongoing injustice undisturbed; this quality of their solution is highlighted and cited as an advantage that makes it more likely to be implemented. While disadvantages in the life opportunities otherwise provided by wealth do have a substantial impact on the value of citizenship rights (as Shachar and Hirschl acknowledge, autonomy presumes a certain degree of citizen capacity), the more fundamental injustice associated with contemporary citizenship practice is its arbitrary effects on the rights of insiders and outsiders. Noncitizens affected by national policies are unable to have a say in policies that constrain their own opportunities; this is a violation of the principle of affected interest. And citizens' opportunities are also arbitrarily restricted, in that they are prevented from free association with those not in the group. A global tax might well lessen the undeserved burden of poverty on many in the world, and this is of course a good thing. Such a tax has no fundamental connection, however, with the injustices perpetrated specifically by the institution of birthright citizenship within arbitrary territorial boundaries.

Provisional Citizenship

What alternative proposal might provisional theory offer? As we have seen, provisional theory seeks to promote the preconditions of political agency and plurality in context, multiplying rather than restricting political possibilities. Without paternalistically calculating specific policies, which should be the province of empowered citizens themselves, provisional theory can criticize existing institutions that reduce political possibility and can suggest types of institution that might encourage agency and plurality to flourish. Though these suggestions are not conclusive, as we saw in chapter 3, some of the candidate institutions likely to promote agency and plurality in a number of contexts are overlapping institutions, protected enclaves for the development of alternative discourses and the empowerment of citizens within their political contexts. Provisional theory takes political principles as hypothetical imperatives, asking what policies might promote them in context. By avoiding conclusive judgments, provisionalism should be able to avoid what Shachar and Hirschl rightly call "naturalizing" assumptions that take existing institutions or popular principles as normative.

Across a number of philosophical commitments, arguments for bounded communities of interest make the reasonable point that such groups make meaningful self-rule possible. Taking the most abstract version of the democratic perspective—the principle of affected interest—

as a hypothetical imperative, and discounting the many would-be conclusive arguments for nationality or other forms of group identity, we still require some political subject and object of rule. We may accept the commonsense notion that the group encompassing all of humanity is too unwieldy a subject and object of political agency, at least in most cases. Even if we do not accept this commonsense view, we would still be selecting the subset of human beings currently able to have a say in the policies that affect them, knowing that many others (young, unborn, disabled, distracted . . .) will be objects of policy without having been subjects. Therefore, some delimited group of agents and objects is necessary for meaningful political action.

This determination of a necessary condition of political agency substantively limits political possibility. A determination that specific subjects and objects of political agency are necessary, however, is not at all the same as a determination that contemporary citizenship practices are necessary. There is no determinative reason in principle, for example, that the target groups of various policies *must overlap* to form a single territorially delimited entity. All the principle of affected interest and the necessity of delimited subjects and objects tell us is that members of those groups affected by a policy ought to have a say in its determination. Although provisional theory's antipaternalism would not allow a substantive determination against people's organizing themselves into national states, neither would membership in a national state be seen as a general condition of political agency.

In fact, a possible way to serve both the principle of affected interest and the need for delimited objects of agency would be a fluid system of participatory rights based on standing rather than arbitrary geography. Replacing citizenship with standing would delimit groups for each policy decision, and those groups would sometimes overlap, but no ossified set of qualifications for permanent enfranchisement would exist. Instead, political agents could have the standing to participate in decisions based on the likelihood that it would affect them. Rather than exclude, for example, those downwind of acid-rain-producing power plants from regulatory decisions based on a boundary that divides citizens by nationality but not according to the results of emissions policy, affected people could be enfranchised to join with those affected by such policies regardless of accidents of birth. There are many precedents for this kind of standing-based enfranchisement; the dominance of territory-based political agency is an artifact of the peculiar history of the national state, of course. In the legal sphere, for example, litigants must prove that they have standing based on the reality or significant possibility of injury related to the case. The right to sue is a political right, distributed by the state to those deemed to have a substantial interest due to real or anticipated losses. In the public comment phase of the promulgation of some regulations in the United States, interested parties express themselves regarding the policies that affect them, and the regulatory agency must at least respond to those expressions of political will. Elections by stockholders or members of organizations of boards of directors are still other instances of collective decision-making on a nonterritorial basis. And, as I discussed earlier in this chapter, noncitizen voting in parts of the United States and elsewhere ensures that those with a stake in outcomes like local school boards may be enfranchised without respect to birthright citizenship.

The policy appropriate to a particular context ought to be determined not by conclusive theorizing but by the participants themselves; this antipaternalist rule of thumb applies even to policies as general as the determination of the subjects and objects of political agency itself. We ought, however, to seek out practices that promote the conditions of political agency and plurality in the abstract, and to imagine what their implementation as hypothetical imperatives in context might look like. Moreover, provisional right as Kant understood it often leads to gradualist rather than revolutionary policies, since overturning the basis of the rule of law in political stability tends to retard rather than promote progress toward the establishment of conditions of justice. Thus even if implementation of the democratic hypothetical imperative in the context of present-day global politics would mean a shift from citizenship as membership in national states with hard borders to citizenship as standing, distributed according to affected interests without regard for territoriality, in practice such a shift would have to take into account transition costs and the value of stability. The *justification* for enfranchisement by membership in a territorial state, however, would have to be very different under provisional right, however. No longer could exclusion of some people from a say in the decisions that affect them be justified with reference to the conclusive legitimacy of historically arbitrary borders. Instead, the continued policy of exclusion could only be justified insofar as its short-term persistence contributes to the possibility of its own obsolescence. This, by the way, is how Kant justifies the continuing presence of so-called enlightened absolutist monarchs in late eighteenth-century Europe.[48]

5

provisional and conclusive
environmental politics

The coastal California gnatcatcher (*Polioptila californica californica*) has the wrong personality for an endangered species.[1] It is loud, easy to find, and friendly. California gnatcatchers reside in the same small area over long periods of time, reappearing regularly to amuse the watcher with mewing calls and tail flips. To experience the presence of a member of an endangered species at first hand, one might be supposed to have to trek far into the wilderness, scale hundred-foot trees (for a spotted owl), risk one's neck on precipice (for a peregrine falcon), or at least get pretty well torn up by chaparral (as I once did, chasing what I thought was a least Bell's vireo). You can find gnatcatchers, though, by pulling off the freeway near the ocean anywhere in Southern California, looking for a patch of coastal sage scrub on a moderate slope, and standing still to listen. If you are quiet and just a little lucky, within a few minutes you can hear what sounds like an unhappy cat with a sort of perky undertone: that's your bird. Gnatcatchers are small and not particularly good looking. Nevertheless, the birds engage your attention; they are appealing, fearless, and quick. No one watching a gnatcatcher is likely to start quoting John Muir or talking about majestic creation. But the gnatcatcher, residing in its expensive coastal sage scrub habitat, has managed to receive the timely official notice it took to precipitate a whole series of institutional shifts in the management of the environment.

In the previous four chapters, I discussed the necessity of provisionality for moral-political argument; the democratic efficacy of provisional theory; the usefulness of provisional reasoning both for exposing reified conditions masquerading as natural property rights and for suggesting contexts in which provisional respect for property might be useful; and the enhanced clarity provisional reasoning brings to arguments about citizenship. After examining the discursive dynamics around the concept of emancipation, I proposed three candidate institutions for the general promotion of agency and plurality (overlapping institutions, protected enclaves, and citizen leverage), and we saw that sometimes these political structures are able to enhance political possibilities. With this final chapter on provisionality in environmental politics, we reach our toughest case.

One might think that the huge challenge of global warming would represent a limit of political possibility within environmental thought, but this turns out not to be the case. As Kant's writings on international right suggest, peoples enjoying basic conditions of agency and plurality are likely to be able to work out the problems that result from sharing the globus terraqueus in some principled, if always imperfect, fashion.[2] Surprisingly, however, the *relatively* minor environmental problem of species conservation presents the more serious challenge to provisional politics. Here we find that the structural dynamics of the policy area of species conservation tend inexorably to limit the sphere of political possibility. Provisionalism's surprising finding in this area of environmental politics, then, is that species conservation policy may represent a conclusive limit to human political power.

I take the gnatcatcher and two species of tiny, pool-dwelling invertebrates called the Riverside and the San Diego fairy shrimp as the unlikely representative objects of provisionality's ultimate policy challenge. In what follows, I tell the part of the story of the development of species protection policy in the United States, from the codification in 1973 by means of the Endangered Species Act (ESA for short) of a national refusal to allow preventable extinctions, to the revision of the ESA in the 1980s and the implementation in the 1990s of a new kind of species protection policy called "habitat conservation plans" (HCPs for short). The ESA as originally formulated was clumsy in its means and conclusive in its principles. Once a species was "listed" as endangered or threatened, non-context-sensitive governing principles came into force; their translation into practice succeeded in preventing some extinctions but also led to numerous irrational and unintended consequences, just as provisional theory would have predicted. The revision of the ESA in the direction of HCPs retained the original value of species preservation while taking into account dynamic conditions, changing scientific evidence, and local stakeholders; at first, it seemed tailor-made to satisfy provisionality's demands for successful politics. However, as we shall see, the revised policy is thus far a failure, even compared to its clumsy predecessor. Species like the San Diego and the Riverside fairy shrimp are closer to extinction under the HCP regime than they were under the original ESA, and the structural dynamics of the revised policy seem likely to drive them to extinction no matter what changes in political will or scientific knowledge take place.

THE SPECIAL PROBLEM OF EXTINCTION FOR PROVISIONAL THEORY

There are two main sorts of environmental problem that matter for our purposes. First, there are sustainability problems centered around realizing long-term general human interests over shorter-term particular human interests; an example would be the difficulty of regulating global emissions of greenhouse gases in the interest of minimizing future climate volatility. Second, we need to consider the kinds of preservationist problems that have to do with minimizing human-caused extinctions. The first problem is an extreme example of a collective action problem, while the second operates according to a sort of irreversible *ratchet effect.* The basic argument in the second case of human-caused extinctions is as follows: Provisional theory refuses to apply conclusive principles to policy problems, since the vindication of hypothetical goods is enabled by different conditions under differing circumstances. Thus the rule of thumb for provisional theory is to expand rather than foreclose the sphere of political possibilities as much as possible. Policies under such provisional conditions will necessarily fluctuate, since to make a conclusive policy determination is to reduce the scope of future political agency. Kant made this argument as early as "An Answer to the Question: What Is Enlightenment?" (1784), where he argued that no one could rightly be bound by another generation's determination of the rules of religious piety. "One age cannot bind itself and conspire to put the following one into such a condition that it would be impossible for it to enlarge its cognitions . . . and generally to make further progress in enlightenment. This would be a crime against human nature, whose original vocation lies precisely in such progress."[3]

The structural dynamics of species preservation, however, militate against Kant's admirable reasoning. Presume a medium-term context of representative democratic decision-making in which there are two main competing views: "develop" and "preserve." If we imagine conservation politics as a game in which players alternatively compete for rights of policy determination and, further, if we presume that the game is played in a democratic context in which at least some alternation in power is the norm, then we can see that for this policy area the policy outcome is not left open but is *structurally predetermined*. Every win for the "develop" team will be a permanent win, while every win for the "preserve" team only temporarily protects the resource in question. The policy area of species conservation imposes a kind of ratchet effect on political decision; even in a context of democratic contest, the policy over the long term can only move in one direction: toward extinction.

In what follows, I address many of the nuances of this general pattern, while demonstrating that this ratchet effect does in fact exist with the case of the two fairy shrimp species in Southern California. Of course, species preservation is an extreme case within environmental policy generally. The alternating pattern of democratic decision combined with the kind of discursive dynamics discussed in chapter 2 could well lead to policy regimes in the future that are far more "environmentally friendly" than those we now enjoy. Moreover, the present policy regimes are more preservationist than other past policies; thus we know from experience that politics is capable of moving in a preservationist direction. However, in the extreme case of species preservation, as we shall see, politics finds its limits.

The problem of the limits that environmental policy imposes on human agency is bound up with the general Kantian problem of autonomy and heteronomy. The collective results of countless individual acts, each of which ought to be morally coherent, confront the recipients not as injury but as nature. This is not peculiar to environmental policy, but the problem is especially acute in this case. In Kantian moral theory, the problem is relatively simple: moral agents, necessarily ignorant of the long-term consequences of their actions, are responsible for the will with which they act. But Kantian provisional politics cannot dispose of the problem in similar fashion, since recklessly disposing of the preconditions of another's autonomy is an injury for which the group doing the disposing is responsible. Even though perfect control of collective outcomes is impossible, institutions are responsible for what can be known of their outcomes, and even for what is probable.

One might get around this problem by taking a quasi-Stoic attitude toward the natural limits of autonomy. It is certainly possible to hold the position: I had to accept the world as it was when I was born, and my successors will do the same. But this is a description of physical reality that does not affect the normative status of one's current actions. To leave it at this would be *to treat oneself as a mere force of nature,* without the capacity to realize one's will, without autonomy, and thus without responsibility, to be sure, but also without rights or freedom. Since provisional politics seeks to maximize the conditions of possibility of political agency and plurality, the provisional theorist cannot accept this sort of Stoic view of human political capacity as regards policies that are empirically within its grasp. As we shall see, the protection of species is to a very large extent scientifically possible under current conditions and with current knowledge. Recovery plans of the sort commissioned by the U.S. Fish and Wildlife Service and other agencies describe the relatively simple steps required to prevent the extinction of endangered and threatened species. The barriers to species preservation are not technical but political. This makes it all the more astonishing for provisional theory to recognize that even under conditions maximizing political possibility, prevention of a large number of extinctions may be impossible.

Two Classes of Problem

Though there are many other ways to characterize environmental policy issues, I shall divide them according to whether they are in principle reversible or not. The first type of problem, exhibited by such issues as global warming, desertification, and other types of services provided naturally, may in fact include some outcomes that are irreversible. It is possible, for example, that even with the (highly unlikely) immediate cessation of the fossil-fuel economy, the atmospheric dynamics already set in motion by human-added greenhouse gases of the past century will lead to climate change that makes human life impossible. This is an empirical question on which modelers can give us various probabilistic answers, but nothing conclusive. For the purposes of political theory, however, it is enough to know that problems like global warming are at least in principle reversible problems that may be solved with the right sort of collective action even after initial actions have taken place.[4] Therefore, sustainability problems belong generally to the class of ordinary political issues that raise no special problems of reversibility or the limits of the possible. They raise very difficult problems, to be sure, especially problems of the type Garrett Hardin has made famous as tragedies of the commons.[5] Even habitat loss may fall under this class of potentially reversible and politically soluble environmental problems, though the current enthusiasm for "mitigation" through habitat restoration has little basis in science. (Mitigation is often possible under current technological constraints and is always theoretically possible if members of the species survive. However, current practices do little more than pay lip service to the concept of mitigation with regard to species preservation.)[6]

Extinction, however, belongs to an entirely different and very much more difficult class of problems: irreversible political decisions. As in the previous class of cases, it is possible to claim that extinctions are natural, that there is no telling what would have survived without one's action, and that every extant species had to defeat numberless competitors in order to reach our notice in the first place. Again, while this is an accurate physical description, it misses the normative heart of the issue: agency and plurality, though unreachable ideals, may be provisionally realized through conditions that are sensitive to context. Prevention of extinctions is technically within our grasp, at least over the medium term.

It is also possible, however, that the value of a given species may not exceed the value achieved by its extinction. We can make two sorts of argument in these cases of irreversible extinction: in the first argument, we can simply presume that the species in question has overriding value, either on account of its uniqueness or because it is in principle impossible to determine what value the species might have to future generations (in this case, all irreversible environmental decisions are normatively similar, regardless of outcome); in the second argument, we can make no such presumption, leaving the question of the value of the object of an irreversible environmental decision open. It is possible that some decisions that remove species from existence, thus reducing future political agency, are nevertheless legitimate. The eradication of smallpox, for example, would not in principle be mistaken, though decisions by the American and Russian governments to keep samples available despite the risk underscores a common understanding of the value of reversibility in political decision-making. As with the earlier case of transborder politics, however, it is not possible to argue that decisions made without consideration of known likely consequences are legitimate because they were made in self-determined isolation. Just as the rich democracies ought to be willing to acknowledge that their policies effectively limit many life chances for those residing legally within their borders, local development agencies ought to acknowledge that they would rather have strong sales and property tax streams than the continued existence of particular (usually uncharismatic) species. Such a position at least has potential (though by no means assured) provisional legitimacy, while the usual declarations of accident or ignorance do not.

Environmental Politics and Provisionality as a Second-Order Theory

For Arne Naess and many other deep ecologists, the kind of policy question I discuss in this chapter is beside the point. Deep ecologists, and not only deep ecologists, argue against anthropocentrism as a philosophical point of view. We ought, they argue, to recognize ourselves as part of nature and to view reality through an "ecocentric" lens. For many such scholars of environmental political thought, no significant policy change will be possible without a global shift in belief systems, on the order of a religious transformation. One might reasonably ask why, then, I am not talking about consciousness-raising in this chapter. The answer is that provisionalism, as a second-order theory of the type Amy Gutmann and Dennis Thompson discuss, should be able to accommodate multiple ethical systems. Though provisionalism presumes that moral argument is ubiquitous in political discourse, it remains a mode of political analysis, not a moral theory. Thus provisional theory makes use of anthropocentric arguments not because they are necessarily true but because they are common to any point of view valuing agency and plurality. There are some moral points of view that provisional theory cannot accommodate (for example, the quasi-Stoical view described earlier in this chapter), but provisional theory attempts to secure the political conditions in which arguments from many different moral points of view may compete, rather than choose among them.

For similar reasons, my case for species preservation does not include any arguments from the point of view of animal rights. One might find Peter Singer's arguments for respect on the basis of sentience rather than arbitrary anthropocentrism compelling as philosophy, but in the sphere of politics such conclusive moral determinations are for citizens, not theorists, to make.[7] If Singer's arguments eventually carry the day, it will be thanks not only to what Jane Mansbridge would call a "logic of formal justice" but also to the availability of the institutions necessary to guarantee agency and plurality in politics. One might put this distinction into Rawlsian language: Animal rights and deep ecology are perfectly legitimate comprehensive doctrines that may well be admitted into general discourse. They cannot, however, accommodate the kind of plurality that provisionalism requires.

Anthropocentric Arguments for Species Preservation

Before we can discuss the policy arena of its preservation, we need to consider the fairy shrimp's potential value from an anthropocentric point of view. I have already argued from a provisional point of view that any political decision that reduces future publics' scope of choice is suspect, and thus that choices reducing the number of extant natural species are always subject to extra scrutiny. Now I would like to add a few more arguments in support of the potential value of each protectable species.[8] One might argue, for example, that the mere existence of a unique species provides irreplaceable potential aesthetic benefits to current and future generations. These benefits are potential because they require work and sensibility on the part of the human beings who are to enjoy them, but they also depend on the existence of the species in question. A species (say, the Riverside fairy shrimp) illustrates a mode of being, provides potential opportunities for observation and interaction, and enriches the category of living things in ways that cannot be reproduced by anything else; thus the Riverside fairy shrimp is uniquely potentially aesthetically valuable. To illustrate this point, think of the way the poet John Keats interacted aesthetically with the nightingale in his famous ode (though of course aesthetic benefits need not be drawn via poetry or any other conventionally aesthetic activity):

> *Thou wast not born for death, immortal Bird!*
> *No hungry generations tread thee down;*
> *The voice I hear this passing night was heard*
> *In ancient days by emperor and clown.*[9]

Keats treats the nightingale as immortal because so long as its species persists, nightingale song of the kind an individual nightingale happens to be providing will continue to exist.

A more concrete argument for the potential anthropocentric value of a single species like the San Diego fairy shrimp is this: each species, as the product of very many years of adaptive evolution, contains within itself unique solutions to problems that independent research might never uncover. To take a recent example, in 2005, the U.S. Food and Drug Administration approved the first of a new class of drugs for type II (adult onset) diabetes. These drugs, which aim to stabilize blood sugar with less risk and volatility than insulin or other existing alternatives, were developed after a scientist working with Gila monster (*Heloderma suspectum*) saliva noticed a similarity in one of its short proteins to a human counterpart. Gila monsters are large, venomous lizards found in the Sonoran Desert of the southwestern United States and northwestern Mexico. Though far too little is known about the internal chemistry of the Gila monster, its life history provides suggestive details for those searching for diabetes drugs: the animal eats only a few huge meals per year, spending the majority of its time underground in a near-dormant state, and thus (considered as a species) has evolved a possibly unique biochemical response to the problem of stability in blood chemistry.[10] The Gila monster is listed as endangered by the New Mexico Game and Fish Department; the state of Utah has listed it as a "species of concern," but not as endangered or threatened. The United States does not list the Gila monster, but the international Convention on International Trade in Endangered Species lists it in "Appendix II," which is analogous to the ESA's "threatened" level. Gila monster habitat in the deserts of the American southwest is under pressure from urbanization and from recreational activities, among other threats. Loss of the species before its biochemistry has been understood would mean loss of a potentially valuable class of diabetes drugs, in addition to the aesthetic and ecological losses extirpation of the species would entail.

The case of diabetes drugs based on Gila monster saliva recalls the more famous cases of drugs based on rain forest species and the efforts of international drug companies to patent them. But the practical benefits to human beings from the existence of unique species are not exhausted by aesthetic or medicinal services. As a thriving literature in ecological economics has been confirming, the economic value of naturally provided services is both enormous and grossly undercalculated by conventional accounting methods. Though we now know enough to make educated guesses about the environmental services provided by the atmosphere generally, by intact watersheds to prevent flooding, by the soil and ocean in providing food, and so forth (and in fact some of these kinds of values are beginning to be included in cost-benefit analyses by governments and international agencies), the state of knowledge on the environmental services provided by the overwhelming majority of extant species is near zero. Few would have guessed that Gila monster biochemistry might lead to an important new drug to fight diabetes, though of course the success or failure of that drug is still unknown. In sum, unique species provide potential value to humanity in at least three ways: aesthetically, as informational and direct resources themselves, and as part of service-providing ecosystems.

So much for arguments for the value of species preservation. Provisional politics should admit such arguments into the arena of public discourse but refrain from making conclusive claims for the political justice or injustice of policies protecting the members of any nonhuman species. The conundrum, to repeat, that the particular case of species preservation presents us with here is that it seems that the provisional stance paradoxically leads to a specific conclusion, namely, that biodiversity will not be protected. This result persists even if conclusive arguments for species protection carry many days in many political arenas, because each moment of flux in environmental policy (a flux, it should be remembered, that makes up an essential element in provisional politics) reduces irretrievably the biological diversity available for argument in the next round.[11] This irreversible ratchet effect in policies relating to species preservation suggests that provisional politics, even politics itself, has some concrete and unavoidable policy outcomes. There are, it seems, limits to the Promethean capacities of political humanity.[12] We may not be free to protect some species from an extinction of our own making.

SPECIES PRESERVATION IN THE CASE OF THE RIVERSIDE AND THE SAN DIEGO FAIRY SHRIMP

The case of species preservation presents a particularly difficult problem for provisional politics. Provisional theory aims to broaden political possibility; by identifying the preconditions of human agency and plurality in various political contexts, provisionality does not seek to define ideal institutions for all times, places, and policy arenas, it seeks to make repeated expressions of political agency and plurality through institutions possible. Provisional theory does not presume that history moves from bad to good through ever-increasing human enlightenment. Even so, it is fundamentally optimistic in one sense: it presumes that given the bare preconditions of agency and plurality, human beings will find ways to practice legitimate self-rule in any number of contexts. The more agency and plurality are enhanced, the more politics should be able to achieve. In the case of species preservation, however, the underlying structure of the policy area seems to restrict the range of available options for self-rule at the outset.

Provisional politics runs up against quasi-natural limits in this case: there are some kinds of sovereign political decisions that are ruled out by the very nature of the policy. Of course, nature always provides limits to potential political sovereignty: no polity can effectively will a longer solar year or human immortality. However, human actions have accelerated the natural rate of extinction by many orders of magnitude.[13] But in this case, the limits faced by provisional policy-makers in the area of species preservation are only quasi-natural; they are the result of the structure of politics, not of physical laws.

Human laws, such as the U.S. Endangered Species Act, and international efforts like the Convention on International Trade in Endangered Species and the U. N. Convention on Biological Diversity, have announced a political will to decrease the rate of human-caused extinctions. Over the medium term of a period of decades, these laws have undoubtedly made a difference; in the years since the ESA was passed (in 1973), far fewer documented extinctions have occurred in the United States than would have otherwise.[14] Of course, some species thrive under human-dominated conditions, and new ones, especially micro-organisms like drug-resistant bacteria, are evolving every day. It is possible to imagine policies that would reduce the *rate* of human-caused loss of biological diversity. As we shall see in this chapter, however, ending the loss itself seems beyond our power, given the ratchet effect and the permanence of political plurality.

Vernal Pools

In trying to come to grips with the conundrum presented to provisional politics by environmental policy, I shall examine a particularly extreme example: the protection of vernal pools and their endemic species like the Riverside and the San Diego fairy shrimp in coastal Southern California. Vernal pools are rare and isolated seasonal wetlands scattered throughout the world's Mediterranean climate regions; they bloom after winter rains in the spring—thus the name—and then gradually dry up during the summer and fall. The past few decades of policy regarding vernal pools (and other endangered habitats and species) is of great interest to the student of provisional politics, since policy-making institutions in this area have moved in an ever more deliberative direction, with decision-making often devolved to the local level. I shall not be able to tell the end of the story in this case (and that is fortunate, at least from the point of view of the conservationist), but I shall endeavor to describe the discursive and institutional dynamics of recent vernal pool preservation efforts in coastal Southern California.

To simplify the story, I have selected a couple of closely related animal species endemic to a few vernal pool complexes in Southern California, whose fates at the hands of bureaucrats, developers, scientists, and members of the public will lead us through the general story: the Riverside fairy shrimp (*Streptocephalus woottoni*) and the San Diego fairy shrimp (*Branchinecta sandiegoensis*). Each of these is a small freshwater crustacean that spends its brief active life swimming upside down in a temporary pool, using its many pairs of legs to catch some of the tiny animals and plants with which it shares its refuge.[15] After mating, fairy shrimp females let their eggs fall to the muddy bottom of this vernal pool, where they develop into what biologists call "encysted embryos."[16] These encysted embryos remain buried in the dirt as the vernal pool dries up during the summer drought; some of them are blown with dust to other areas, some (biologists have speculated) may be carried on birds' feet to other vernal pools, and the rest stay in place during the dry period.[17] Come winter rains, a small portion of the available embryos will emerge to begin the fairy shrimp life cycle anew. Though much remains to be learned about fairy shrimp ecology, biologists have identified some remarkable adaptations by the shrimp to their difficult environment, in-

cluding unusual systems for regulating their internal chemistry to withstand the volatile hydrology of vernal pools.[18]

The preservation of these two species of fairy shrimp presents enormous biological and political challenges. Of the two species, the Riverside
fairy shrimp is the more imperiled; the U.S. Fish and Wildlife Service has
not simply listed it as endangered but classified it as a "5C" case, under
high threat, with low chances for recovery, and subject to an unusually
high level of potential conflict with development projects.[19] The San
Diego fairy shrimp is also endangered, but classified 2C, with high threat
and conflict potential but also a high potential for recovery. One bright
spot for fairy shrimp conservation comes from the unusual life history of
the shrimp; since fewer than 10 percent of encysted embryos in a vernal
pool's "egg bank" hatch during a given period of inundation, fairy shrimp
are better able than many other rare and endangered species to maintain
the genetic diversity on which their long-term survival depends.[20] The
fairy shrimp are unlikely to become objects of public attention, except as
a nuisance to developers, since they are not only tiny (less than an inch
long) but also absent for most of the year.[21] Their vernal pool habitat can
be beautiful in the early spring, when the pools are surrounded by bloom-
ing native plants and attract graceful birds; during the dry season, however, the pools are essentially dirt patches or mud holes of exceptional,
though temporarily invisible, biological value.

What environmental or other services might be provided by the
Riverside and the San Diego fairy shrimp are unknown; it is certain, however, that such services are potentially substantial. Like the Gila monster,
fairy shrimp have had to adapt to an unusually volatile environment; perhaps their status as "osmoregulators" or some other as yet undiscovered
adaptation will prove to be of direct use to human beings (osmoregulators "maintain consistent internal chemical concentrations" despite in-
habiting the extremely volatile vernal pool environment).[22] Fairy shrimp
are an important food source for other species in the Southern California
bioregion.[23] Environmentalists have also claimed that the fairy shrimps'
vernal pool habitats themselves provide substantial and undervalued environmental services, "such as their ability to retain stormwater and filter
pollutants."[24] In short, even a hard-line anthropocentric point of view,
one that excludes the value of potential informational and aesthetic ben-

efits, must still recognize that the two species of fairy shrimp have some indeterminate but real and irreplaceable value.

Vernal pools hospitable to San Diego and Riverside fairy shrimp have always been rare. Even before the arrival of the first Spanish settlers to the region hundreds of years ago, the pools probably existed only over an area of about two hundred square miles.[25] To develop, vernal pools require very specific soil types (relatively impermeable), climate conditions (seasonal rainfall and mild temperatures), and just the right topography (ideally, a mesa or table-top formation within coastal sage scrub). Between the first Western settlement and the present day, scientists estimate, between 95 and 97 percent of the already rare vernal pools in the region were destroyed.[26] Probably not many more than two thousand vernal pools remain in the region, all of them threatened either directly by development or indirectly by habitat fragmentation, edge effects, everyday pollution, emergencies like air crashes or toxic spills, and other sources of damage incidental to coexistence with a growing region of nearly three million people.[27]

This combination of rare microhabitats and rapid development has made the state of California a national laboratory for species conservation (it has the second-largest number of threatened and endangered species—291 at this writing; only Hawaii has more). California's San Bruno mountain was the location for the U.S. Fish and Wildlife Service's first experiment with habitat conservation plans, in 1980, and the California Department of Fish and Game's Natural Community Conservation Planning program became the model for HCPs on a national scale.[28]

Provisionalism's suggested mechanisms for the promotion of agency and plurality—protected enclaves, overlapping institutions, and citizen empowerment—are all present in the HCP debate in Southern California. Players on all sides of these debates, including developers, environmentalists, and other interested groups, are well endowed with the financial and informational resources necessary to compete in the regulatory and legislative arenas. Multiple agencies at many different levels of government take an interest in environmental policy there. Our results from chapter 1 suggest that we should be able to see the political agency, expressed through laws declaring popular support for species preservation and through institutions like public comment, realized in policies that

preserve the possibility of plural outcomes. Before embarking on the recent history of Southern Californian HCPs with regard to the conservation of fairy shrimp, however, I need to backtrack a few years to the establishment of the ESA regulatory regime in the 1970s.

The Original ESA Regulatory Regime

In 1973, the U.S. Congress passed the ESA, which provided powerful federal protection for endangered and threatened species in the United
States. "The Congress finds and declares that—(1) various species of fish,
wildlife, and plants in the United States have been rendered extinct as a
consequence of economic growth and development untempered by adequate concern and conservation; (2) other species of fish, wildlife, and
plants have been so depleted in numbers that they are in danger of or
threatened with extinction; (3) these species of fish, wildlife, and plants
are of esthetic, ecological, educational, historical, recreational, and scientific value to the Nation and its people." The act also mentions the country's international obligations and declares that Congress intends "to provide a means whereby the ecosystems upon which endangered species
and threatened species depend may be conserved."[29] The ESA, administered mainly by the U.S. Fish and Wildlife Service (FWS), provides for the
identification and listing of species as threatened or endangered; once a
species becomes listed, a whole series of activities aimed at preventing its
extinction comes into play. Under the ESA as passed in 1973, not only did
federal agencies have to initiate efforts at recovery of the listed species,
ranging from habitat protection to captive breeding programs, but private citizens were forbidden to "take" any individual members of the
species or to destroy their habitat (though these protections are stronger
for animals than for plants, and nonnatives and pest insects are excluded).[30] About thirteen hundred species are now listed by the FWS;
seventeen species have been officially declared "recovered," while nine of
the listed species have been declared extinct.[31]

Although a former chairman of the House Resources Committee,
Richard Pombo (R-CA), has called the ESA a failure, the scientific consensus considers it a qualified success.[32] The longer a species is protected
under the ESA, the more likely it is to recover.[33] Far too little is known
about the status of listed species, not to mention the many imperiled but
unlisted species (twenty-seven species have gone extinct while on the

waiting list for the FWS to decide about their status). However, of those species with known circumstances, most are improving.[34] In a context of population growth, intensive development, and chronic underfunding of the agencies entrusted with its enforcement, the ESA should be evaluated in light of its record of "only" nine extinctions of listed species, rather than in terms of a "mere" seventeen recorded recoveries. Without the ESA, loss of biodiversity over the past thirty years would surely have been much higher; such a result would be contrary to the expressed will of the people, as recorded, at least, in the text of the act.

"Ever since the U.S. Supreme Court, in *TVA* v. *Hill,* held that the protection of a three-inch fish, the endangered snail darter, precluded completion of a dam for which Congress had expended more than $100 million, no one has doubted that the [Endangered Species] act has sharp teeth."[35] Though only seventeen of the nearly thirteen hundred listed endangered species have crossed the threshold to recovery, the ESA has some spectacular records of success, including prevention (thus far) of the seemingly inevitable extinction of such "charismatic megafauna" as the California condor. Other prominent recoveries include the gray whale, the peregrine falcon, and the bald eagle.[36] The FWS claims on its Web site that "in concert with our many partners, we have prevented the extinction of approximately 900 listed species and stabilized or improved the status of at least 350 species."[37] Once listed, a species (and its constituency of biologists, environmentalists, nongovernmental agencies, and agency managers) gains access to significant federal moneys for research and conservation; furthermore, "taking" of the species or its habitat becomes a serious crime subject to substantial penalty. Massive recovery efforts for individual species have had some positive ancillary effects for nonlisted species and for wildlife in general, since every species exists within ecological systems composed of interdependent members (how interdependent, of course, is a matter of some knowledge and much intense speculation for each species in question, particularly our own).

The Revised ESA Regulatory Regime: HCPs

Nevertheless, toward the end of the twentieth century, interested parties across the political landscape, from land developers to conservation biologists, began to agree about some general weaknesses of the ESA regulatory regime. From the point of view of property holders and development interests, the strong protection provided to a species once it became listed translated into an atmosphere of uncertainty in which to make their investment decisions. Not only was the regulatory process long and difficult (not an unusual complaint in any policy area), its outcome was far from certain, since new knowledge and a changing environment could bring new environmental regulations into effect at any time. As political scientist Craig W. Thomas reports, at stake in ESA reform was "what all developers, landowners, and agency line managers wanted. They wanted certainty."[38]

From the point of view of environmentalists, the ESA enjoyed intermittent success at the species level but failed to preserve unfragmented, viable habitat. A new consensus among biologists emphasized the conditions necessary not simply to support a population's immediate needs (food, territory, and so forth) but to enable a species to survive the inevitable shocks that challenge its survival. In 1967, Robert H. Macarthur and Edward O. Wilson published their now-famous theory of island biogeography, arguing that biodiversity (the number of different species) varies according to an island's size and proximity to a larger landmass. Both of these aspects of habitat—nearness to a large area and its own size—affect the ability of a new population within a species to recolonize an appropriate habitat vacated by a population that had suffered a natural shock, such as excess predation, a weather event, disease, or some other difficulty.[39] This theory was soon applied in conservation science; increasing suburban and exurban development left the remaining patches of natural habitat in conditions not unlike those of islands surrounded by the sea. The biologist Michael Soulé (among others) further applied these ideas by proposing the concept of "wildlife corridors" among fragmented and otherwise isolated areas of natural habitat. By traversing the corridors between areas of otherwise fragmented habitat together, dispersed members of species would gain some of the benefits in terms of repopulation and migration that are no longer available in the form of large, undisturbed areas of wilderness. For example, a wildfire that might extirpate a species endemic to an isolated area surrounded by development might not do so if the area were connected by wilderness corridors to places undamaged by the fire and populated with members of the same species. Additional research emphasized newly understood genetic viability thresholds for species populations, migration patterns essential to

some species survival, the threat posed by edge effects to otherwise protected areas, and the massive territories required by many of the large
predators anchoring whole ecological systems. The upshot of all these
ideas for people interested in conservation was that preservation of individual endangered and threatened species could be managed only within
a broader program of preservation of as much unfragmented, interconnected habitat as possible. Advances in computer modeling and geographic information systems (GIS) allowed scientists and bureaucrats to
calculate and map the preserve systems that would maximize probable
habitat and species preservation while allowing for (the politically inevitable) continued development of previously natural habitat.

As scientific consensus grew around the need for large areas of unfragmented habitat and an ecosystem rather than a species-based approach to conservation, the law provided instead for piecemeal preservation of the isolated areas in which members of listed species had been
discovered. The FWS, strapped for resources and only rarely able to take a
proactive approach to habitat conservation, found itself driven by litigation rather than any overarching rational principles. Regarding the law-
suit-driven nature of the work done at the Carlsbad (California) Field
Station of the FWS, for example, spokeswoman Jane Hendron said, "We
are almost totally hamstrung in terms of setting our own priorities."[40]

A revision of the ESA to allow for "habitat conservation plans" thus
proposed to serve the interests of developers and environmentalists simultaneously. In 1982, Congress amended Section 10 of the ESA to allow
"incidental take permits"—that is, permission to kill some individual
members of the species—to be granted to holders of federally certified
habitat conservation plans. Though the program advanced in fits and
starts, with early HCPs failing due to lack of interest from developers and
lack of public resources, by the turn of the century more than four hundred HCPs had been approved by the FWS and state regulatory agencies.[41] These agreements generally exchanged a long-term, blanket incidental take permit granted to local authorities by federal and state wildlife
agencies for a comprehensive local program of habitat conservation. Developers would, within some species-specific limits, be granted permission to develop particularly attractive parcels of land containing populations of endangered species in exchange for biologically significant land
to be used to cobble together a relatively unfragmented wildlife preserve.

Consider the famous example of the coastal sage scrub habitat of the endangered songbird with which we began this chapter, the California gnatcatcher. Biologists estimate that a sustainable chunk of gnatcatcher habitat ought to be able to support at least twenty-five pairs of the birds.[42] According to traditional ESA regulations, a patch of ocean-view, undeveloped coastal sage scrub supporting perhaps five pairs of gnatcatchers would be subject to the most stringent review process. Under such a regime, patches of preserved habitat would be created, none of which would be large enough to withstand the periodic natural (not to mention artificial) shocks that threaten the population's survival. Under a locally administered HCP, however, the owner of this fabulously valuable undeveloped piece of ocean-view property would be able to build on the land, effectively killing a small population of endangered gnatcatchers. This population was probably not viable over the long run anyway, however, and in exchange the developer and the permit-granting government would have to arrange for more viable habitat and populations elsewhere to be preserved. As this sketch should make clear, the HCP concept in its early days seemed like that very rare thing in politics, the win-win situation.

San Diego provided the perfect showcase example of HCPs for Bruce Babbit's Department of Interior under President Bill Clinton.[43] The Southern California region is a biodiversity hotspot, with hundreds of endemic species and a stunning diversity of habitats. Most imperiled of these was coastal sage scrub, which covers bluffs overlooking the ocean and a few miles inland, provides habitat for endangered species like the California gnatcatcher (which breeds nowhere else), and occupies some of the most valuable undeveloped real estate anywhere. In fact, it was the FWS decision to list the gnatcatcher as threatened that finally propelled interested parties in Southern California to commit to HCPs beyond the early "voluntary" and thus toothless first experiments.[44] Habitat loss to development in San Diego County led to "more than 200 species considered imperiled . . . [there are] more endangered and threatened plants and animals in San Diego County than in any other place in the lower forty-eight states."[45]

Although the concept of exchanging takings permits for land to develop large, viable reserves had been around for years, the program existed only in voluntary form until the California gnatcatcher was listed as endangered in 1993.[46] Under California protections for the gnatcatcher habitat, no more than 5 percent of still-undeveloped coastal sage scrub in an area could be released for development; add to this the new federal restrictions associated with the now officially threatened gnatcatcher's status, and you have a strong incentive for developers to find some way to escape from these constraints on their business. By 1998, the city of San Diego had approved a massive Multiple Species Conservation Program (MSCP), which meant that the city, as holder of a blanket incidental take permit from the FWS, could grant permission to develop previously protected areas, so long as it pursued the plan of habitat-wide conservation outlined in its federally approved management plan. A similar plan was developed for northern San Diego County; the city of Carlsbad was the first of the northern subarea cities to gain approval for its part of the Multiple Habitat Conservation Plan (MHCP); it was granted an incidental take permit by the FWS in November of 2004. Though the details are still being litigated, in the main the area covered by an HCP is exempt from previous regulations like the 5 percent limit on loss of coastal sage scrub habitat, the prohibition against taking any endangered species or harming its habitat, and possibly from the strictures of critical habitat designation or other coverages. In exchange, permit holders like the cities of Carlsbad and San Diego promise to carry out the projects listed in their HCPs of acquiring and maintaining viable habitats. The permits are theoretically revocable if the FWS determines that permit holders have not fulfilled their obligations.

San Diego County's HCPs

Advances in GIS technology and "gap analysis," plus still-inadequate but ongoing efforts at data collection, made it possible for the MSCP and MHCP planners (I'll refer to them collectively as HCP planners) to construct patterns of habitat conservation that created the largest feasible unfragmented habitats connected by "wildlife corridors," to allow individuals to migrate according to their needs, and to allow extirpated populations to be replaced by remaining viable populations from elsewhere in the HCP area. The HCP did not create much new, fully protected preserve area, nor did it directly effect any transfer of land from private to public hands. Instead, the HCPs aimed to identify remaining areas of viable habitat and encourage their protection, while streamlining the process of economic development for governments and private citizens. The city of Carlsbad's long-planned municipal golf course, for example, was unable to receive the state and federal permissions required for construction before the city's HCP was approved; upon the final approval of the MHCP by the state Coastal Commission, and with a few more concessions to ecological necessity, the city was able to begin building the course. The developer's photographic projections of the future golf course clearly show destruction of coastal sage scrub habitat; without the MHCP, and its plan for the conservation of habitat elsewhere and adjacent to it, Carlsbad's municipal golf course would likely have remained mired in environmental regulation.[47] Instead, the city set aside half of the course's four hundred acres for "protected habitat" and planned to open The Crossings golf course to the public in July 2007.[48]

The North County MHCP (of which Carlsbad is a subarea) is a commitment on the part of permit holders "to protect viable populations of key sensitive plant and animal species and their habitats, while accommodating continued economic development and quality of life for residents of the north county region."[49] Implementation of the plan depends on many contingencies, including especially funding by local and other governments. The consultants who developed the plan tried to balance many different considerations in addition to species preservation, and thus the plan contains numerous references to the difference between ideal and planned habitat development. Regarding the habitat of the California gnatcatcher within the plan area, for example, the MHCP relates that the holder of the largest undeveloped area of unfragmented gnatcatcher habitat has already been granted a take permit under Sections 7 and 10(a) of the ESA, and thus the plan will have to rely on "stepping-stone" reserves of lower quality, with the expectation that the nearby larger areas controlled by the Marine Corps at Camp Pendleton and elsewhere will sustain the population.[50] This provision of the MHCP is typical of a dynamic that we shall see in more detail toward the end of this book. First, note that the HCP tends to rely on outside agencies to secure the preservation of the protected species, although the clear intent of the ESA is directly to promote the recovery of listed species. Second, much of the language of these documents is devoted to lamenting the *future loss,* treated as inevitable, of a population of a listed species that is at the writing of the

HCP *still viable.* In Carlsbad's MHCP there is a marked pattern of irresponsibility consistent with this type of environmental discourse.

The MHCP envisions a combination of "hard-line" and "soft-line" reserves, with the former having at least 90 percent of their area reserved for wildlife habitat; these reserves are estimated to preserve a bit less than three-quarters of the remaining natural habitat in a subsection of the MHCP region identified through GIS as the "biological core area." Rather than attempt to build large, unfragmented reserves through any large-scale transfer of land, the MHCP proposes a network of existing reserves, supplemented with land exchanged by developers for take permits (and managed by a combination of private trusts and public agencies), and made up mostly of "stepping-stone" and "postage stamp" preserves, with a few larger, already preserved areas less vulnerable to edge effects.[51]

Although even the destruction of vernal pools is explicitly allowed by the MHCP if the preservation of such pools would reduce the value of the property in question to zero, the plan envisions "no net loss" of wetlands.[52] The MHCP specifically addresses the question of preservation of vernal pools and fairy shrimp: "All vernal pools and their watersheds within the MHCP study area must be 100% conserved, regardless of occupancy by this species and regardless of location inside or outside of the FPA [focused planning area], unless doing so would remove all economic uses of a property." In such cases, the MHCP calls for mitigation with no net loss.[53] The authors of the plan note that although one prominent area of vernal pools at the Poinsettia train station is protected within the plan's focused planning area, most vernal pool habitat is not. The persistence of the Riverside fairy shrimp within the MHCP area will depend, the authors argue, on "intensive management and monitoring."[54]

It is hard to see how the writers of the MHCP can square these two statements, one of no net loss, and the other of allowable take in case of loss of property value. Perhaps the authors relied on the atmosphere of uncertainty surrounding responsibility for wetlands under the Clean Water Act (1977). After the 2001 decision by the United States Supreme Court in *Solid Waste Agency of North Cook County (SWANCC) v. United States Army Corps of Engineers,* the jurisdiction of the corps (ACOE) over isolated wetlands has been unclear. Litigation is ongoing, but the SWANCC decision almost certainly eliminates ACOE responsibility to enforce the Clean Water Act in cases of isolated wetlands used by migratory birds, and possibly eliminates ACOE responsibility for vernal pools in general. The MHCP authors do not, however, provide any scientific evidence that mitigation efforts to replace vernal pools destroyed under the allowance for property loss would have any positive effect on the survival of the listed species in question. One wonders, then, how the no-net-loss standard would be met.

By the time the U.S. Fish and Wildlife Service issued the permit granting the city of Carlsbad its incidental take permit (November 12, 2004), two further regulatory issues affecting the Riverside and the San Diego fairy shrimp had emerged: critical habitat designation, and the "no surprises rule." The Endangered Species Act as currently revised provides multiple tools for protection of listed species. On the one hand, "take" of the protected species is prohibited unless special permitting within a habitat conservation plan allows it. Even within areas covered by HCPs, however, other designations can trump local authorities' incidental take permits. The Riverside and the San Diego fairy shrimp, for example, may also be covered under vernal pools' wetlands protection, though, as we have seen, recent court rulings have thrown this regulatory area into confusion.[55] On the other hand, the ESA provides that listed species have their "critical habitat" identified, and that once habitat critical to the recovery of a species is designated, additional protection applies to those lands.

At present, the FWS maintains that critical habitat designation is redundant, adding useless layers of regulation to species that are already otherwise protected.[56] Curiously, they also maintain that critical habitat designation will result in additional economic costs; the service has estimated that the designation of critical habitat for vernal pools in California and Oregon, for example, would result in nearly $1 billion in "lost development opportunities," including about sixteen hundred homes that would not be built.[57] Designation of an area as critical habitat provides that decisions regarding development must take into account not simply the direct effects on an endangered species but also its potential effects on the recovery of the species. As we shall see by the end of this chapter, this distinction matters a great deal.

As the present administration views critical habitat designation as unnecessary, most critical habitat designation and revision of designation is being done under court order, after litigation is brought by environmental groups. The current dispute over critical habitat designation for the fairy shrimp and other vernal pool endemics stems from litigation brought by an environmental-advocacy group, the Center for Biological Diversity, to force the FWS to designate critical habitat for the animals. The FWS ultimately designated twenty-two acres in northern San Diego County, and three acres in southern San Diego County, as critical habitat for the Riverside fairy shrimp.[58] Though the question of redundancy remains open, there is some support in the scientific literature for the view that critical habitat designation, in addition to other ESA protections, enhances an endangered species' chance of recovery. Though the authors of one study emphasize the short amount of time the ESA has been in effect (with an average of 15.5 listed years per species) and the lack of data generally, they conclude that "species with critical habitat for two or more years were more than twice as likely to have an improving population trend in the late 1990s, and less than half as likely to be declining in the early 1990s, as species without."[59]

From a provisional point of view, critical habitat designation is important because it requires policy-makers to consider not just the present effect of actions but also the potential for an action to promote eventual recovery of a species. Moreover, it provides for overlapping authorities to pursue a goal; here, the FWS would be forced to retain some of the permit-granting authority it intended to devolve to the city of Carlsbad. However, the precariousness of any such strong protection for endangered species is illustrated by the recent (2004) exemption of all Defense Department–managed lands from critical habitat designations (specifically, the conservation benefits must be weighed against national security costs unless an approved management plan exists). A substantial portion of the region's Riverside and San Diego fairy shrimp, for example, inhabit vernal pools located on lands managed by the Department of the Navy. It is easily conceivable that future security concerns or other compelling interests could arise to override the preservation of two endangered species of fairy shrimp inside these critical habitats. Another key consideration with regard to critical habitat designation is the locus of final decision-making. Though HCP plans are subject to federal and state review, the bureaucrat issuing the permit that will result in habitat loss in the case of HCPs probably works for a city, whereas the bureaucrat issuing such a

permit in the case of critical habitat exemptions or standard ESA procedures probably works for the federal government. Therefore, as a policy
for which the federal government retains discretionary authority, the
critical habitat designation process should be better able to discount
the pressure for generating local revenue through development than the
process of granting incidental take permits, which though federally su-
pervised occurs mostly at the local level. As we shall see, this apparently
minor distinction ends up making a big difference.

A second recent regulatory challenge for the endemic fairy shrimp of
northern San Diego County concerns the so-called no surprises rule. Also
highly litigated, the no surprises rule as it stands at this writing allows the
FWS to provide an extra guarantee of certainty to property developers by
assuring them that the discovery of any new threats to endangered species
in the area granted an incidental take permit will not result in revocation
of that permit. As part of the rule-making the FWS was required to undergo before the rule passed muster in the federal courts, the service included commitments to "adaptive management" of HCPs, which the
FWS claims will sufficiently contain unforeseen threats to wildlife. Theoretically, adaptive management incorporates the results of new species
and habitat-specific data into the preservation process. Since the assurances granted to the permittee prevent the FWS from requiring any new
mitigation, or funding, or habitat acquisition, however, it is hard to see
how adaptive management is to be implemented in practice. The no surprises rule currently constrains the FWS from doing more than encouraging the managers of HCPs to respond to dynamic conditions affecting
listed species by using adaptive management techniques. A robust set of
overlapping institutions might yet constrain property owners, even those
under HCPs. Even as the FWS exempts HCPs from critical habitat protection and grants its take permit holders assurances of no surprises, other
agencies remain at least potentially interested in the protection of vernal
pools and their endemic endangered species.

San Diego Area HCPs from a Provisional Point of View

Depending on the season and year in which you are reading this book,
then, there may well be living representatives of the San Diego and the
Riverside species of fairy shrimp still swimming in a few vernal pools in
Southern California. Some of the pools are located in northwestern San

Diego County near the Poinsettia train station, where local residents can catch a "Coaster" commuter train from the northern city of Carlsbad into downtown San Diego. These pools have been made into a "postage stamp preserve," about five acres of vernal pool habitat surrounded by development, vulnerable to edge effects, and largely isolated from other populations of San Diego and Riverside fairy shrimp. The beautifully designed commuter station includes pedestrian bridges to protect the pools, which are located between the parking lot and the train tracks. Large signs provide information about vernal pool ecology and the efforts being made to protect the pools.

Protection of these few acres of pool habitat and their resident fairy shrimp is mandated by several different and overlapping federal, state, and local regulatory regimes. The city of Carlsbad, the U.S. Fish and Wildlife Service, the California Coastal Commission, and the California Department of Fish and Game have all committed themselves to protecting these fairy shrimp and their habitat.[60] The final (2003) Multiple Habitat Conservation Program document covering these animals states that "all vernal pools and their watersheds within the MHCP study area must be 100% conserved, regardless of occupancy [by the Riverside fairy shrimp] and regardless of location inside or outside of the Focused Planning Area, unless doing so would remove all economic uses of a property." In the case of total loss of economic value, the program requires mitigation with "no net loss."[61]

A variety of regulatory regimes cover and have covered the Riverside and the San Diego fairy shrimp; since the passage of the federal Endangered Species Act in 1973, most have aimed squarely at the strongest possible protection and recovery of the animals. Moreover, as regulation in this area has evolved, it has become more attractive from a provisional point of view. The ESA as originally written provided inflexible, conclusive principles that managers on the ground could not hope to follow. Whole sections of the ESA are routinely ignored unless litigation or powerful interest groups raise the issue.[62] Federal mandates met the strong resistance of local stakeholders who had not been involved in the conservation decisions that deeply affected their livelihoods. The ESA policy regime, as I have noted, has had some success in preventing otherwise likely extinctions from taking place. Nevertheless, from a provisional point of view, its institutions were likely to fail. Under the HCP regime, by contrast, government efforts to protect the fairy shrimp have gradually incorporated a number of principles recommended by provisional politics, including overlapping authority, revisability, maximum information under an empirically guided, flexible stance, increased public participation, and even, if often indirectly, empowerment of the stakeholders toward active citizenship. Ironically, the same changes that make the recent evolution of environmental regulation attractive from a provisional point of view have led to a *narrowing* of choice available to future publics, rather than the expected preservation of broad policy choice.

Almost as soon as the San Diego MSCP was approved, stories of its failure began to appear. In 1998, city authorities, backed by the Army Corps of Engineers, ignored their commitments to the FWS and issued permits to allow the destruction of all but one of sixty-six vernal pools in a protected area, to allow for the development of a strip mall and condominium complex. The remaining vernal pool, fenced off in front of the Legacy condominium housing development, is unlikely to remain viable, not least due to the hostility it elicits from its human neighbors.[63] The MSCP's language and apparent commitment to preserving, among other species, the endangered San Diego fairy shrimp at the site notwithstanding, local officials were able to exercise broad discretion regarding the final decision about development of the project. That they chose the development of relatively redundant shopping centers like Cousins Market and condominium complexes like Legacy over the relatively irreplaceable vernal pools should not surprise us. The short-term incentive horizon of city council members, for whom property and sales tax revenue are overwhelmingly important, makes them unlikely agents of species preservation.[64]

In Carlsbad, local officials are subject to the same overwhelmingly short-term sets of incentives. City council member Ramona Finnila speaks plainly about her support for MHCP goals: she supported the plan only because it would make it easier to approve development projects. Confronted with delays in the municipal golf course project, Finnila lamented the city's prompt approval of its part of the MHCP: "Being on the leading edge of this process turned out to be on the bleeding edge." [65] City officials' chances of reelection depend upon provision of local services and implementation of popular development plans such as golf courses; governance of a city is far easier in the context of growing sales and property tax revenues than in a slow or no-growth environment. The threat of permit revocation by the FWS is a long-term and distant one compared with near-term electoral prospects for a local elected official (while for the FWS bureaucrat, central sanctions are likely to be far more efficacious).

In this context, it is not surprising that environmental groups have continued to rely on court orders and ongoing litigation to advance the preservation agenda that comes from the state and federal levels rather than the municipal level. The chair of the Working Group that hammered out the San Diego MSCP, Karen Scarborough, has expressed frustration at the continued use of a litigation strategy by environmental groups: "We had hoped to change the environmentalist vs. builder paradigm."[66] The crucial flaw in the HCP regime has been its reliance on the discretion of local officials to implement an expensive program serving long-term goals with nearly invisible short- and medium-term results.

The implementation of HCPs, as all the literature and plans recognize, depends on adequate funding, both initially for the development of the conserved areas and indefinitely for monitoring and management. Inadequate funding is a constant across the ESA and HCP regimes, and thus cannot itself account for the different outcomes. However, the HCPs as enacted have shown less resilience to underfunding and funding shocks than the ESA. Both San Diego area HCPs discussed here depend on voter-granted endowments that have not materialized. Since the late 1990s, the city of San Diego has been involved in the worst financial scandal in the city's history and may not be able to fund its employee pension plans, much less the loosely mandated and distant goal of species preservation.[67] Despite the city's insistence that it is committed to the MSCP, recent spending on land acquisition was near zero.[68] Both the HCPs and the scientific literature agree that both land acquisition and land management are essential elements of a successful habitat conservation effort. Much of the land in San Diego's MSCP is left to private management companies, whose performance over the long haul is untested. One of the most important private holders of conservation easements and managers of HCP property, Environmental Trust, Inc., went into bankruptcy in 2005, leaving acres of habitat formally conserved but unmanaged and thus unprotected.[69]

San Diego area vernal pools remain vulnerable to both natural and political shocks; given the fragility of species involved, over time these shocks are likely to result in irreversible policy failure. For example, although the project has thus far been resisted by both voters and San Diego's military establishment, it is likely that the largest remaining area of relatively undisturbed vernal pools will be destroyed to make way for a new municipal airport in the next decade or two. Growth in the San Diego metropolitan region has been limited by the capacity of the city's downtown airport; the San Diego County Regional Airport Authority has designated the military facility at Miramar as the most promising location for a new, multirunway facility to accommodate future demand. The airport authority's own study neglects even to discuss the project's potential impact on the Riverside and the San Diego fairy shrimp, while making the odd claim that little information on the Miramar pools is available.[70]

Meanwhile, environmentalists and scientists have expressed shock and dismay at the idea of a new airport on the site. David Hogan, of the Center for Biological Diversity, opposes the plan's likely destruction of Southern California's largest remaining vernal pool area: "You cannot deal with this. This project will result in the extinction of seven species— off the face of the planet. They're gone. They're dead."[71] Even normally cautious biological scientists have used strong language in this case. San Diego State University's Ellen Bauder has predicted the extinctions of vernal pool endemic species should the airport plan go forward. "It [the proposed destruction of the vernal pools at Miramar] cannot be mitigated. Period. . . . That's like saying you'll build a new Grand Canyon somewhere or a new Yosemite. This may not be as charismatic and flashy, but it is very important—and it is the only piece that is left."[72]

THE CONCLUSIVE LIMITS OF PROVISIONAL POLICY IN THE CASE OF SPECIES PRESERVATION

The political scientist Nicholas R. Miller has written a beautiful description of the role of reversibility in democratic practice: a "pluralist political system does *not* authoritatively allocate values in a stable fashion. Rather, it sets political competitors—who might otherwise be bashing heads instead of (repeatedly) counting them (and seemingly getting different counts every time)—running around. . . . Not only does each competitor 'win some and lose some,' but most wins and losses are themselves reversible. Thus the competitors can never be confident of their victories, nor need they resign themselves to their defeats. Of course, since considerable resources are devoted to this competitive treadmill, pluralist politics are somewhat inefficient in economic terms. But the state of affairs associated with severe political instability is far more profoundly inefficient."[73] Policy reversibility of this type is essential to democratic politics in a provisional mode.

Perhaps, then, provisional theory should take a conclusive stand against all potentially irreversible policies? (At least, against those that are irreversible on a social scale, since considered individually, all policies are in some sense irreversible.) Imagine such a strong stance: provisional theory would then counsel preservation at all costs of irreplaceable species, regardless of the opportunity costs or other considerations. This would indeed be a conclusive policy that reduces the scope of future generations' political agency, though it would preserve the existence of the species, thereby enhancing the scope of agency with regard to biodiversity and its concomitant values. If we imagine instead of this conclusive policy a set of institutions that mandates consideration of potential trade-offs, however, we are also led to unfortunately conclusive results. Take an imaginary policy that would allow the eradication of a tiny fish, very like similar species, in order to provide continued basic subsistence for local people. Thinking about the conditions of the continued possibility of democratic self-rule, one might weigh the loss of the fish (a scope-reducing act) against the wealth and health that increase citizen capacity. In fact, we do not need imaginary examples to understand this dynamic. The residents of one neighborhood in San Diego have been waiting for decades for a planned school, Jonas Salk Elementary School, to be built. The land was set aside by a developer in 1980, and the bond to fund construction was passed in 1998. However, the presence of vernal pools on the site and the uncertainty about whether mitigation would be adequate or even possible have thus far prevented construction. Many local people do not see the issue in terms of flexible school locations in conflict with potentially irreversible species eradication. Instead, some reason as Ted Brengel, chairman of the Mira Mesa Community Planning Group, does: "What's more important? The children or the fairy shrimp?"[74]

There are many ways to achieve wealth and health, and only a few ways to preserve a unique species. Each policy has its own set of possibility enhancing and reducing consequences. In a context of democratic give and take, over time policy choices will fluctuate between preserving the unique values associated with each species and promoting some people's interests in wealth and health. Long-term discursive developments could change the degree and path of that fluctuation; perhaps over time in a certain context, policy might grow steadily more preservationist, or steadily less so. Because species loss is irreversible, however, the provisional commitment to agency and plurality in practice amounts to a preemptive, substantive decision against species preservation. Since provisional politics ought to promote the exchange of office among groups, reversible policies, and the freedom that comes from a nonossified system, presumably environmental policies will fluctuate, too. But unlike the case of, say, tax policy, where individuals are irreversibly harmed or benefited, but the society as a whole can make a policy one year and repeal it the next, in species preservation any switch to nonpreservation is permanent. How can this promote reversibility?

The answer is that it cannot. The claim that policies affecting species extinctions are provisionally legitimate because they are reversible is like the claim that a natural right to property prevents change to the status quo in economic relations. The latter claim, I argued in chapter 3, is flawed on account of its reification of the conditions of a principle's vindication. The indiscriminate application of such conditions regardless of context or political result is a mistake, and thus legitimate property rights rules vary according to circumstance. Declaring oneself a conclusive supporter of the minimalist version of the right to property, then, amounts to declaring oneself a partisan of the status quo. Similarly, but at a further level of abstraction, declaring oneself a supporter of provisionality in the case of species protection, since each case presents unique consequences for the conditions of political freedom, actually amounts to declaring oneself in favor of eventual species destruction, since the ratcheting effect of each fluctuation in the policy environment inevitably leaves the world with less biodiversity.

The problem, then, with species conservation and politics is that provisionalism cannot specify a particular outcome, even one that seems structurally required. Morality remains within politics as part of the system, but the moral arguments themselves must be made by citizens over time, evolving into discourses that constrain political possibility, rather than be made by theorists and enforced from the center. As we have seen,

Kant argues that it is an illegitimate reduction of the scope of future free-dom to restrict the political possibilities of future generations. Thomas Jefferson argues similarly that each generation should set its own consti-tutional rules. Even Gutmann and Thompson argue that restricting the scope of democratic decision-making is, for the most part, illegitimate (which is why they insist that moral questions be on the table); the kinds of things they are willing to exclude are things that violate the conditions of just political activity as such, like slavery. Could any of these republi-can, democratic, or liberal theorists possibly argue that one generation may willfully remove a large part of future generations' discretion by nar-rowing their available options? After all, this is one description of the sub-stantive, preemptive result we reached in our consideration of species preservation under conditions of agency and plurality.

Mostly, political theorists do not think about these kinds of things. Hobbes describes the legacy of civilization as a precious good, echoing Thucydides in his emphasis on great worth of the fruits of cooperation. Locke, as is well known, argues for the enclosing (that is, the develop-ment) of as much wilderness as possible, but he does include his famous proviso that "enough and as good" be left for posterity.[75] Arguably, Locke among all of the classic sources has the most coherent, if not the most pleasant, response to this question of environmental uncertainty. We can find it in paragraphs 240–242 of the *Second Treatise,* where Locke asks how one is to know whether rebellion against a given authority is justi-fied. One reading of his response is that since we cannot possibly know for certain, we must rely on our own reason, our "only star and compass" (*First Treatise*), and trust that the general outcome will be satisfactory from God's point of view.[76]

"Let God be judge" could be the ironical motto for the outcome reached in the case of species conservation by provisional theory: agency and plurality require us to insist on reversibility, on empowering citizens to make their own policy decisions, and on enabling moral argument to affect politics not by imposing undemocratic restrictions but by encour-aging public discourse to influence political outcomes through protected enclaves, overlapping institutions, and citizen leverage. These elements are in fact present in the MSCP cases, and becoming ever more present even in the global sustainability case. Sadly, the structure of these kinds of policies in the present context, unimagined by our classical authors in their contexts, means that species extinction on a large scale is the over-whelmingly likely outcome.

Contrary to the view of many environmental theorists, the problem does not lie with public opinion: the ESA has withstood repeated attacks in the U.S. Congress, and international institutions have expressed a global interest in species preservation through treaties and resolutions. Even the people of Texas have been discovered, through deliberative polling, to be more committed to the preservation of the environment than one might have thought.[77] Rather, the problem is one of the irreversible ratcheting structure of this particular policy area: the institutions through which legitimate political will can be expressed are not capable of achieving species preservation over the long run; the timescale over which public discourse influences political culture in a way that would alter this dynamic is far too slow to matter for many of the species in question. I hope that I am wrong, but the analysis of this chapter leads me to conclude that agency and plurality in the present context means living in an ever more biologically impoverished environment.

Even the wilderness preserves that are the best chance for long-term sustainability of many species are vulnerable to this dynamic. Take the earlier example of the conversion of Miramar air station into a municipal airport for the city of San Diego. Though there is broad recognition that the Miramar vernal pools complex contains one of the very few remaining potentially sustainable habitats for endemic species like fairy shrimp that are narrowly adapted to those conditions, and even though the people, globally, nationally, and even locally, have repeatedly expressed their desire to preserve endangered species, this airport could always be built. What could possibly prevent this event, which we can say with relatively little uncertainty brings us very close to losing several endemic vernal pool species, any one of which could be of enormous practical value, and all of which are uniquely valuable qua species? Each successful prevention of the airport, through lawsuits, referenda, or any other means, political or otherwise, only puts off the day when short-term interest prevails. And when it does, it prevails permanently.

EPILOGUE

On October 13, 2006, U.S. Senior District Judge Rudi M. Brewster ruled in the case of *Southwest Center for Biological Diversity v. Bartel* that the

U.S. Fish and Wildlife Service had not fulfilled either the letter or the spirit of the ESA with regard to protection of vernal pools and their endemic endangered species in granting San Diego an incidental take permit and approving its MSCP.[78] The judge granted an injunction halting current and planned development affecting vernal pool habitat. Construction of at least one road, a church, and a housing project has been delayed; more significantly, the FWS has been ordered to review its planned protection of vernal pool species in San Diego.[79] As reported in the local newspaper, the ruling "heartened conservationists, even though they said much of the habitat they sued to protect has been paved over."[80]

Brewster's ruling represents only one event in the fluctuating history of vernal pool protection in Southern California. Its concrete effects will be negotiated among lawyers, bureaucrats, and representatives of the many interested parties in the suit; subsequent court actions will enhance or diminish its influence. For our purposes, however, the ruling is interesting not only as an event in the preservation history of fairy shrimp but also as an instance of public reason in the provisional mode. Brewster does not reach the conclusion of this chapter, that species preservation policy in a context of agency and plurality inevitably tends toward extinction. Brewster reasons, in a sort of American legal version of the hoary ethical principle that "ought implies can," that the explicit intent of Congress in the ESA is the prevention of extinction and therefore that the duty of the state is to realize this goal. However, in his analysis of the case of the San Diego MSCP, Brewster identifies dynamics akin to what I call the "ratchet effect," "policy irreversibility," and the tendency on the part of HCP authors toward irresponsibility.

Almost as soon as he has introduced the topic, Brewster complains about the structure of the policy envisioned by the MSCP. By granting an incidental take permit to the city in exchange for vague promises that funding for acquisition and monitoring will be found, the FWS has "virtually guaranteed development" and permitted "monumental destruction" of vernal pool species (3). Though the nearly invisible fairy shrimp may not strike many people as significant, Brewster continues, "if this type of destruction is treated on a case-by-case basis as an unimportant loss, it does not take long before life on this planet is in jeopardy" (4). The dynamics of species extinction is such that incremental losses may not be noticed until severe damage has been done. This same pattern is institutionalized in the MSCP process on an individual-species basis. By relying on outside agencies which may not in fact have authority (13), and on vague promises by players with little interest in species preservation (28), the FWS pushes its moments of responsibility forward, to a time when "it may have lost the opportunity to protect the vernal pool species from extinction" (32). Though the FWS claims that permits are revocable, no net loss is anticipated, and mitigation is required, Brewster counters that "the destruction is permanent and the 'mitigation' is illusory" (30).

As we have already seen, the SWANCC decision (2001) calls into question the FWS assumption that the Army Corps of Engineers will protect vernal pools as part of its mandate under the Clean Water Act to protect wetlands. Brewster notes that even though this safeguard has been removed, the FWS has proceeded to grant assurances to holders of take permits that no new requirements beyond those initially undertaken will be added in the future (27). The FWS undertook this obligation despite the fact that it had no reason to believe that vernal pool species would not be driven to extinction by development of those areas allowed under the MSCP and not in fact protected by ACOE or other agencies (27, 36). Brewster lists some of the many weakness of the FWS's plan for protection: the MSCP includes an arbitrary measure of allowable loss of vernal pool habitat (12 percent), calculates losses by pool surface area while measuring mitigation according to the much larger vernal pool basin area measure, includes no evidence that fairy shrimp even occupy those areas anticipated as mitigation for losses of occupied pools, and offers no reason to believe that the city's "shaky pledge" to find essential funding for the plan will be met (39–53). Rather than constructing a plan that promotes the ESA's mandate of making the changes needed to move endangered species out of jeopardy, San Diego's MSCP seems to be memorializing species that are not yet extinct (34).

Brewster's strong condemnation of the FWS's shirking of its clear mandate under the ESA indicates his belief that enforcement of the law protecting species from extinction is possible, and thus that the San Diego MSCP's shortcomings are remediable bureaucratic and political failures rather than reflections of an inherent structural problem with species preservation. He notes, for example, that the ESA's dual mechanisms of enforcing direct species protections, on the one hand, and of designating critical habitat for some listed species, on the other, provide a helpful set of overlapping institutions that would have helped the vernal pool species, had critical habitat designations been in place as they should have been (43). Had the FWS fulfilled its mandate, it would not have granted the assurances to permit holders that were allowed in the San Diego MSCP without having stronger reasons to believe that San Diego would in fact successfully protect endangered vernal pool species. Thus for Brewster the permit-granting process, overlapping institutions, the process of accumulating and responding to scientific data on the species, and other accountability measures are presumably sufficient at least to fulfill the ESA mandate of moving species out of jeopardy.

Even so, in the case of this MSCP, Brewster identifies the same troubling policy dynamics that I have identified with species protection under conditions of agency and plurality in general. The irreversibility of development's effects on fragile species like the fairy shrimp, combined with a process that ensures periodic "take" and no reliable mitigation, creates a ratcheting effect moving the species toward extinction. The process moves in one direction, despite the "plain intent of Congress . . . to halt and reverse the trend toward species extinction" (5, quoting *Tennessee Valley Authority v. Hill* [1978]). As Brewster memorably puts it, "The species are left in a 'heads I lose, tails you win' position" (4).

6

conclusions

Fiat iustitia, pereat mundus.
—Kant

Fiat iustitia, ut duret mundus.
—Ellis

Environmental policy is a limit case for provisional right. Provisional theory contends that the facts of agency and plurality lead to a politics of permanent contestation. Adam Przeworski's remark about democracy applies to provisional politics as well: "The essential feature of democracy is
that nothing is decided definitively."[1] As we have seen, this leads provisional theory to prioritize battles for substantive citizenship and other
preconditions of agency and plurality, over battles for particular policy
outcomes. On this understanding of politics, neither individual rights
nor democratic justice are given absolute priority: everything is always at
least potentially on the political table, since anything removed in theory
reduces the sphere of potential political agency and plurality. While provisional theory recognizes, for example, that individuals in order to exercise substantive freedom must have some independent access to their
means of subsistence, and thus that some private property rights ought to
be protected in order to render citizen autonomy practicable, it does not
grant any *a priori* status to property rights as such. Limited property
rights—how limited is a political question to be left open by provisional
theory—are justified provisionally and hypothetically in the name of the
complex imperatives of modern politics. On the other hand, even the

most compelling democratically legitimate public good cannot become a permanent policy implemented by an absolutely empowered central state. Moral judgments about political questions are not to be prejudged by political theorists, who in any case are unlikely to agree.

This approach worked well with most of my case studies. However, the presumption of permanent contestation, which Kant and others argue is essential for preserving each generation's political freedom, is much more difficult to sustain with regard to the preservation of endangered species. If, as the political scientist Nicholas R. Miller argues, legitimate politics and ultimately political stability depend on the *reversibility* of political wins and losses, then clearly environmental issues pose a difficult conundrum. There is a long tradition in political thought of resorting to absolute rule in the face of necessity. However, the contemporary situation in the case of species preservation is less one of necessity (imminent collective ruin) than of uncertainty: potential collective ruin.[2] Garrett Hardin challenges his readers with just this problem, and he concludes that if the choice is between freedom and survival, humanity ought to choose survival.[3] Hardin's dichotomy is not exhaustive, however. Even if it were, provisional right cannot promote species preservation at the expense of limiting possible future agency and plurality through autocratic governance. Conclusive theoretical determinations of policy, even such morally defensible ones as the preservation for posterity of a unique and irreplaceable form of life, cannot coexist with agency and plurality.[4]

It is an interesting question whether the defense of vulnerable species is beyond the power not only of politics that values agency and plurality but also of politics as such. Hardin thought not, and he argued for privatization in cases where those institutions would solve collective action problems (such as pollution), but for near-authoritarian measures when liberal ones are not effective (as in the case of overpopulation). One wonders about the potential effectiveness of such measures, even if they were to be justified by environmental emergency. James Scott, for example, gives us reason for doubt with his demonstration that authoritarian governments attempting to institute absolute policies can certainly disrupt preexisiting social institutions but have always failed in their "schemes to improve the human condition."[5]

Hardin's intuition that one should resort to absolutist measures in the face of catastrophe is given a different formulation by the philosopher

Peter Singer in his famous example of the drowning child.[6] When faced with an overwhelmingly compelling moral good, such as saving a drowning child, preventing mass starvation, or ensuring air and water for coming generations, argues Singer, we must do whatever is necessary to ensure the achievement of the moral good. Even if we are not directly responsible for the present situation—the child's being in the water or the injustice suffered by most of the world—we would be as wrong to ignore the one as the other. Singer's drowning child example has real moral power. Provisional theory does not deny that those claims ought to be taken seriously. It does claim, however, that the proper venue for such claims is the political sphere: political theorists in their offices, would-be guardians of the public good in their think tanks, and absolutist "servants of the people" in their palaces may believe that the potential for enacting an apparently superior set of policy prescriptions excuses or even demands their imposing a policy outside the political process. But citizens cannot so easily transfer the burden of the drowning child's claims to scholars, technocrats, or tyrants. Moral claims in the public sphere are the people's responsibility. Citizens cannot shuck off their agency and plurality in the face of difficult questions.

Neither can they retreat into moral rigorism. Political agents' first responsibility is for the discovery, promotion, and maintenance of the conditions of political possibility, rather than for any more specific political end, however compelling. Moral rigorism's attraction stems from its promise of certainty: even if I cannot control the circumstances in which I make my decision, or the consequences of it in the world, at least I can calculate whether my maxim accords with whatever ethical principle is authoritative for me. Without making a determination of the appropriateness of moral rigorism as a personal ethic, I can say that for politics it cannot be the right attitude. As I have argued throughout this book, taking political principles to be conclusive statements of right is a mistake.

Given the endemic uncertainty of political life, its shifting conditions, and the dependence of moral argument in any given context on its peculiar discursive history, claims of political right must necessarily be provisional. Again, as I have argued, 'provisional' does not mean 'illegitimate' or 'relative' or 'arbitrary'. On the contrary, provisional arguments for political right must not only succeed as exemplars of a particular moral-political language but must also not contradict the conditions of their own existence. Over the course of this book I have explored some general conditions of the production of provisionally legitimate political arguments and have found a few candidates, including overlapping institutions, citizen empowerment, and protected enclaves. This list, however, is hardly conclusive, as the examples from property rights, boundary politics, and environmental policies have shown. Instead, what these case studies demonstrate is that despite the many challenges to moral legitimacy faced by arguments about politics, claims of right may be made in any context that does not utterly deny the possibility of agency and plurality for those involved. Though ordinary political arguments almost always follow the norms of conclusive claims, and though many if not most of the people making them believe that their claims are conclusively true, political arguments cannot be stripped of their enabling contexts: they are always provisional, never really conclusive. Politics is unlikely to come to an end any time soon; furthermore, the absence of politics would not mean the advent of a universally agreed comprehensive moral doctrine but would far more likely mean the imposition of conditions that render agency and plurality impossible.

KANT'S INCONCLUSIVE LEGACY FOR PROVISIONAL POLITICS

In chapter 1, I argued against Sissela Bok and others that Kant's "fiat iustitia" is a call not for an anticonsequentialist moral rigorism but rather for empowering citizens' moral judgments of political life, even at the price of reduced power for the sovereign. Kant's fiat iustitia demands that the conditions of moral politics be promoted by those in power regardless of the consequences for themselves. At the conclusion of our investigations of moral politics in practice, we have an opportunity to reflect on the Kantian legacy for politics. Can provisional theory now endorse Kant's "fiat iustitia, pereat mundus"? Even once we have dismissed readings like Bok's that read the motto as a sign of Kant's moral-political fanaticism, the properly interpreted position remains only partly defensible. Kant presumes that the price of justice will always be paid by those rulers who are powerful obstacles to progress, by "all the rogues in the world." He switches back and forth between the supposition that "everything that happens or can happen is . . . the mere mechanism of nature" (8:372; 340) and the alternative supposition that freedom and morality are active in the physical world.[7] And while he sometimes trusts nature and sometimes calls for rational reform, in both cases Kant insists on a single model for a just constitutional regime, a model toward which all politics necessarily, if slowly, tends. Though he frequently reminds us of the fragile theoretical basis for such a view, and though his pessimism regarding human nature tempers it somewhat, overall Kant's politics are infused with the idea that progress toward just arrangements is a necessary feature of human life. It cannot be accidental, for example, that unlike his predecessors in British contractarian thought, Kant did not include a chapter on the dissolution of government in any of his political works.[8]

Though I have kept my distance from Kantian teleology in this book, I have retained a measure of Kant's faith in the power of public discourse to effect political change. As we saw in chapter 1 and elsewhere, there is plenty of empirical evidence for the hypothesis that moral judgments collected into public arguments about the right can, under many conditions, move an otherwise stable world to change. Both Kantian and contemporary provisional theory rely on institutions that promote the conditions of public discourse to make efficacious moral arguments possible. Kant did not worry too much about the specific mechanisms that might transform public judgment into political reality. For him, what matters most is that the discourse itself be enabled, putting pressure in myriad ways on those empowered to make the many small and large changes that would promote gradual reform. Now that I have completed the case studies for this book, it seems to me that Kant did not foresee the most dangerous threat to the power of public discourse to effect political change. He did anticipate the dangers associated with regimes that would prevent political arguments from being expressed in the first place, and thus argued strongly for those minimal rights that would create a viable public sphere even under authoritarian conditions. However well Kant appreciated the need for gradualism in the name of the stable conditions of progress toward a just state, though, he missed the dangers associated with gradualism as a means of disarming the power of public judgment. Put bluntly, too many potentially efficacious political judgments are rendered useless by delay, eventually serving only a sort of mourning or lamentation function as latecoming publics attempt to reconcile irreversible injustices with admissions of judgment against them.

Kant comes close to recognizing this danger in *Toward Perpetual Peace*, where he argues against allowing states to use assassination under any circumstances because such means poison the possibility of future peaceful relations. Though he does not divide policy areas according to whether they are reversible or not, he does make a similar argument that policies that undermine the long-term prospects for peace are inherently worse than similarly unjust policies whose harm is confined to the present. Later, in *Conflict of the Faculties,* Kant argues for the extraordinary authority of moral arguments made by spectators powerless to affect the outcome of a policy, on the grounds that since no interest could reasonably move a powerless spectator, their arguments must be based in judgments of right. His example here, the Prussian sympathizers with the French Revolution who risked retribution from their own absolutist regime for expressing such views, indicates that Kant does not have a self-governing public in mind when he argues for spectator disinterest. Even so, these expressions of political judgment, impotent by definition, were supposed by Kant to have the effect of swaying the public sphere and eventually of altering the conditions under which even absolutist rulers make their policy decisions.

Kant does not, however, consider a problem that has arisen repeatedly over the course of this book, which is that arguments for the right frequently arrive too late to make any concrete difference to the irreversible policy in question. In this sense, contemporary political moralists are like the backward-looking "angel of history" that Walter Benjamin imagines depicted in a painting by Paul Klee: "This is how one pictures the angel of history. His face is turned toward the past. Where we perceive a chain of events, he sees one single catastrophe which keeps piling wreckage and hurls it in front of his feet. The angel would like to stay, awaken the dead, and make whole what has been smashed. But a storm is blowing in from Paradise; it has got caught in his wings with such a violence that the angel can no longer close them. The storm irresistibly propels him into the future to which his back is turned, while the pile of debris before him grows skyward. This storm is what we call progress."[9]

We cannot compare everyone who makes public political judgments with Benjamin's spectator-angel. Some policy contexts encourage prospective judgment. A society, for example, may engage in public debate on whether to expand a class of protected social categories to include previously excluded ones; an example of this type from the present-day United States is public discussion about how to protect those suffering from discrimination according to sexual orientation. Other policy contexts, however, make it difficult for the public to engage in discourse that could actually affect the policy. I am not arguing that such retrospective debates are thereby rendered meaningless: a particularly clear example is offered by the debate in the second half of the twentieth century in Germany over public judgments concerning the Holocaust. Those genocidal policies could be ended but not reversed; those killed could not be returned to life; the reparations offerable were not insignificant to the living, but they were generally recognized as in principle incapable of anything like just compensation for injuries suffered. The focus of those debates, however, was less policy than public attitude. As titles like Alexander and Margarethe Mitscherlich's *Inability to Mourn* attest, insofar as the debate was not merely retrospective, it centered on contemporary citizens' *attitudes* toward the horror of the past.[10]

Similarly, the arguments offered in many of the cases studied in this book served a social-psychological function rather than being a source of prospective principles for reform. In the case of arguments for exclusive citizenship, for example, mainstream embrace of the legitimacy of native cultures tends to arise only after the native culture is reduced to a powerless remnant. Though arguments for the sanctity of wildlife certainly predate the establishment of "Earth Day" in the United States in 1970, it is notable that the Endangered Species Act was passed only after most of the continent had been rendered inhospitable to wildlife by Western settlement. There is even an element of mourning rather than of collectively deciding connected with the present-day debate over what to do about global inequality. Only now that the international economic system seems retrospectively inevitable do arguments that the present state of global inequality is unjust, and ought to be ameliorated somehow, enjoy much discursive success among the better-off. As I argued in chapter 4, however, the various proposals for taxation of the rich countries and transfer to the poor ones have more value as absolution than as redistribution. Fortunately for morality in politics, political arguments do not always restrict themselves to this function of lamentation. Retrospective justification of policies pursued for the sake of raw interests will always be with us, of course, and I suspect that this style of argument is more prevalent with regard to some types of policy than to others.

A PROVISIONALLY KANTIAN PERSPECTIVE

We cannot, therefore, adopt a Kantian optimism with regard to the inevitability of progress, whether it is guaranteed by the hidden hand of nature or the beneficial effects of public discourse. But perhaps Kant himself is less optimistic than he is usually supposed to be. There is, in fact, significant tension in Kant's view as he expounds it in *Toward Perpetual Peace.* The work opens, for example, with the story of the Dutch tavern called Zum ewigen Frieden (Toward Perpetual Peace); the sign over the door depicts the peace of the graveyard. Kant gestures toward his own ambiguous referent, saying that it remains to be seen whether the sign depicts the fate of humanity, of war-hungry leaders, or just of dreamy philosophers (8:343; 317). He admits that his progressive view is not the only potentially legitimate one, but he argues that we face a strictly dichotomous choice between assuming that "pure principles of right have objective reality, that is, that they can be carried out," on the one hand, and a deep pessimism that would condemn creation itself (8:380; 346).

Seen in this context, Bok's and other rigoristic interpreters' contention that Kant's view of progress rests on faith in divine providence is plausible, though I agree with Allen Wood that the larger context of Kant's theory of history is in tension with such an interpretation. Wood rightly emphasizes the empirical conditions that determine what political ends are to be pursued by moral citizens. Even such Kantian goals as the establishment of just civil constitutions and peace among sovereign nations are moral ends "conditioned by empirical contingencies highlighted by Kant's philosophy of history."[11]

The specific contents of political justice are empirically conditioned, but they always refer to morality. This is what Kant means when he writes that "true politics can therefore not take a step without having already paid homage to morals," and also that "all politics must bend its knee before right" (8:380; 347). Actual people express their moral judgments in public; the resulting public sphere reflects universal moral commitments as they are judged by speakers to determine specific maxims appropriate to the local context.[12] Kant is not here referring to any specific content that moral reason might provide to all political actors, he is referring to the bald fact that "the moral principle in the human being never dies out"

(8:380; 346). People judge politics according to morality, and these public judgments affect and condition political possibility. Kant even hints that this aspect of politics leads inevitably if slowly to universal peace and justice (8:380; 347).

We need not be so bold. Where Kant would have "fiat iustitia, pereat mundus," we need only "fiat iustitia, ut duret mundus" (let there be justice, so that the world may endure). A gloss of the provisional motto in the Kantian style would take the usual explanatory liberties: "Let there be provisional right, so that the possibility of politics in the world endures."

NOTES

Note. References to Kant's works are designated by the volume and page numbers in the standard Prussian Academy edition, followed by the page number of the English translation. In English, the Cambridge University Press editions of Kant's works include the standard pagination. The translations given here are from Mary J. Gregor's volume in the Cambridge edition, *Kant's Practical Philosophy,* unless otherwise noted.

CHAPTER 1 Introduction to Provisional Theory

1 Kant, *Metaphysics of Morals,* 6:347; 485.

2 Sandel, *Liberalism and the Limits of Justice.*

3 Kuehn, *Kant,* 396. For a detailed account of my interpretation, see Ellis, *Kant's Politics.*

4 Kant explicitly introduces the concept of provisional right two years later, in the *Metaphysics of Morals* (1797). I have argued elsewhere that he makes implicit use of the concept in *Toward Perpetual Peace* (1795). See Ellis, *Kant's Politics,* ch. 3.

5 For a different view, see Ishay, *The History of Human Rights.*

6 "Inuit, as Miners' Canary, Lead Fight for World," Knight-Ridder Newspapers, January 4, 2006.

7 Arendt, *The Human Condition,* 322.

8 On this topic see Walzer, *Just and Unjust Wars,* ch. 1.

9 Ellis, *Kant's Politics;* this section is based on part of my article "Citizenship and Property Rights: A New Look at Social Contract Theory."

10 Some recent exceptions include: Shaw, "Rawls, Kant's Doctrine of Right, and Global Distributive Justice"; LaVaque-Manty, *Arguments and Fists;* Muthu, "Justice and Foreigners: Kant's Cosmopolitan Right"; Flikschuh, *Kant and Modern Political Philosophy;* Cavallar, *Kant and the Theory and Practice of International Right;* and Laursen, *The Politics of Skepticism in the Ancients, Montaigne, Hume, and Kant.*

11 In this regard, see Thomas Pogge's interesting critique of Rawls's interpretation of Kant. Pogge argues that Kant's politics can accommodate Kantian morality as a comprehensive doctrine but need not exclude other comprehensive doctrines. As Pogge summarizes his argument, Kant's liberalism is "if anything, *more* freestanding than Rawls's" (Pogge, http://www.columbia.edu/~tp6/index.html; see Pogge, "Is Kant's *Rechtslehre* a 'Comprehensive Liberalism'?"; see also Ellis, *Kant's Politics*).

12 Provisional arguments take the form of hypothetical imperatives: if we are committed to x, then y and such follows in z and such a context. Arguments with conclusivist ambitions—based on divine right, the ideal speech situation, rational choice, biological imperatives, and the greatest happiness of the greatest number, to take a few examples—aim for universal application.

13 Beiser, *The Fate of Reason;* Beiser, *Enlightenment, Revolution, Romanticism.*

14 Riley, *Will and Political Legitimacy,* 125.

15 Kant's views on the importance of freedom of the pen were radical, original, and even "subversive" in their historical context, as John Christian Laursen has established (Laursen, "The Subversive Kant"; *The Politics of Skepticism in the Ancients, Montaigne, Hume, and Kant;* "Kant on Book Piracy"). However, it is Kant's hypotheses about the role of press freedom as a social agent of change that distinguish his theory from more general arguments for freedom of expression, and these hypotheses form an essential part of his dynamic theory of provisional right.

16 Habermas, *The Structural Transformation of the Public Sphere.*

17 Sissela Bok, "Kant's Arguments in Support of the Maxim 'Do What Is Right Though the World Should Perish.'"

18 Ibid., 7. Ferdinand's adoption of the motto is ironic: he began his career as an uncompromising fighter for Roman Catholicism but ended up being remembered for his achievements as a peacemaker who allowed religious plurality to flourish within his realm. "Ferdinand I." *Encyclopædia Britannica.* 2007. Encyclopædia Britannica Online. 30 May 2007. http://www.search.eb.com/eb/article-9034006.

19 Slovoj Žižek, "Robespierre of the 'Divine Violence' of Terror," on Lacan.com, www.lacan.com/zizrobes.htm.

20 Bok, "Kant's Arguments," 24.

21 Ibid., 11–15.

22 Ibid., 10–11.

23 Kant insists on this "policy/practice" distinction a paragraph later: "Thus objectively, or in theory, there is no conflict between morals and politics. Subjectively, however, in the selfish propensity of men (which should not be called 'practice,' as this would imply that it rested on rational maxims), this conflict will always remain."

24 Bok, "Kant's Arguments," 16.

25 Kant, "On the Supposed Right to Lie from Philanthropy" (8:425–430; 611–615). Bok rightly notes that Kant does sometimes use consequentialist arguments in *Perpetual Peace,* but she mistakenly claims that at these points he is "crossing over to the terrain of his adversaries." Bok, "Kant's Arguments," 18.

26 I look forward to receiving corrections on this point, if I am in error: ellis@politics.tamu.edu.

27 Klosko, "Provisionality in Plato's Ideal State."

28 Ibid., 175.

29 Ibid., 175.

30 Ibid., 178; 175–178.

31 Ibid., 179.

32 Ibid., 183.

33 Walzer, *Just and Unjust Wars,* 20.

34 The term 'realism' is difficult here, since I am arguing for a realistic approach to the world of political argument, one that recognizes the empirical reality of moral argument. See Shapiro, "Realism in the Study of the History of Ideas."

35 Gutmann and Thompson, *Democracy and Disagreement.*

36 Walzer, *Just and Unjust Wars,* xxi.

37 Ibid., xx.

38 Taylor, *Sources of the Self.*

39 Again, see Pogge, "Is Kant's *Rechtslehre* a 'Comprehensive Liberalism'?"

40 Pettit, "Resilience"; Pettit, "Democracy and Punishment."

41 Mansbridge, "Cracking through Hegemonic Ideology."

42 Kant, "Theory and Practice," 8:290; 291.

CHAPTER 2 Provisionalism and Democratic Theory

1 Antipaternalism, however, does not exclude such time-honored republican and democratic practices as temporary dictatorship in the face of emergency. I thank a very helpful anonymous reviewer for this important point.

2 Ackerman and Fishkin, *Deliberation Day,* 3.

3 Fung, "Review of *Deliberation Day*"; Ryfe, "Review of *Deliberation Day* and *Reflective Democracy*"; Shapiro, "The State of Democratic Theory: A Reply to James Fishkin."

4 On this literature, and on criticism of aggregative democracy from other points of view, see Shapiro, *The State of Democratic Theory,* ch. 1. See also Knight and Johnson, "Aggregation and Deliberation: On the Possibility of Democratic Legitimacy." In their 1996 work, *Democracy and Disagreement,* Gutmann and Thompson differentiate their position mainly from proceduralist and constitutionalist views. In later work, however, Gutmann and Thompson focus on alternative conceptions of democratic legitimacy (their deliberative conception versus conventional aggregative democracy). See Gutmann and Thompson, *Why Deliberative Democracy?,* 13 and n. 13, 190–191.

5 See Robert Sugden's remarks on baseline problems in "The Contractarian Enterprise." See also Gutmann and Thompson, *Why Deliberative Democracy?,* 16.

6 Cass R. Sunstein, *The Partial Constitution,* 68–92. Thanks to Andy Sabl for this reference.

7 Ibid., 72–73.

8 Dewey quoted in ibid., 79.

9 Ibid., 84–85.

10 Gutmann and Thompson, *Why Deliberative Democracy?;* Gutmann and Thompson, *Democracy and Disagreement.*

11 Ackerman and Fishkin, *Deliberation Day,* 7.

12 Gutmann and Thompson, *Why Deliberative Democracy?,* 13–15.

13 Gutmann and Thompson, *Democracy and Disagreement,* 98; Karpowitz and Mansbridge, "Disagreement and Consensus: The Importance of Dynamic Updating in Public Deliberation."

14 Sanders, "Against Deliberation"; Shapiro, "Enough of Deliberation: Politics Is about Interests and Power"; Young, *Inclusion and Democracy.*

15 Gutmann and Thompson, *Democracy and Disagreement,* ch. 6, esp. p. 220; Fishkin, *The Voice of the People: Public Opinion and Democracy.*

16 I am using the term 'discursive' differently from John Dryzek's pioneering use in *Discursive Democracy*. For me, study of discursive dynamics traces developments in public discourse on political right, identifying changing constraints on what it is possible to argue in any given context.

17 Koselleck, *The Practice of Conceptual History;* Richter, *The History of Political and Social Concepts;* Pagden, ed., *The Languages of Political Theory in Early-Modern Europe;* Foucault, *Language, Counter-Memory, Practice;* Kant, *Practical Philosophy;* Habermas, *The Structural Transformation of the Public Sphere;* Mansbridge, "Using Power / Fighting Power."

18 See Richter *The History of Political and Social Concepts;* Palonen, "The History of Concepts as a Style of Political Theorizing"; Martin, "Context and Contradiction."

19 In this section, I take Gutmann and Thompson's work as the main representative of deliberative democracy, recognizing that there are quite significant differences between their work and that of other theorists in the tradition, especially those following the legacies of the Frankfurt School of critical theory.

20 For their clearest statements yet on provisionality and democratic theory, see ch. 3 of Gutmann and Thompson, *Why Deliberative Democracy?*

21 Ibid., 4.

22 Iris Marion Young, *Inclusion and Democracy,* 16–17.

23 Gutmann and Thompson, *Democracy and Disagreement.*

24 Gutmann and Thompson, *Why Deliberative Democracy?,* 97.

25 In this regard, deliberative democrats may be able at least partly to bridge the gap between critics and practitioners of democratic theory, since such a theory would not address well-known problems like the legitimacy of interests as observed through elections or survey research.

26 Gutmann and Thompson, *Democracy and Disagreement; Why Deliberative Democracy?*

27 Gutmann and Thompson, *Democracy and Disagreement,* 143.

28 In this case, Gutmann and Thompson focus on the reciprocity- and accountability-enhancing effects of "reiterated deliberation, punctuated by periodic elections," rather than on the specific linguistic constraints faced by individual political actors. For their account of speaker-level constraint, see Gutmann and Thompson, *Democracy and Disagreement,* ch. 3.

29 Gutmann and Thompson, *Why Deliberative Democracy?,* 19.

30 See Gutmann and Thompson, "Why Deliberative Democracy Is Different," 13; see also Thomas Pogge's brilliant account of Kant's politics as a second-order, "free-standing" conception, in contrast to Kant's comprehensive ethical doctrine ("Is Kant's *Rechtslehre* a 'Comprehensive Liberalism'?").

31 Lying is of course a problem, but one that my mid-range focus largely diffuses. Lying in the short run can be highly effective, of course. "Torture is not a part of United States policy." The sentence can free up the government for a time. But over the longer run, such policies tend to be self-defeating. "We pretend to work, and they pretend to pay us."

32 Kant, *The Conflict of the Faculties;* Ellis, *Kant's Politics,* ch. 5.

33 Kant, *The Conflict of the Faculties.*

34 Here I can only gesture at the shortcomings of mainstream democratic theory that lead me to suggest the inclusion of reason-giving practices.

35 On this topic see my book chapter, "Provisionalism in the Study of Politics."

36 Young, *Inclusion and Democracy.*

37 Mansbridge, "Using Power / Fighting Power."

38 Mansbridge and Flaster, "The Cultural Politics of Everyday Discourse."

39 I do not mean an isolated public sphere, of course, but one tightly integrated with other political and social institutions. Others have argued along the same lines: Kant in his political work and Habermas in *Structural Change* both make similar claims.

40 Mansbridge, "Everyday Talk in the Deliberative System," 219.

41 Generally, I argue for research into and promotion of 'discursive dynamics', a term of art I use to include a number of separate efforts to integrate discourse analysis into democratic life. Here, however, I am focusing on a particular school, the *Geschichtliche Grundbegriffe* group led by Koselleck, Conze, and Brunner in Germany and introduced into the United States by Melvin Richter.

42 Though I seek to appropriate their insights for democratic theory, I have a set of goals very different from those of the intellectual historians whose models I propose to appropriate. In this case, I am not interested in improving reading of classic texts, though thanks to, for example, the work of Cambridge School historians better readings are now available. Nor am I at all interested in teleological readings of the necessary pattern of history, even if the dynamic at work can properly be called "dialectical" (see Farr, "Understanding Conceptual Change Politically").

43 For a general introduction to this literature, see Richter, *The History of Social and Political Concepts.*

44 Brunner et al., eds., *Geschichtliche Grundbegriffe.*

45 Richter, *The History of Social and Political Concepts,* 36

46 Koselleck, *The Practice of Conceptual History,* 254

47 Ibid., 128–129.

48 Ibid., 129.

49 Ibid., 129.

50 Ibid., "Linguistic Change and the History of Events," 659.

51 Koselleck, *The Practice of Conceptual History.*

52 Ibid., 252.

53 Ibid., 261.

54 Ibid., 253.

55 Ibid., 249.

56 Ibid., 256.

57 Ibid., 257.

58 Ibid., 256.

59 Ibid., 260.

60 Ibid.

61 Ibid., 264.

62 Mansbridge, "Using Power/Fighting Power"; Mansbridge, "Cracking Through Hegemonic Ideology."

63 Ibid. (both works).

64 Mansbridge, "Cracking Through Hegemonic Ideology," 338.

65 Ibid., 345.

66 Ibid.,

67 Ibid., 339.

68 Sunstein, *Why Societies Need Dissent,* 165.

69 On this topic, see Ayelet Shachar's excellent *Multicultural Jurisdictions.*

70 Mansbridge, "Cracking Through Hegemonic Ideology," 346.

71 Ibid., 339.

72 Mansbridge "Everyday Talk in the Deliberative System," 220.

73 Mansbridge, "Using Power/Fighting Power," 58.

74 On this topic see Laursen, "Kant on Book Piracy"; see also ch. 1 of Ellis, *Kant's Politics.*

75 Kant, "An Answer to the Question, What Is Enlightenment?" (8:33–42; 15–22). Other, more famous institutions recommended by Kant in this essay include freedom of conscience and freedom of expression. These, however, do not apply directly to this second issue of citizen political leverage.

76 Reich, *The Work of Nations.*

77 Hacker and Pierson, "Abandoning the Middle"; Skocpol, *Diminished Democracy.*

78 See Scott, *Seeing Like a State.*

79 See Shapiro, *Democratic Justice;* Shapiro, *The State of Democratic Theory.*

80 Karpowitz and Mansbridge, "Disagreement and Consensus."

81 Ibid.

82 Ibid., 243.

83 Ibid., 241.

84 Ibid., 246.

85 I am interested here in the case of downtown redevelopment described by Karpowitz and Mansbridge, not in evaluating the organization as a whole. For more on the Princeton Future effort, see the Web site at http://www.princetonfuture.org/.

86 Karpowitz and Mansbridge, "Disagreement and Consensus," 244.

87 Ibid., 240.

88 Shapiro, *The State of Democratic Theory.*

89 Ibid., 47.

90 Ibid.

91 Ibid.

92 Richter, *The History of Social and Political Concepts.*

93 For example, see Ball, Farr, and Hanson, eds., *Political Innovation and Conceptual Change.*

94 Martin, "Context and Contradiction"; Koselleck, *Critique and Crisis;* Palonen, "The History of Concepts"; Ball, "Green Democracy."

95 I do not mean to suggest that democratic politics ought to be seeking any permanent consensus. Deliberative democrats should be seeking not consensus but the expansion of political possibilities. Insofar as political discourse reveals some political
possibilities while it forecloses others, it might be seen to lead to single "correct" outcomes for policy debates. This would be a mistake. Even after the use of the concept
of self-determination made a revival of the old regime linguistically unlikely, republicanism was far from the only remaining option. Nor should this view be considered teleological. Discursive dynamics may look progressive because discourse perspective requires us to take the long view. But instead of looking backward from our
current policy perspective and defining everything that made it possible in reverse
according to the outcome, we should look at political universe as a sort of fluctuating band, widening and narrowing as the relationship between discursive and political possibility varies. The result of these discursively dynamic modifications of present-day democratic theory should be a political theory that can accommodate the
demands of public reason without paying an antidemocratic price in paternalism.

96 See Ellis, *Kant's Politics,* ch. 5.

97 Gutmann and Thompson, *Why Deliberative Democracy?,* 18.

98 Ibid., 15.

CHAPTER 3 Provisionality and Property

1 Kant, *Metaphysics of Morals.*

2 Shapiro, *The State of Democratic Theory;* Nussbaum, "Beyond the Social Contract."

3 Provisionalism has recently been given a thoughtful treatment in Gutmann and
Thompson's collection of essays on deliberative democracy, *Why Deliberative
Democracy.* Though Rawls constructs a Kantian contractarianism, he does not ad-
vocate provisional right; nor is Rawls much influenced by Kant's political, as op-
posed to his ethical, ideas. See Shaw, "Rawls, Kant's Doctrine of Right, and Global
Distributive Justice."

4 The following section is based on part of my article "Citizenship and Property
Rights: A New Look at Social Contract Theory."

5 Braybrooke, "Social Contract Theory's Fanciest Flight," 750.

6 In a similar vein, Adam Przeworski calls for putting "the consensualist theory of
democracy where it belongs—in the Museum of Eighteenth-century Thought"
(Przeworski, "Minimalist Conception of Democracy"). As we shall see, however,
Przeworski's minimalism is very different from David Gauthier's minimalism; in
fact, Przeworski's minimalist democratic theory exemplifies an appropriate use of
contractarian thought in political science, as he does not confuse historically particular enabling conditions with democracy itself. For the purposes of this chapter,
'minimalism' refers to contractarian thought that would limit realization of the
principle of government by consent by means of the conditions of that consent, including not only Gauthier but also Buchanan and Tullock, *The Calculus of Consent,*
and Nozick, *Anarchy, State, and Utopia.*

7 On this see chapter 2 and Sunstein, *The Partial Constitution,* 68–92.

8   David Hume famously lampoons the idea of an historical social contract in his 1748 essay "Of the Original Contract": "The face of the earth is continually changing, by the encrease of small kingdoms into great empires, by the dissolution of great empires into smaller kingdoms, by the planting of colonies, by the migration of tribes. Is there anything discoverable in all these events, but force and violence?" (Hume, *Political Essays*, 190).·

9   This is the choice to which Rawls refers near the end of his *Lectures on the History of Moral Philosophy*, where he argues against Hegel that one need not choose between the priority of either "single individuals as atoms" or "the state as a concrete whole." Instead, Rawls points to Kant's contractarian theory, of which he says that "it is different from starting with single individuals as atoms independent from all social ties and then building up from them as a basis. And it does not use the idea of the state as spiritual substance and individuals as mere accidents of its substantiality; the state is the arena in which individuals can pursue their ends according to principles each can see are reasonable and fair" (364–365). See also Morris and Oppenheimer, "Rational Choice and Politics," 7.

10 Gauthier, *Morals by Agreement*, 17. The exclusive consequences of this view of contractualism are agreed upon by minimalist contractualists and their many critics; by contrast, I hold that exclusivity is one of two possible solutions to the problem of autonomous citizen consent, and the less attractive of the two. Gauthier even suggests that social contract theory as an ideology is undermined by the inclusion of previously excluded groups ("The Social Contract as Ideology," 160–163).

11 Burns, Schlozman, and Verba, *ThePrivate Roots of Public Action;* Fraser, "After the Family Wage"; Orloff, "Gender and the Social Rights of Citizenship"; Putnam, *Bowling Alone;* Skocpol, *Diminished Democracy.*

12 Gauthier, "The Social Contract as Ideology," 141.

13 Gauthier, *Morals by Agreement*, 258.

14 Flikschuh, *Kant and Modern Political Philosophy*, 118.

15 Locke, *Two Treatises;* Flikschuh, *Kant and Modern Political Philosophy.*

16 Rosen, *Kant's Theory of Justice.*

17 Wolff, "Completion of Kant's Moral Theory."

18 Gauthier, *Morals by Agreement;* Gauthier, "Between Hobbes and Rawls."

19 In fact, there is no consistent lesson to be drawn from the political science literature on the wisdom of maintaining strict respect for property rights across political transitions. For an interesting take on the evidence from the Latin American cases, see Mason, "Take Two Acres."

20 On this dynamic with regard to affirmative action and other policy areas, see Sunstein.

21 Emily Wax, "A Place Where Women Rule: All-Female Village in Kenya Is a Sign Of Burgeoning Feminism Across Africa," *Washington Post*, Saturday, July 9, 2005; p. A1.

22 Agence France-Presse, July 21, 2005; *Korea Herald*, September 2, 2005.

23 For an excellent description of the state of pluralism in the present-day United States, see Hacker and Pierson, "Abandoning the Middle.".

24 *New York Times*, May 5, 2003, 10.

25 President Mwai Kibaki, who came to office on a reform platform, failed to garner a majority for his draft constitution. Thus the old postcolonial constitution, and with it a legal structure that often relies on nineteenth-century British law combined with local customary practice, remains at least nominally in force at this writing. For a general introduction, see Chanock, *Law, Custom, and Social Order.*

26 Walsh, *Double Standards.*

27 Quoted in "Rights Group Urges New Government to Adopt and Implement Laws Protecting Women's Rights to Property in Kenya and Africa," by Susan Linnee, Associated Press, March 4, 2003, accessed with Lexis-Nexis Academic Universe.

28 See, for example, World Bank, "The Kenyan Strategic Country Gender Assessment."

29 Shachar, *Multicultural Jurisdictions.*

30 See Mwangi, "Subdividing the Commons"; Francis and Amuyunzu-Nyamongo, "Bitter Harvest"; Aliber et al., "The Impact of HIV/AIDS on Land Rights."

31 Aliber et al., "The Impact of HIV/AIDS on Land Rights," 85; Mwangi, "Subdividing the Commons," 9.

32 Walsh, *Double Standards.*

33 "The Future is Orange," *The Economist* (London). November 26, 2005. Vol. 377, no. 8454: 70.

34 Francis and Amuyunzu-Nyamongo, "Bitter Harvest," 2.

35 Aliber et al., "The Impact of HIV/AIDS on Land Rights," x, 1. On p. 6 of its report HRW says, "Though difficult to quantify, experts say that women's property rights abuses are widespread and increasing." Later the report cites an editorial that quotes a figure of one in three widows having been forced to undergo "cleansing." Walsh, *Double Standards,* 13.

36 *New York Times,* March 5, 2003, p. 10; *Washington Post,* August 18, 2003, p. A12; *Christian Science Monitor,* May 15, 2003, p. 7; Amnesty International, "Women, HIV/AIDS, and Human Rights."

37 United Nations Human Rights Committee, "Concluding Observations," 2.

38 Aliber et al., "The Impact of HIV/AIDS on Land Rights," 89.

39 Walsh, *Double Standards,* 44.

40 From *Africa News,* November 22, 2004, via Lexis-Nexis, "Customary Law on Trial": The "Judicature Act, Chapter 8 of the Laws of Kenya, Section 3(2) provides, 'The High Court, the Court of Appeal and all subordinate courts shall be guided by African Customary Law in civil cases in which one or more of the parties is subject to it or affected by it. So far as it is applicable and is not repugnant to justice and morality or inconsistent with any written law, and shall decide such cases according to substantial justice without undue regard to technicalities of procedure and without undue delay.'"

41 Human Rights Watch enumerates the following international treaties against discrimination valid in Kenya: Convention on the Elimination of All Forms of Discrimination against Women (CEDAW), G. A. Res. 34/180, U.N. Doc. A/34/46 (1981; Kenya 1984); International Covenant on Civil and Political Rights (ICCPR), 999 U.N.T.S. 171, (1976; Kenya 1972); International Covenant on Economic, Social, and Cultural Rights (ICESCR), G. A. Res. 2200 (XXI), 21 U.N. GAOR Supp. (No.

16), U.N. Doc. A/6316 (1976, Kenya 1972); Universal Declaration of Human Rights (UDHR), G.A. Res. 217A (III), U.N. GAOR, #d. Sess., pt. 1, at 71, U.N. Doc. A/810 (1948); African (Banjul) Charter on Human and Peoples' Rights (African Charter), June 26, 1981, OAU Doc. CAB/LEG/67/3 rev. 5, 21 I.L.M. 58 (1982) (1986; Kenya 1992). Walsh, *Double Standard*, 44, n. 214. The report provides ample documentation that Kenya is in violation of all these treaties (45ff.).

42 See also Benschop, *Rights and Reality*, 152.

43 Walsh, *Double Standards*, 3–5.

44 Better studies sought to investigate representative samplings of potentially affected citizens, rather than interviewing victims and asking people about their impressions of the problem. They also used research methods such as participatory mapping, focus groups, surveys, and key informant interviews. See Aliber et al., "The Impact of HIV/AIDS on Land Rights," 148; Benschop, *Rights and Reality*.

45 Aliber et al., "The Impact of HIV/AIDS on Land Rights," 63.

46 Keck and Sikkink call this the "boomerang effect." *Activists beyond Borders*.

47 This would not have surprised Kant, who is critical of the view that property rights are relations between individuals and property, rather relations among agents. He makes fun of the view thus: "Someone who thinks that his right is a direct relation to things rather than to persons would have to think (though only obscurely) that since there corresponds a right on one side a duty on the other, an external thing always remains *under obligation* to the first possessor even though it has left his hands. . . . So he would think of my right as if it were a *guardian spirit* accompanying the thing, always pointing me out to whoever else wanted to take possession of it" (6:260; 413).

48 Women's secondary rights to cattle are gained in myriad ways: some may be allocated to a woman's household by her husband or his family; some may be brought from her natal home; women may be able to purchase them outright themselves.

49 Aliber et al., "The Impact of HIV/AIDS on Land Rights," 88, 119–20.

50 Ibid., 123.

51 Walsh, *Double Standards*, 34.

52 Another unintended consequence has been the neglect of common resources such as roads and byways, which were formerly maintained locally and collectively; see also Benschop, *Rights and Reality*, 146.

53 Aliber et al., "The Impact of HIV/AIDS on Land Rights," 3, 64, 117–118, 136.

54 Mwangi, "Subdividing the Commons."

55 On cadastral mapping generally, see Scott, *Seeing Like a State*. Scott's arguments about the inflexibility of regimes based on such maps, as well as the incentives that states have to remake society in the maps' images, are certainly relevant here. On the other hand, if the only institutions ready to coordinate development and provide vindication of women's rights are states acting under pressure from liberal international organizations, it is hard to argue that citizens should undermine them by resisting mapping. Provisional theory would remind us: it is not the taxation, state sovereignty, or mapping policies that are worthy of support in every case; these have been conditions of the vindication of rights and the provision of development aid in

some cases. The question should be which policies would promote these good things in this case.

56 Benschop, *Rights and Reality,* 151.

57 Aliber et al., "The Impact of HIV/AIDS on Land," 136.

58 Ibid.

59 Mwangi, "Subdividing the Commons," 42.

60 Benschop, *Rights and Reality,* 152–153.

61 Aliber et al., "The Impact of HIV/AIDS on Land," 159.

62 Walsh, *Double Standards,* 2–3.

63 Francis and Amuyunzu-Nyamongo, "Bitter Harvest" 2; Bates, *Markets and States in Tropical Africa.*

64 On this point, see Tocqueville, *The Old Regime and the French Revolution.*

65 The HRW report remarks that "community sympathy sometimes helps minimize women's property rights violations. Human Rights Watch encountered one case where sympathy for a disabled widow—not respect for her rights—led to reinstatement in her home after an in-law evicted her." Walsh, *Double Standards,* 21.

66 Benschop, *Rights and Reality,* 143.

67 For similar arguments see Pettit on resilience and Mansbridge on the evolution of discourses. Pettit, "Resilience in Social Science and Political Philosophy." Mansbridge, "Cracking Through Hegemonic Ideology."

68 *Africa News,* November 22, 2004, via Lexis-Nexis, "Customary Law on Trial."

69 Mwangi, "Subdividing the Commons," 17.

70 Marshall, *Class, Citizenship, and Social Development.* Koselleck, *The Practice of Conceptual History.*

71 Aliber et al., "The Impact of HIV/AIDS on Land," 29ff., 86; Benschop, *Rights and Reality,* 144.

72 Benschop, *Rights and Reality,* 148–149.

CHAPTER 4 Citizenship and Provisional Right

1 See, for example, Benhabib, *The Rights of Others* and *The Claims of Culture;* Flikschuh, *Kant and Modern Political Philosophy;* Muthu, "Justice and Foreigners."

2 The arguments in the first part of this section of the chapter are based on my "Citizenship and Property Rights: A New Look at Social Contract Theory."

3 Marshall, "Citizenship and Social Class," in *Class, Citizenship, and Social Development;* Huntington, *The Clash of Civilizations and the Remaking of World Order;* Mill, *On Liberty.*

4 In his *Rechtslehre,* Kant distinguishes between general philosophical argument, which he puts into the main text, and particular empirical remarks, which he indents. Noting that the study of politics inevitably involves historical, empirical facts and their relation to commonly held moral principles, Kant concludes that a perfectly formal, example-free metaphysics of right would be impossible and necessarily incomplete; this is why he called his first section "metaphysical *first principles* of the Rechtslehre" instead of the more elegant "metaphysics of right."

5 The distinction between active and passive citizenship is only one of several mutu-

ally incompatible arguments Kant attempts in his effort to establish the best possible political judgment among limited rational beings. Elsewhere in his writings, Kant argues variously for disinterested spectators or deliberative scholars to play this role (7:84–89; 150–161; see also 8:41–42; 21–22).

6   Burns, Schlozmann, and Verba, *Private Roots of Public Action.*

7   See Danilovic and Clare, "The Kantian Liberal Peace (Revisited)."

8   On the globus terraqueus, see especially Flikschuh, *Kant and Modern Political Philosophy.*

9   See Pitts, *A Turn to Empire;* and Muthu, *Enlightenment against Empire.*

10   See Thornton, *American Indian Holocaust and Survival.*

11   But see Ellis, *Kant's Politics;* Muthu, "Justice and Foreigners," and Flikschuh, *Kant and Modern Political Philosophy.*

12   Benhabib, *The Claims of Culture,* 160.

13   Cited in Benhabib, *The Claims of Culture,* 168; Kymlicka, "Territorial Boundaries," 252; and many others.

14   Benhabib, *The Claims of Culture,* 169.

15   Thane Burnett, "RCMP Turban, 15 Years After," *Toronto Sun,* March 5, 2006, p. 8.

16   A similar dynamic applies to the controversy around gays in the military in the present-day United States, though in that case, conditions of service continue at this writing to be reified into matters of principle. See the preface to Ellis, *Kant's Politics;* see also Kymlicka, "Territorial Boundaries."

17   Thane Burnett, "RCMP Turban, 15 Years After," *Toronto Sun,* March 5, 2006, p. 8.

18   Jill Young Miller, "Photo ID Hot Topic," *Atlanta Journal-Constitution,* July 19, 2006, p. 6D.

19   Editorial, "Georgia's New Poll Tax," *New York Times,* September 12, 2005, p. 20.

20   Tim Becker, quoted in Miller, "Photo ID Hot Topic" (see n. 18 above).

21   Edwards, *Why the Electoral College Is Bad for America;* Dahl, *How Democratic Is the American Constitution?*

22   Edwards, *Why the Electoral College Is Bad for America,* 33.

23   Hayward, "The Difference States Make," 504–505.

24   Ibid., 511.

25   Ford, "The Boundaries of Race," 1905.

26   Ibid., 1909 (emphasis added).

27   See Weber, *Peasants into Frenchmen.*

28   In recent years, German citizenship law has been relaxed slightly, to allow native-born children of non-German parents a path to citizenship under some conditions. Note that provisional theory would not presume to determine what the appropriate immigration policy for contemporary Germany should be. However, reified conditions should be replaced with provisional principles in the justification of policy. Many policies, from totally open to totally closed borders are possible under provisionalism, but the *real* arguments for them ought to be given, as a condition of future political possibility.

29   Harper-Ho, "Noncitizen Voting Rights."

30   Miller, *On Nationality.*

31 Schuster and Solomos, "Rights and Wrongs across European Borders"; Vertovec, "Multicultural Policies and Modes of Citizenship."

32 Kymlicka, "Territorial Boundaries," 249.

33 Lomasky, "Toward a Liberal Theory of National Boundaries," 55–61.

34 Kymlicka, "Territorial Boundaries," 250–253.

35 Lomasky, "Toward a Liberal Theory of National Boundaries," 72–23.

36 See, for example, the nice enumerations in Shachar and Hirschl, "Citizenship as Inherited Property."

37 Kymlicka, "Territorial Boundaries," 266.

38 Ibid., 269.

39 Ibid., 267–269.

40 Ibid., 271. See also Shachar and Hirschl, "Citizenship as Inherited Property," Steiner, "Hard Borders, Compensation, and Classical Liberalism," and Risse, "Is There a Human Right to Free Movement?," among others.

41 Lomasky, "Toward a Liberal Theory of National Boundaries," 70.

42 "Like most inheritance liability in the domestic arena—which is shouldered by a tiny percentile of the total population, namely, the ultra-rich—the birthright levy would best be designed as a steeply progressive tax. . . . [T]he liability for the collective would effectively be borne by a small echelon of the most well-established citizens/title holders." Shachar and Hirschl, "Citizenship as Inherited Property," 281.

43 Hardin, "Group Boundaries, Individual Barriers," 277.

44 Of course arguments in defense of hard boundaries beyond this simplistic kind of pragmatism are possible. But as we have seen, they tend to amount to the reification of imaginary identities. In some cases, hard boundaries are justifiable in the name of cultural survival, but, as we shall see, such justifications, defensible as they most certainly are, must always point beyond themselves (they must take provisional form).

45 Shachar and Hirschl, "Citizenship as Inherited Property," 255.

46 See Hardin, ""Group Boundaries, Individual Barriers," 277.

47 Singer, *One World*.

48 Kant, "An Answer to the Question: What Is Enlightenment?" See also Ellis, *Kant's Politics*, ch. 1.

CHAPTER 5 Provisional and Conclusive Environmental Politics

1 This subspecies of gnatcatcher is currently listed by the federal government as "threatened." Its listing in 1993 precipitated the events culminating in the establishment of the habitat conservation plan that is the focus of this chapter. There is some controversy among ornithologists about the classification of the bird, since the subspecies distinctions are based more on geography and morphology than on genetics. Mock, "California Gnatcatcher (*Polioptila californica*)."

2 Of course I am no judge of the *technical* difficulties regarding global warming, only of the political ones. It is certainly a theoretical possibility that the changes in climate chemistry related to the industrial revolution are such that human extinction in the relatively near term is inevitable. Politically, however, the collective action problem represented by global warming is in principle soluble.

3 Kant, "An Answer to the Question: What Is Enlightenment?," 8:39; 20.

4 On current approaches to global warming, see Kolbert, "The Climate of Man," and Soulé, "Conservation"; see also Ehrlich and Wilson, "Biodiversity Studies."

5 Hardin, "The Tragedy of the Commons." See also Hardin, "Extensions of 'The Tragedy of the Commons.'"

6 "Mitigation solutions are often arbitrary, lacking an empirical foundation in the species' life history requirements." Bingham and Norton, "Mitigation of Habitat 'Take'" 127. The scientific consensus on adaptive management is that it is possible but rarely used appropriately. Wilhere, "Adaptive Management in Habitat Conservation Plans." See also Rahn et al., "Species Coverage in Multispecies Habitat Conservation Plans." For a good summary, see *Southwest Center for Biological Diversity v. Bartel.*

7 Singer, "Utilitarianism and Vegetarianism." See also Singer, *Animal Liberation.*

8 I am aware that the concept of 'species' is somewhat controversial, in that divisions among designated species are made according to shifting and sometimes even arbitrary standards. As Peter Singer has made plain, there are other ways to categorize members of the family of living things that might serve certain purposes better. See Singer, *Animal Liberation.* For purposes of arguing for provisionality in politics, however, I shall take 'species' to designate a mode of being that is unique.

9 Keats, "Ode to a Nightingale," www.bartleby.com/101/624.html.

10 Andrew Pollack, "Lizard-Derived Diabetes Drug is approved by the FDA," *New York Times,* April 30, 2005, p. C3.

11 Of course this dynamic is open-ended. It is conceivable that there is a level of biological diversity at which the conflict between political flux and species persistence would disappear or even reverse. Some biologists speculate, plausibly I think, that certain types of species particularly adapted to coexistence with human society are likely to flourish while the others become extinct. New species are always emerging, though too slowly to be relevant for the purposes of this argument, and at unpredictably volatile rates of emergence. Even in the unlikely event of a new human ability to repopulate the world with biological diversity equivalent to what has been lost since industrialization, or the even less likely event of a natural acceleration in the emergence of new species, human publics inheriting contemporary extinctions lose their political opportunities to benefit from, and to make choices about, those species that are lost.

12 For an excellent account of Prometheanism in environmental discourse, see Dryzek, *The Politics of the Earth.*

13 Wilson, *The Future of Life.*

14 Lee, "Protection in Jeopardy."

15 Colburn, *Vernal Pools,* 105.

16 Bauder et al., *Recovery Plan,* 31.

17 *Final MHCP Plan,* vol. 2, 4–182.

18 Richard J. Gonzalez et al., "Physiological Correlates of Water Chemistry Requirements in Fairy Shrimps (*Anostraca*) from Southern California." *Journal of Crustacean Biology* 16, no. 2 (1996): 315–322. Cited in Bauder et al., *Recovery Plan,* 30.

19 Bauder et al., *Recovery Plan,* 17.

20 Ibid., 31; Fugate, "Branchinecta of North America," 140.

21 *Pace* Belk, who gamely advocates allowing take of up to fifty individual endangered fairy shrimp at a time from their natural environment for purposes of study and observation, in the hope that public enthusiasm for them will grow. Belk, "Global Status and Trends in Ephemeral Pool Invertebrate Conservation," 149.

22 Bauder et al., *Recovery Plan,* 30.

23 Witham et al., eds., *Ecology, Conservation, and Management.*

24 According to Barbara Vlamis, executive director of the Butte Environmental Council, quoted in Eryn Gable, *Land Letter,* June 30, 2005, vol. 10, no. 9 (Washington, D.C.: Environment and Energy Publishing).

25 Bauder and McMillan, "Current Distribution and Historical Extent of Vernal Pools," 56.

26 Bauder et al., *Recovery Plan,* iii.

27 Ibid., 47; it is possible that off-road vehicle activities and bike trenches sometimes create the conditions for new vernal pools, but these have not been shown to be sustainable; see Helen Gao, "Finding of Shrimp Delays Opening of New School," *San Diego Union-Tribune,* August 1, 2005.

28 Layzer, *The Environmental Case,* 322, 326.

29 *The Endangered Species Act of 1973,* www.fws.gov/endangered/esa.html#lnk02, secs. 2–3.

30 www.fws.gov/endangered; accessed July 13, 2006.

31 Lee, "Protection in Jeopardy."

32 "The Pombo Report," 2005, accessed at www.house.gov/pombo/pomboreport/2005/050930.htm; Lee, "Protection in Jeopardy."

33 Male and Bean, "Measuring Progress in U.S. Endangered Species Conservation," 986.

34 Schnoor, "Endangered Species Act Revisited," 63.

35 *Legal Intelligencer,* December 16, 2004, vol. 231, no. 117, p. 5.

36 Taylor et al., "The Effectiveness of the Endangered Species Act," 360–367.

37 U.S. Fish and Wildlife Service, http://www.fws.gov/endangered/, accessed July 10, 2006.

38 Thomas, *Bureaucratic Landscapes,* 213. Of course, certainty is not an option for scientists seeking to preserve species in a dynamic landscape; "as a general rule, the scientific understanding of an environmental problem is highly uncertain." Layzer, *The Environmental Case,* 6.

39 MacArthur and Wilson, *The Theory of Island Biogeography.*

40 Lee, "Plight of Tiny Fairy Shrimp."

41 By 2006, there were more than six hundred such plans. Lee, "Judge Assails S.D.'s Landmark Habitat Plan."

42 *Final MHCP Plan,* vol. 1, 2–12.

43 Thomas, *Bureaucratic Landscapes,* ch. 6.

44 Layzer, *The Environmental Case.*

45 Ibid., 321.

46 Thomas, *The Bureaucratic Landscape;* Layzer, *The Environmental Case.*

47 http://www.carlsbadca.gov/parks/golf.html; accessed July 13, 2006; Rodgers, "Habitat Plan," and Hala Ali Aryan, "Carlsbad OKs Revised Plans for Golf Course," *San Diego Union-Tribune,* February 6, 2003.

48 "Out of the rough; It's been a rough road for Carlsbad's ocean-view golf course, but city officials are better the $68 million investment pays off as a first-class amenity," by Michael Burge, *San Diego Union-Tribune,* November 26, 2006, N1.

49 *Final MHCP Plan,* vol. 1, $^{1-1.}$

50 Ibid., 2–12.

51 Ibid., 3–17.

52 Ibid., 3–7; 4–178.

53 Ibid., 4–178.

54 Ibid.

55 *Solid Waste Agency of Northern Cook County (SWANCC) v. United States ACOE,* 531 U.S. 159 (2001); *Rapanos v. United States,* Nos. 04–1034, 04–1384 (2006).

56 U.S. Fish and Wildlife Service, *Federal Register* 70, no. 154, Thursday, August 11, 2005; accessed at: www.fws.gov/policy/library/05–15569.pdf.

57 Mary Lynn Vellinga, "Adding Vernal Pool Species Would be Costly, U.S. Says," *Sacramento Bee,* July 14, 2005, p. B1; Gable, *Land Letter* (see n. 24 above).

58 U.S. Fish and Wildlife Service, *Federal Register* 70, no. 154, Thursday, August 11, 2005; accessed at: www.fws.gov/policy/library/05–15569.pdf.

59 Taylor et al., "The Effectiveness of the Endangered Species Act," 360.

60 In this chapter I consider the fairy shrimp in their official designation as endangered species and the vernal pools in their possible official designation as critical habitat. I do not explore the politics of wetlands protection, because the pools' status as wetlands is too uncertain at this writing. See SWANCC (2001); see also *Rapanos v. United States,* Nos. 04–1034, 04–1384 (U.S. Supreme Court, June 19, 2006), in which the Court held that to qualify as wetlands under the Clean Water Act, an area must have contiguous connection to a free-flowing waterway.

61 *Final MHCP,* vol. 2, 4–178.

62 Thomas, *The Bureaucratic Landscape,* 18.

63 Layzer, *The Environmental Case,* 337.

64 This dynamic is similar to the one Mwangi describes in the case of Kenyan property rights: "Where systems in the wider social and political order are not accountable, it is unlikely that decentralized policy reforms will be accountable. This lack of accountability creates opportunity for rent-seeking behavior among rational actors. ... This, and other, studies demonstrate that the move to private, individualized land holdings, that have been so important in the economic development of the West is fraught with problems that could undermine the potential economic gains that had been hoped for" (Mwangi, "Subdividing the Commons," 42).

65 Hala Ali Aryan, "Carlsbad OKs Revised Plans for Golf Course," *San Diego Union-Tribune,* February 6, 2003.

66 Quoted in Layzer, *The Environmental Case,* 339.

67 Moody's Investors Service, February 16, 2006, "Ratings Update: San Diego (City of) CA," at http://www.sandiego.gov/press/060216.pdf; accessed July 13, 2006.

68 Lee, "Habitat Ruling Clouds Development Picture."

69 Lee, "Land Trust's Bankruptcy."

70 June 19, 2006, www.voiceofsandiego.org, Rob Davis, "Miramar's Ecological Price Tag."

71 Ibid.

72 Ibid.

73 Miller, "Pluralism and Social Choice."

74 Helen Gao, "Endangered shrimp delaying new school; District must make up for destroying habitat," *San Diego Union-Tribune,* March 4, 2007, B1.

75 On this see Liebell, *Environmental Liberalism.*

76 Locke makes a similar argument in the *Essay,* in a discussion of whether to hang a criminal of uncertain guilt.

77 By James Fishkin and his colleagues, in the late 1990s. "Texas Electric Utilities," accessed July 27, 2006 at http://cdd.stanford.edu/polls/energy/index.html.

78 *Southwest Center for Biological Diversity v. Bartel,* Case no. 98-CV-2234-B(JMA) Decision and Injunction [Doc. Nos. 174, 181, 189, and 197], October 13, 2006, United States Senior District Judge Rudi M. Brewster, United States District Court, Southern District of California.

79 Lee, "Habitat Ruling Clouds Development Picture."

80 Lee, "Judge Assails S.D.'s Landmark Habitat Plan"

CHAPTER 6 Conclusions

1 Przeworski, "Minimalist Conception of Democracy."

2 Seen from the perspective of the contemporary United States, environmental protection seems like a problem in paternalism. How can the state protect citizens' long-term interest in clean air and water and other sustainable resources from the citizens' own short-term interests in unlimited consumption? Considerations like these have prompted many if not most American theorists of environmental politics to focus on consciousness-raising rather than institution-building. Taking the perspective of the globus terraqueus, however, may well diminish the paternalism problem (or it may not: it is an empirical question). From this broader view, high-consuming populations look like Lockean outlaws who ought to be subject to the discipline of the majority in a civil society. Wars over the right to consume natural resources, including the global emissions atmospheric sink, are not unthinkable in this context.

3 Hardin, "The Tragedy of the Commons."

4 It is possible that this same dynamic exists for cultural preservation as it does for species preservation. Hardin, for example, argues that the policies that bolster minority cultures against majority ones tend to do so by sacrificing the freedom of choice of younger members of the group. See Hardin, "Group Boundaries, Individual Barriers."

5   Scott, *Seeing Like a State*.

6   Singer, "The Drowning Child and the Expanding Circle."

7   Kant is relying on his discussion of these alternatives in the Third Antinomy of the *Critique of Pure Reason;* see my treatment of the topic in *Kant's Politics*.

8   Instead, revolution is treated primarily as a naturally occurring event, while gradual reform under conditions of political stability is the preferred course for rational agents.

9   Walter Benjamin, ninth thesis, "Theses on the Philosophy of History," accessed June 2007 at: http://www.leedstrinity.ac.uk/depart/media/staff/ls/WBenjamin/CONCEPT2.html.

10 Mitscherlich, *The Inability to Mourn*.

11 Wood, "Kant's Theory of History," 256.

12 For a more detailed description of this dynamic, see chs. 1 and 5 of Ellis, *Kant's Politics*.

SELECTED BIBLIOGRAPHY

Ackerman, Bruce, and James S. Fishkin. *Deliberation Day.* New Haven: Yale University Press, 2004.

Aliber, Michael, Cherryl Walker, Mumbi Machera, Paul Kamau, Charles Omondi, and Karuti Kanyinga. "The Impact of HIV/AIDS on Land Rights: Case Studies from Kenya." Cape Town, South Africa: Human Sciences Research Council and the Food and Agriculture Organisation, 2004.

Amnesty International. "Women, HIV/AIDS, and Human Rights." Document released November 24, 2004, online at http://web.amnesty.org/library/Index/ENGACT770842004?open&of=ENG-347, accessed on July 8, 2006.

Arendt, Hannah. *The Human Condition.* Chicago: University of Chicago Press, 1958.

Arrow, Kenneth, et al. "Economic Growth, Carrying Capacity, and the Environment." *Science,* n.s., 268 (1995): 520–521.

Ball, Terence. "Green Democracy: Problems and Prospects." Typescript, 2005.

———, ed. *Idioms of Inquiry: Critique and Renewal in Political Science.* Albany: State University of New York Press, 1987.

———. *Transforming Political Discourse.* Oxford: Basil Blackwell, 1988.

Ball, Terence, James Farr, and Russell Hanson, eds., *Political Innovation and Conceptual Change* Cambridge: Cambridge University Press, 1989.

Bates, Robert H. *Markets and States in Tropical Africa: The Political Basis of Agricultural Policies.* Berkeley: University of California Press, 1981.

Bauder, Ellen T., and Scott McMillan. "Current Distribution and Historical Extent of Vernal Pools in Southern California and Northern Baja California, Mexico." In Carol Witham et al., eds., *Ecology, Conservation, and Management of Vernal Pool Ecosystems: Proceedings from a 1996 Conference.* Sacramento: California Native Plant Society, 1998: 56–70.

Bauder, Ellen, et al. *Recovery Plan for the Vernal Pools of Southern California.* Portland, Ore.: U.S. Fish and Wildlife Service, 1998.

Beiser, Frederick C. *Enlightenment, Revolution, Romanticism: The Genesis of Modern German Political Thought.* Cambridge, Mass.: Harvard University Press, 1992.

———. *The Fate of Reason: German Philosophy from Kant to Fichte.* Cambridge, Mass.: Harvard University Press, 1987.

Belk, Denton. "Global Status and Trends in Ephemeral Pool Invertebrate Conservation: Implications for California Fairy Shrimp." In Carol Witham et al., eds., *Ecology, Conservation, and Management of Vernal Pool Ecosystems: Proceedings from a 1996 Conference.* Sacramento: California Native Plant Society, 1998: 147–150.

Benhabib, Seyla. *The Claims of Culture: Equality and Diversity in the Global Era.* Princeton: Princeton University Press, 2002.

————. *The Rights of Others: Aliens, Residents, and Citizens.* Cambridge: Cambridge University Press, 2004.

Benschop, Marjolein. *Rights and Reality: Are Women's Equal Rights to Land, Housing and Property Implemented in East Africa?* Nairobi: UN-HABITAT, 2002.

Bingham, Bruce B., and Barry R. Norton. "Mitigation of Habitat 'Take': Application to Habitat Conservation Planning." *Conservation Biology* 11, no. 1 (February 1997): 127–139.

Black, Charles, and Paul H. Zedler. "An Overview of 15 Years of Vernal Pool Restoration and Construction Activities in San Diego County, California." In Carol Witham et al., eds., *Ecology, Conservation, and Management of Vernal Pool Ecosystems: Proceedings from a 1996 Conference.* Sacramento: California Native Plant Society, 1998: 195–205.

Bohman, James, and William Rehg. *Deliberative Democracy: Essays on Reason and Politics.* Cambridge, Mass.: MIT Press, 1997.

Bok, Sissela. "Kant's Arguments in Support of the Maxim 'Do What Is Right Though the World Should Perish.'" *Argumentation* 2, no. 1 (February 1988): 7–25.

Braybrooke, David. "Social Contract Theory's Fanciest Flight." *Ethics* 97 (July 1987): 750–764.

Brunner, Otto, Werner Conze, and Reinhard Koselleck, eds. *Geschichtliche Grundbegriffe: Historisches Lexikon zur politischen-sozialen Sprache in Deutschland.* Stuttgart: Klett-Cotta, 1972–.

Buchanan, James, and Gordon Tullock. *The Calculus of Consent: Logical Foundations of Constitutional Democracy.* Ann Arbor: University of Michigan Press, 1962.

Burns, Nancy, Kay Lehman Schlozman, and Sidney Verba. *The Private Roots of Public Action: Gender, Equality, and Political Participation.* Cambridge, Mass.: Harvard University Press, 2001.

Cavallar, Georg. *Kant and the Theory and Practice of International Right.* Cardiff: University of Wales Press, 1999.

Chanock, Martin. *Law, Custom, and Social Order: The Colonial Experience in Malawi and Zambia.* Portsmouth, N.H.: Heinemann, 1998.

Colburn, Elizabeth A. *Vernal Pools: Natural History and Conservation.* Blacksburg, Va.: McDonald and Woodward, 2004.

Dahl, Robert A. *How Democratic Is the American Constitution?* New Haven: Yale University Press, 2002.

Danilovic, Vesna, and Joe Clare. "The Kantian Liberal Peace (Revisited)." *American Journal of Political Science* 51, no. 2 (April 2007): 397–414.

Dobson, Andrew. *Citizenship and the Environment.* Oxford: Oxford University Press, 2003.

Dryzek, John S. *Deliberative Democracy and Beyond: Liberals, Critics, Contestations.* Oxford: Oxford University Press, 2000.

———. *Discursive Democracy: Politics, Policy, and Political Science.* Cambridge: Cambridge University Press, 1990.

———. *The Politics of the Earth: Environmental Discourses.* Oxford: Oxford University Press, 1997.

———. "Strategies of Ecological Democratization." In *Democracy and the Environment.* Cheltenham, U.K.: Edward Elgar, 1996.

Edwards, George C. *Why the Electoral College Is Bad for America.* New Haven: Yale University Press, 2004.

Ehrlich, Paul R., and Edward O. Wilson, "Biodiversity Studies: Science and Policy." *Science,* n.s. 253 (1991): 758–762.

Ellis, Elisabeth. "Citizenship and Property Rights: A New Look at Social Contract Theory." *Journal of Politics* 68 (August 2006): 544–555.

———. *Kant's Politics: Provisional Theory for an Uncertain World.* New Haven: Yale University Press, 2005.

———. "Provisionalism in the Study of Politics." In Ian Shapiro, Rogers M. Smith, and Tarek E. Masoud, eds., *Problems and Methods in the Study of Politics.* Cambridge University Press, 2004: 350–377.

Farr, James. "Understanding Conceptual Change Politically." In Terence Ball, James Farr, and Russell Hanson, eds., *Political Innovation and Conceptual Change.* Cambridge: Cambridge University Press, 1989: 24–49.

Final MHCP Plan. 2 vols. Prepared for the Cities of Carlsbad, Encinitas, Escondido, Oceanside, San Marcos, Solana Beach, and Vista. San Diego: San Diego Association of Governments, March 2003.

Fishkin, James. *Democracy and Deliberation: New Directions for Democratic Reform.* New Haven: Yale University Press, 1991.

———. *The Voice of the People: Public Opinion and Democracy.* New Haven: Yale University Press, 1991.

Flikschuh, Katrin. *Kant and Modern Political Philosophy.* Cambridge: Cambridge University Press, 2000.

Ford, Richard Thompson. "The Boundaries of Race: Political Geography in Legal Analysis." 107 Harv. Law. Rev. 1843 (1994).

Foucault, Michel. *Language, Counter-Memory, Practice: Selected Essays and Interviews.* Edited by Donald F. Bouchard. Translated from the French by Donald F. Bouchard and Sherry Simon. Ithaca: Cornell University Press, 1977.

Francis, Paul, and Mary Amuyunzu-Nyamongo. "Bitter Harvest: The Social Costs of State Failure in Rural Kenya." Conference paper given at the Arusha Conference, New Frontiers of Social Policy, December 12–15, 2005.

Fraser, Nancy. "After the Family Wage: Gender Equity and the Welfare State." *Political Theory* 22 (1994): 591–618.

Fugate, Michael. "Branchinecta of North America: Population Structure and Its Implication for Conservation Practice." In Carol Witham et al., eds., *Ecology, Conservation, and Management of Vernal Pool Ecosystems: Proceedings from a 1996 Conference.* Sacramento: California Native Plant Society, 1998: 140–146.

Fung, Archon. "Review of *Deliberation Day,*" *Journal of Policy Analysis and Management* 24, no. 2 (2005): 472–476.

Gastil, John, and Peter Levine, eds. *The Deliberative Democracy Handbook: Strategies for Effective Civic Engagement in the 21st Century.* San Francisco: Jossey-Bass, 2005.

Gauthier, David. "Between Hobbes and Rawls." In David Gauthrier and Robert Sugden, eds., *Rationality, Justice and the Social Contract.* Ann Arbor: University of Michigan Press, 1993: 24–39.

———. *Morals by Agreement.* Oxford: Clarendon Press, 1986.

———. "The Social Contract as Ideology." *Philosophy and Public Affairs* 6, no. 2 (1977): 130–164.

Ginsburg, Ruth Bader. "In Pursuit of the Public Good: Access to Justice in the United States." *Washington University Journal of Law and Policy* 7 (2001): 1–15.

Gutmann, Amy, and Dennis Thompson. *Democracy and Disagreement.* Cambridge, Mass.: Harvard University Press, 1996.

———. "Why Deliberative Democracy is Different." *Social Philosophy and Policy* 17, no. 1 (2000): 161–180.

———. *Why Deliberative Democracy?* Princeton: Princeton University Press, 2004.

Habermas, Jürgen. *The Structural Transformation of the Public Sphere: An Inquiry into a Category of Bourgeois Society.* Translated by Thomas Burger, with Frederick Lawrence. Cambridge, Mass.: MIT Press, 1989 [1962].

———. "Wahrheitstheorien." In *Wirklichkeit und Reflexion: Festschrift für W. Schultz,* edited by H. Farhenbach. Pfüllingen, 1973.

Hacker, Jacob, and Paul Pierson. "Abandoning the Middle: The Revealing Case of the Bush Tax Cuts." *Perspectives on Politics* 3 (March 2005): 33–53.

Hardin, Garrett. "Extensions of 'The Tragedy of the Commons.'" *Science,* n.s., 280 (May 1, 1998): 682–683.

———. "The Tragedy of the Commons," *Science,* n.s., 162 (Dec. 13, 1968): 1243–1248.

Hardin, Russell. "Group Boundaries, Individual Barriers." In David Miller and Sohail H. Hashmi, eds., *Boundaries and Justice: Diverse Ethical Perspectives.* Princeton: Princeton University Press, 2001: 276–295.

Harper-Ho, Virginia. "Noncitizen Voting Rights: The History, the Law, and Current Prospects for Change." *Law and Inequality* 18, no. 2 (2000): 271–322.

Hayward, Clarissa Rile. "The Difference States Make: Democracy, Identity, and the American City," *American Political Science Review* 97, no. 4, 2004: 501–514.

Hirschl, Ran. *Towards Juristocracy: the Origins and Consequences of the New Constitutionalism.* Cambridge, Mass.: Harvard University Press, 2004.

Hobbes, Thomas. *Leviathan.* Edited by Edwin Curley. Indianapolis: Hackett, 1994.

Hölscher, Lucien. "Öffentlichkeit." In Otto Brunner, Werner Conze, and Reinhard Koselleck, eds., *Geschichtliche Grundbegriffe: Historisches Lexikon zur politischen-sozialen Sprache in Deutschland.*Stuttgart: Klett-Cotta, 1975: vol. 4, 413–467.

Hume, David. *Political Essays.* Edited by Knud Haakonssen. Cambridge: Cambridge University Press, 1998.

Huntington, Samuel. *The Clash of Civilizations and the Remaking of World Order.* New York: Touchstone, 1996.

———. "Democracy for the Long Haul." *Journal of Democracy* 7, no. 2 (1996): 3–13.

Ishay, Micheline R. *The History of Human Rights: From Ancient Times to the Globalization Era.* Berkeley: University of California Press, 2004.

Ivison, Duncan. "The Secret History of Public Reason: Hobbes to Rawls." *History of Political Thought* 18 (1997): 125–147.

Kant, Immanuel. *The Conflict of the Faculties (Der Streit der Fakultäten).* Translated by Mary J. Gregor. Lincoln: University of Nebraska Press, 1979.

———. *Kant's gesammelte Schriften.* Preussischen Akademie der Wissenschaften. Berlin: Walter de Gruyter, 1902–.

———. *Practical Philosophy.* Edited and translated by Mary J. Gregor. Cambridge: Cambridge University Press, 1996.

Karpowitz, Christopher F., and Jane Mansbridge. "Disagreement and Consensus: The Importance of Dynamic Updating in Public Deliberation." In John

Gastil and Peter Levine, eds., *The Deliberative Democracy Handbook: Strategies for Effective Civic Management in the Twenty-first Century.* San Francisco: John Wiley and Sons, 2005: 237–253.

Keck, Margaret E., and Kathryn Sikkink. *Activists beyond Borders: Advocacy Networks in International Politics.* Ithaca: Cornell University Press, 1998.

King, Jamie L. "Loss of Diversity as a Consequence of Habitat Destruction in California's Vernal Pools." In Carol Witham et al., eds., *Ecology, Conservation, and Management of Vernal Pool Ecosystems: Proceedings from a 1996 Conference.* Sacramento: California Native Plant Society, 1998: 119–123.

Klosko, George. "Provisionality in Plato's Ideal State." *History of Political Thought* 5, no. 2 (1984): 171–193.

Knight, Jack, and James Johnson. "Aggregation and Deliberation: On the Possibility of Democratic Legitimacy." *Political Theory* 22, no. 2 (May 1994): 277–296.

———. "Inquiry into Democracy: What Might a Pragmatist Make of Rational Choice Theories?" *American Journal of Political Science* 43, no. 2 (April 1999): 566–589.

Kolbert, Elizabeth. "The Climate of Man," parts 1–3. *New Yorker,* vol. 81, nos. 10–12 (2005): 52-63, 56-63, and 52-63, respectively.

Koselleck, Reinhard. *Critique and Crisis: Enlightenment and the Pathogenesis of Modern Society.* Oxford: Berg, 1988.

———. "Einleitung." In Otto Brunner, Werner Conze, and Reinhard Koselleck, eds., *Geschichtliche Grundbegriffe: Historisches Lexikon zur politisch-sozialen Sprache in Deutschland.* Stuttgart: Ernst Klett Verlag, 1972–: vol. 1, xiii–xxvii.

———. *Futures Past: On the Semantics of Historical Time.* Translated by Keith Tribe. Cambridge, Mass.: MIT Press, 1985.

———. "Linguistic Change and the History of Events." *Journal of Modern History* 61 (1989): 649–666.

———. *The Practice of Conceptual History: Timing History, Spacing Concepts.* Translated by Todd Samuel Presner et al. Foreword by Hayden White. Stanford: Stanford University Press, 2002.

Kuehn, Manfred. *Kant: A Biography.* New York: Cambridge University Press, 2001.

Kymlicka, Will. *Politics in the Vernacular. Nationalism, Multiculturalism and Citizenship.* Oxford: Oxford University Press, 2000.

———. "Territorial Boundaries: A Liberal Egalitarian View." In David Miller and Sohail H. Hashmi, eds., *Boundaries and Justice: Diverse Ethical Perspectives.* Princeton: Princeton University Press, 2001: 249–275.

Laursen, John Christian. "Kant on Book Piracy." In Elisabeth Ellis, ed., *Kant's Po-*

litical Theory: Interpretations and Applications. State College: Pennsylvania State University Press, forthcoming.

———. *The Politics of Skepticism in the Ancients, Montaigne, Hume, and Kant*. Leiden: E. J. Brill, 1992.

———. "The Subversive Kant." *Political Theory* 14, no. 4 (1986): 584–603.

LaVaque-Manty, Mika. *Arguments and Fists: Political Agency and Justification in Liberal Theory*. New York: Routledge, 2002.

———. "Kant's Children." *Social Theory and Practice* 32, no. 3 (July 2006): 365–388.

Layzer, Judith A. *The Environmental Case: Translating Values into Policy*. Washington, D.C.: CQ Press, 2002.

Lee, Mike. "Habitat Ruling Clouds Development Picture; Vernal Pool Protections Must Be Readdressed," *San Diego Union-Tribune*, October 23, 2006.

———. "Judge Assails S.D.'s Landmark Habitat Plan; Ruling Orders Portion of Blueprint to Be Revised," *San Diego Union-Tribune*, October 14, 2006.

———. "Protection in Jeopardy? Federal Officials Say They Cannot Determine Effectiveness of Endangered Species Act," *San Diego Union Tribune*, April 3, 2006.

———. "Land Trust's Bankruptcy Raises Range of Questions," *San Diego Union-Tribune*, September 20, 2005.

———. "Plight of Tiny Fairy Shrimp Is a Symbol of Crisis; Federal Effort to Save Threatened Species Is Hobbled by Lawsuits," May 1, 2005.

Liebell, Susan. "Environmental Liberalism: The Values and Mechanisms of a Principled Political Theory." Dissertation. University of Chicago, 2001.

———. "The Rules of the Game: Contract Theory, the Rule of Law and the Problem of Ecology." Paper delivered at the 2001 annual meeting of the American Political Science Association, San Francisco.

Locke, John. *"Two Treatises of Government" and "A Letter Concerning Toleration."* Edited by Ian Shapiro. New Haven: Yale University Press, 2003.

Lomasky, Loren. "Toward a Liberal Theory of National Boundaries." In David Miller and Sohail H. Hashmi, eds., *Boundaries and Justice: Diverse Ethical Perspectives*. Princeton: Princeton University Press, 2001: 55–78.

MacArthur, Robert H., and Wilson, Edward O. *The Theory of Island Biogeography*. Princeton: Princeton University Press, 1967.

Macedo, Steven. *Deliberative Politics: Essays on Democracy and Disagreement*. New York: Oxford University Press, 1999.

Mackie, Gerry. *Democracy Defended*. Cambridge: Cambridge University Press, 2003.

Male, Timothy D., and Michael J. Bean. "Measuring progress in US endangered species conservation." *Ecology Letters* 8, no. 9 (September 2005): 986.

Mansbridge, Jane. "Cracking through Hegemonic Ideology: The Logic of Formal Justice." *Social Justice Research* 18, no. 3 (September 2005): 335–347.

———. "Everyday Talk in the Deliberative System." In Steven Macedo, ed., *Deliberative Politics.* Oxford: Oxford University Press, 1999: 211–242.

———. "Rethinking Representation." *American Political Science Review* 97 (November 2003): 515–528.

———. "Using Power/Fighting Power: The Polity." In Seyla Benhabib, ed., *Democracy and Difference: Contesting the Boundaries of the Political.* Princeton: Princeton University Press, 1996: 46–66.

Mansbridge, Jane, and Katherine Flaster. "The Cultural Politics of Everyday Discourse: The Case of 'Male Chauvinist.'" *Critical Sociology* 33, no. 4 (2007): 627–660.

Marshall, T. H. *Class, Citizenship, and Social Development: Essays.* Garden City, N.Y.: Doubleday, 1964.

Martin, Robert W. T. "Context and Contradiction: Toward a Political Theory of Conceptual Change." *Political Research Quarterly* 50 (1997): 413–436.

Mason, T. David. "'Take Two Acres and Call Me in the Morning': Is Land Reform a Prescription for Peasant Unrest?" *Journal of Politics* 60, no. 1 (1998): 199–230.

Mill, John Stuart. *On Liberty.* Edited by Stefan Collini. Cambridge: Cambridge University Press, 1989.

Miller, David. "Group Rights, Human Rights, and Citizenship." *European Journal of Philosophy* 10, no. 2 (2002): 178–195.

———. *On Nationality.* Oxford: Oxford University Press, 1995.

Miller, David, and Sohail H. Hashmi, eds. *Boundaries and Justice: Diverse Ethical Perspectives.* Princeton: Princeton University Press, 2001.

Miller, Nicholas R. "Pluralism and Social Choice." *American Political Science Review* 77, no. 3 (1983): 734–747.

Minteer, Ben A., and Bob Pepperman Taylor. *Democracy and the Claims of Nature: Critical Perspectives for a New Century.* Lanham, Md.: Rowman and Littlefield, 2002.

Mitscherlich, Alexander, and Margarete Mitscherlich. *The Inability to Mourn: Principles of Collective Behavior.* Grove, 1984.

Mock, P. "California Gnatcatcher (*Polioptila californica*)." In *The Coastal Scrub and Chaparral Bird Conservation Plan: A Strategy for Protecting and Managing Coastal Scrub and Chaparral Habitats and Associated Birds in California.* California Partners in Flight. http://www.prbo.org/calpif/htmldocs/scrub.html. 2004.

Morris, Irwin L., and Joe A. Oppenheimer. "Rational Choice and Politics." In Irwin L. Morris, Joe A. Oppenheimer, and Karol Edward Soltan, eds., *Politics from Anarchy to Democracy: Rational Choice in Political Science*. Stanford: Stanford University Press, 2004: 1–36.

Muthu, Sankar. *Enlightenment against Empire*. Princeton: Princeton University Press, 2003.

———. "Justice and Foreigners: Kant's Cosmopolitan Right." *Constellations* 7, no. 1 (2000): 23–45.

Mwangi, Esther. "Subdividing the Commons: Distributional Conflict in the Transition to Individual Property in Kenya's Maasailand." Research paper. Bozeman, Mo.: Political Economy Research Center, 2003.

Norton, Anne. *95 Theses on Politics, Culture, and Method*. New Haven: Yale University Press, 2004.

Nozick, Robert. *Anarchy, State, and Utopia*. New York: Basic Books, 1974.

Nussbaum, Martha. "Beyond the Social Contract: Capabilities and Global Justice." *Oxford Development Studies* 32, no. 1 (2004): 4–18.

———. 1997. "Kant and Cosmopolitanism." In James Bohman and Matthias Lutz-Bachmann, eds., *Perpetual Peace. Cambridge, Mass.: MIT Press, 1997: 25–58.*

Orloff, Ann. "Gender and the Social Rights of Citizenship." *American Sociological Review* 58 (1990): 303–328.

Pagden, Anthony, ed., *The Languages of Political Theory in Early-Modern Europe*. Cambridge: Cambridge University Press, 1987.

Palonen, Kari. "The History of Concepts as a Style of Political Theorizing: Quentin Skinner's and Reinhart Koselleck's Subversion of Normative Political Theory." *European Journal of Political Theory* 1, no. 1 (2002): 91–106.

———. "The Politics of Conceptual History." *Contributions to the History of Concepts* 1, no. 1 (March 2005): 37–50.

Pettit, Philip. "Democracy and Punishment: Is Criminal Justice Politically Feasible?" *Buffalo Criminal Law Review* 5, no. 2 (2002): 427–450.

———. "Resilience as the Explanandum of Social Theory." In Ian Shapiro and Sonu Bedi, eds., *Contingency in the Study of Politics*. New York: New York University Press, 2007: 79–96.

Phillipson, Nicholas, and Quentin Skinner, eds. *Political Discourse in Early Modern Britain*. Cambridge: Cambridge University Press, 1993.

Pierson, Paul. *Politics in Time: History, Institutions, and Social Analysis*. Princeton: Princeton University Press, 2004.

Pitts, Jennifer. *A Turn to Empire: The Rise of Imperial Liberalism in Britain and France*. Princeton: Princeton University Press, 2005.

Pocock, J. G. A. "The Concept of a Language and the *métier d'historien:* Some Considerations on Practice." In Anthony Pagden, ed., *The Languages of Political Theory in Early-Modern Europe.* Cambridge: Cambridge University Press, 1987.

———. *Politics, Language, and Time.* Chicago: University of Chicago Press, 1989.

Pogge, Thomas W. "Is Kant's *Rechtslehre* a 'Comprehensive Liberalism'?" Spindel Conference Proceedings, *Southern Journal of Philosophy* 36, supplement (1997): 161–187.

Przeworski, Adam. "Minimalist Conception of Democracy: A Defense." In Ian Shapiro and Casiano Hacker-Gordon, eds., *Democracy's Value.* Cambridge: Cambridge University Press, 1999: 23–55.

Putnam, Robert D. *Bowling Alone: The Collapse and Revival of American Community.* New York: Simon and Schuster, 2000.

Rahn, Matthew E., Holly Roremus, and James Diffendorfer. "Species Coverage in Multispecies Habitat Conservation Plans: Where's the Science?" *BioScience* 56, no. 7 (July 2006): 613–619.

Rawls, John. *Collected Papers.* Edited by Samuel Freeman. Cambridge, Mass.: Harvard University Press, 1999.

———. *Lectures on the History of Moral Philosophy.* Edited by Barbara Herman. Cambridge, Mass.: Harvard University Press, 2000.

———. *Political Liberalism.* 2nd edition. New York: Columbia University Press, 1996.

———. *A Theory of Justice.* Cambridge, Mass.: Harvard University Press, 1971.

Reich, Robert. *The Work of Nations.* New York: Vintage Books, 1992.

Richter, Melvin. *The History of Political and Social Concepts.* Oxford: Oxford University Press, 1995.

———. "More Than a Two-Way Traffic: Analyzing, Translating, and Comparing Political Concepts from Other Cultures." *Contributions to the History of Concepts* 1, no. 1 (March 2005): 7–20.

———. "Understanding *Begriffsgeschichte.*" *Political Theory* 17 (1989): 296–301.

Riker, William. *Liberalism against Populism: A Confrontation between the Theory of Democracy and the Theory of Social Choice.* San Francisco: Freeman, 1982.

Riley, Patrick. *Will and Political Legitimacy.* Cambridge, Mass.: Harvard University Press, 1982.

Risse, Mathias. "Is There a Human Right to Free Movement? Immigration and Original Ownership of the Earth." Paper given at the Center for Human Values, Princeton University, October 12, 2006.

Rosen, Alan D. *Kant's Theory of Justice*. Ithaca: Cornell University Press, 1993.

Ryfe, David Michael. "Review of *Deliberation Day* and *Reflective Democracy*." *Public Opinion Quarterly* 68, no. 4 (2004): 641–650.

Sandel, Michael. *Liberalism and the Limits of Justice*. 2nd edition. Cambridge: Cambridge University Press, 1998.

Sanders, Lynn. "Against Deliberation." *Political Theory* 25, no. 3 (1997): 347–376.

Schnoor, Jerald L. "Endangered Species Act Revisited." *Environmental Science and Technology* 40, no. 3: 63.

Schuster, Liza, and John Solomos. "Rights and Wrongs across European Borders: Migrants, Minorities, and Citizenship." *Citizenship Studies* 6, no. 1 (2002): 37–54.

Scott, James. *Seeing Like a State: How Certain Schemes to Improve the Human Condition Have Failed*. New Haven: Yale University Press, 1998.

Shachar, Ayelet. *Multicultural Jurisdictions*. Cambridge: Cambridge University Press, 1997.

Shachar, Ayelet, and Ran Hirschl. "Citizenship as Inherited Property." *Political Theory* 35, no. 3 (June 2007): 253–287.

Shapiro, Ian. *Democracy's Place*. Ithaca: Cornell University Press, 1996.

———. *Democratic Justice*. New Haven: Yale University Press, 1999.

———. "Enough of Deliberation: Politics Is about Interests and Power." In Stephen Macedo, ed., *Deliberative Politics: Essays on Democracy and Disagreement*. Oxford: Oxford University Press, 1999: 28–38.

———. *The Flight from Reality in the Human Sciences*. Princeton: Princeton University Press, 2005.

———. "Realism in the Study of the History of Ideas." *History of Political Thought* 3, no. 3 (Winter 1982): 536–578.

———. *The State of Democratic Theory*. Princeton: Princeton University Press, 2003.

———. "The State of Democratic Theory: A Reply to James Fishkin." *Critical Review of International Social and Political Philosophy* 8, no. 1 (2005): 79–83.

Shaw, Brian J. "Rawls, Kant's Doctrine of Right, and Global Distributive Justice." *Journal of Politics* 67, no. 1 (2005): 220–249.

Simovich, Marie A. "Crustacean Biodiversity and Endemism in California's Ephemeral Wetlands." In Carol Witham et al., eds., *Ecology, Conservation, and Management of Vernal Pool Ecosystems: Proceedings from a 1996 Conference*. Sacramento: California Native Plant Society, 1998: 107–118.

Singer, Peter. *Animal Liberation: A New Ethics for our Treatment of Animals*. New York: Random House, 1975.

————. "The Drowning Child and the Expanding Circle." *New Internationalist* (April 1997). Accessed at: http://www.utilitarian.net/singer/by/199704—.htm; accessed May 5, 2007.

————. *One World: the Ethics of Globalization.* New Haven: Yale University Press, 2004.

————. "Utilitarianism and Vegetarianism," *Philosophy and Public Affairs* 9, no. 4. (Summer 1980): 325–337.

Skinner, Quentin. "The Empirical Theorists of Democracy and Their Critics: A Plague on Both Their Houses." *Political Theory* 1, no. 3 (1973): 287–306.

Skocpol, Theda. *Diminished Democracy: From Membership to Management in American Civic Life.* Norman: University of Oklahoma Press, 2003.

————. *States and Social Revolutions: A Comparative Analysis of France, Russia and China.* Cambridge: Cambridge University Press, 1979.

Soulé, Michael E. "Conservation: Tactics for a Constant Crisis." *Science,* n.s., 253 (1991): 744–750.

Southwest Center for Biological Diversity v. Bartel. Case no. 98-CV-2234-B(JMA) Decision and Injunction [Doc. Nos. 174, 181, 189, and 197], October 13, 2006, United States Senior District Judge Rudi M. Brewster, United States District Court, Southern District of California.

Steiner, Hillel. "Hard Borders, Compensation, and Classical Liberalism." In David Miller and Sohail H. Hashmi, eds., *Boundaries and Justice: Diverse Ethical Perspectives.* Princeton: Princeton University Press, 2001: 79–88.

Sugden, Robert. "The Contractarian Enterprise." In David Gauthier and Robert Sugden, eds., *Rationality, Justice, and the Social Contract.* Ann Arbor: University of Michigan Press, 1993: 1–23.

————. "Contractarianism and Norms." *Ethics* 100 (July 1990): 768–786.

Sunstein, Cass R. "Incompletely Theorized Agreements." *Harvard Law Review* 108 (1995): 1733–1772.

————. *The Partial Constitution.* Cambridge, Mass.: Harvard University Press: 1993.

————. *Why Societies Need Dissent.* Cambridge, Mass.: Harvard University Press, 2003.

Taylor, Charles. *Sources of the Self: The Making of Modern Identity.* Cambridge, Mass.: Harvard University Press, 1992.

Taylor, Martin F. J., et al. "The Effectiveness of the Endangered Species Act: A Quantitative Analysis," *BioScience* 55, no. 4 (April 2005): 360–367.

Thomas, Craig W. *Bureaucratic Landscapes: Interagency Cooperation and the Preservation of Biodiversity.* Cambridge, Mass.: MIT Press, 2003.

Thompson, Dennis F. *The Democratic Citizen: Social Science and Democratic Theory in the Twentieth Century.* Cambridge: Cambridge University Press, 1970.

Thornton, Russell. *American Indian Holocaust and Survival: A Population History since 1492.* Norman: University of Oklahoma Press, 1990.

Tribe, Keith. "The *Geschichtliche Grundbegriffe* Project: From History of Ideas to Conceptual History." *Comparative Studies in Society and History* 31 (1989):180–184.

Tocqueville, Alexis de. *The Old Regime and the French Revolution.* Translated by Stuart Gilbert. New York: Doubleday, 1955.

United Nations Human Rights Committee. "Concluding Observations," April 29, 2005; CCPR/CO/83/KEN; online at http://www.unhchr.ch/tbs/doc .nsf/898586b1dc7b4043c1256a450044f331/62fd6231f4e490fbc1256ffe004 c06e2/$FILE/G0541383.pdf; accessed July 8, 2006.

U.S. Fish and Wildlife Service. *Recovery Plan for Vernal Pool Ecosystems of California and Southern Oregon.* Portland, Ore., 2005.

Vertovec, Steven. "Multicultural Policies and Modes of Citizenship in European Cities." *International Social Science Journal* 156 (1998): 187–99.

Walsh, Janet. *Double Standards: Women's Property Rights Violations in Kenya.* New York: Human Rights Watch, March 2003 (vol. 15, no. 5 [A]). Accessed at http://www.hrw.org; accessed June 2006.

Walzer, Michael. *Just and Unjust Wars: A Moral Argument with Historical Illustrations.* 3rd edition. New York: Basic Books, 2000 [1977].

Weber, Eugen. *Peasants into Frenchmen: The Modernization of Rural France, 1870–1914.* Stanford: Stanford University Press, 1976.

Wilhere, George F. "Adaptive Management in Habitat Conservation Plans." *Conservation Biology* 16, no. 1 (February 2002): 20–29.

Wilson, Edward O. *The Future of Life.* New York: Knopf, 2002.

Witham, Carol W., et al., eds. *Ecology, Conservation, and Management of Vernal Pool Ecosystems: Proceedings from a 1996 Conference.* Sacramento: California Native Plant Society, 1998.

Wolff, Robert Paul. "The Completion of Kant's Moral Theory in the Tenants of the Rechtslehre." In Jane Kneller and Sidney Axinn, eds., *Autonomy and Community: Readings in Contemporary Kantian Social Philosophy.* Albany: State University of New York Press, 1998.

Wood, Allen W. "Kant's Theory of History." In Immanuel Kant, *"Toward Perpetual Peace" and Other Writings on Politics, Peace, and History,* edited by Pauline Kleingeld. New Haven: Yale University Press, 2006.

World Bank. "The Kenyan Strategic Country Gender Assessment." October 2003.

Young, Iris Marion. *Inclusion and Democracy.* Oxford: Oxford University Press, 2000.

INDEX